Some Place Like Home

Using Design Psychology to Create Ideal Places

Toby Israel

WILEY-ACADEMY

For Sarah and Liam: may you always carry the best of home in your hearts

Published in Great Britain in 2003 by Wiley-Academy, a division of John Wiley & Sons Ltd

Copyright © 2003   John Wiley & Sons Ltd, The Atrium, Southern Gate, Chichester, West Sussex PO19 8SQ, England Telephone (+44) 1243 779777

Email (for orders and customer service enquiries): cs-books@wiley.co.uk
Visit our Home Page on www.wileyeurope.com or www.wiley.com

Other Wiley Editorial Offices

John Wiley & Sons Inc., 111 River Street, Hoboken, NJ 07030, USA

Jossey-Bass, 989 Market Street, San Francisco, CA 94103-1741, USA

Wiley-VCH Verlag GmbH, Boschstr. 12, D-69469 Weinheim, Germany

John Wiley & Sons Australia Ltd, 33 Park Road, Milton, Queensland 4064, Australia

John Wiley & Sons (Asia) Pte Ltd, 2 Clementi Loop #02-01, Jin Xing Distripark, Singapore 129809

John Wiley & Sons Canada Ltd, 22 Worcester Road, Etobicoke, Ontario, Canada M9W 1L1

ISBN 0470849509

Cover design: Artmedia Press Ltd, London
Typeset by Florence Production Ltd, Stoodleigh, Devon, UK, based on a text design by Rita Bartolini

Printed and bound in Italy

Contents

Acknowledgements

Many people deserve thanks for helping this book find a home. Thanks must first go to Michael Graves, Charles Jencks and Andres Duany for contributing their time, resources and, most especially, insights to ensure the successful completion of *Some Place Like Home*. Beyond this, there are two mentors whose influence on my life and work over many years set the stage for my thinking. More than anyone else, Lona Fowler laid the groundwork for this book by contributing to my personal growth and introducing me to the phenomenon of psychology. I am also indebted to Dr. Leanne Rivlin, a founder of environmental psychology. She was a selfless advisor over the years I spent at City University of New York's Environmental Psychology Program, giving generously of her time and enthusiasm to my endeavors.

I am also particularly thankful to Clare Cooper Marcus whose now classic article "The House as Symbol of Self" and subsequent book, *The House as Mirror of Self: Exploring the Deeper Meaning of Home*, inspired me and many other environmental psychologists to probe more deeply into the meaning of home and environmental autobiography. For their enthusiasm, support and willingness to innovate, I also am indebted to Ray Heinrich, Tony Bisogno and all of those from the KSS team, New Jersey City University, and the University Academy Charter School.

Behind the scenes, first and foremost I express my gratitude to Gloria Shapiro not only for her editorial input but for her inspiration and ongoing encouragement, optimism, and love. Similarly, endless thanks goes to Ken and Marian Hamilton for their loving, selfless contributions to my life and efforts. My heartfelt gratitude also to Martin Vaccaro, Mitchell Funk, and Bill Mikesell for contributing their support, time, and talents.

Beyond this I must also thank those on two continents who helped me find some place like home: the friends who waved goodbye to us in our tiny boat as we sailed back from England through the storm; and the friends who waited on shore in America, helping us anchor and build our next settlement.

Of particular importance, also, has been the support received from Haworth, Inc. including the mighty efforts of both Heidi Quellet and Kim Eich in helping me to bring the concept of Design Psychology to designers across the United States and beyond. Thanks also to Looney Ricks Kiss and to the University of Lincoln including especially Derek Crotherell.

I also wish to acknowledge those who helped me navigate the publishing world including Ian Colquhoun, Richard Smith, Karen Franck, and Phyllis Spiegel. Jed Docherty, Constance Forrest, Susan Painter, Sally Augustine, Ahuva Windsor, Felicia Davis and Katherine Ramsland also contributed greatly to the critical reading of the book's manuscript. I could not have obtained all of the photographic documentation and reference material without the assistance of Linda Burton-Hamill, Dodie Colavecchio, and Mark Bujac of Michael Graves' office as well as Lisa Bayne of Eli Lilly and Company and the librarians at both Princeton University's School of Architecture and School of Psychology. For their technical assistance I am most grateful to Peter Smith, Howard Strauss, Steve Albin, and Barbie Freiden. My appreciation also goes to Susan Zalnis for her efforts on my behalf, to Andrea Imredy Saah for her skills as a translator, and to Sue Williamson for her artistic contribution.

Last but by no means least, I thank my children whose wondrous existence reminded daily of the reasons for writing this book.

Introduction

When I began writing this book I had one simple premise in mind: I believed that each of us possesses our own unique environmental autobiography. Each of us has a treasure chest of memories and impressions of places we have lived that includes both past homes and large scale environments (villages, towns, cities, etc.). I believed in the importance of uncovering these riches to reveal how our past environmental experiences laid the foundation for our present and future choices when selecting "Some Place Like Home."

The influence of the past on our present sense of home is not a new idea. In 1964 the French philosopher Gaston Bachelard inspired the imagination when he wrote of the "Poetics of Space":

> An entire past comes to dwell in a new home . . . .. Thus the house is not experienced from day to day only, on the thread of a narrative or in the telling of our own story. Through dreams, the various dwelling-places in our lives co-penetrate and retain the treasure of former days.[1]

During the process of writing this book I was also looking for a house of my own. With Bachelard's words in mind, I decided to explore my own deep notion of home as part of my housing search. In doing so, I found connections between my past, present, and future sense of place that I never dreamed existed. I used these previously undiscovered riches to guide me in my search.

The more meaningful and revealing this search became for me, the more I began to speculate about the importance of environmental autobiography for others. As an environmental psychologist I had been doing exercises for years with art, architecture and psychology students, encouraging them to explore the impact of their own past history of place.[2] These students had been amazed by the richness of their environmental pasts which they had buried and forgotten. However, most of them were in their early twenties, still living in student housing, and not yet designing. The influence of their environmental pasts on their design sense and their notions of home was still undeveloped and uncertain.

Yet, what about older adults with more experience in establishing a home? What about architects involved in house design? In fact, what about the superstar designers of our time who influence our most basic notions of environment, design, and home? Do not they, too, possess personal environmental autobiographies which they then translate as public theory, taste, and style?

Convinced of the profound relevance of our environmental past for our environmental present, I wrote to three of the leading figures in the world of design: architect Michael Graves, architecture critic Charles Jencks, and architect and town planner Andres Duany, all of whom in particular had dedicated substantial thought, time and effort to the creation of their own home place. All agreed to be interviewed.[3]

I embarked upon these interviews optimistic that I would discover with them *some* connection between their past, present, and future sense of environment and home. As the interviews progressed, I think they, too, were surprised to find how deeply they could dig down to the bottom of their environmental sources. In the necessarily brief but intense period I spent with each of them,[4] we uncovered connections that seemed so direct and profound as to be totally enthralling to me and, hopefully, to them. As the environmental stories of all unfolded, I was able to suggest how they had subconsciously reworked their history of places not only to create their own homes but their well-known public buildings and/or architecture/planning philosophies.

In truth almost all of us, designers and non-designers alike, approach the choice and creation of a home place as if we were writing on a blank slate. For example, architecture students arriving in the lecture hall begin on day one to learn about the aesthetic styles of the great architectural gurus past and present. Necessarily they also learn the principles of building technology. Meanwhile the deeper environmental memories that each student carries with them into that hall—the experiences that have the most profound influence on their notion of place—are ignored.

Similarly, this blank slate approach continues when non-designers scan the latest architectural magazines hoping to emulate design trends when creating some place like home. They look outward to these magazines, to architects, to interior designers, to the houses of admired friends for sources of ideas rather than inward to tap their own rich environmental reservoirs. Thus the gap between architects and people over which we often grieve, is really a grieving over the gap that exists for all of us (including architects) between our present sense of house and our buried sense of home.

In taking myself and those whom I have interviewed here through the process of environmental self-reflection, I have engaged in a process similar to that which Bachelard termed "topoanalysis." He defined topoanalysis as ". . . the systematic psychological study of the sites of our intimate lives."[5] For Bachelard, the house itself was the central focus of such study for he believed, "Our soul is an abode. And by remembering 'houses' and 'rooms,' we learn to 'abide' within ourselves."[6] While the house seems the obvious starting point for topoanalysis, I have enlarged such an analysis to encompass other sites beyond the house, large-scale settings, for example, that also hold intimate meaning for us.

As a result of leading my own students, the design figures interviewed here, and myself through a type of topoanalysis in this wider sense, I have come to believe that

1. our sense of self and sense of the environment are intimately and profoundly entwined;

2. the seeds of this connection between self and place are planted in childhood;

3. our sense of self–place connection continues to grow and change throughout our lives;

4. that connection is shaped not only by the physical reality of our environment but by the psychological, social/cultural, and aesthetic meaning that place holds for us;[7]

5. we can become conscious of this meaning that place holds for each of us uniquely;

6. such consciousness can help us create places that express a fulfilling self–place bond;

7. those in the design world who shape our physical environment have a particular responsibility to build places that help us to reinforce this vital bond;

8. design professionals who explore their own self–place connection can more consciously create fulfilling places for themselves and others whose lives they touch.

Thus what began as a personal exploration of my environmental autobiography has ended up as a much broader exploration of the psychological connection between person and place, a connection I will discuss throughout the following pages. As that discussion will show, my theories are based not only on the work of Bachelard, but on the ideas and methods of other colleagues, many of whom were also inspired by Bachelard to journey down the path of environmental meaning.

Environmental psychologists, interdisciplinary professionals who examine the interplay between people and the environment, have particularly contributed to thinking in this area. Yet the challenge for environmental psychologists has always been to see their thinking—their theories and research—*applied* as part of the actual design process.[8] Thus, I present here not only a process by which individuals can gain insight into their self–place connection but a useable programming technique which can help "match" people and place at the deepest possible level. In fact, I have come to refer to this method of working as a new "inner vision" field of design called "Design Psychology." I define Design Psychology as "the practice of planning, architecture and interior design in which psychology is the principal design tool."[9]

Why is this new form of design practice so crucial at this juncture? The tragedy of September 11th underscored, as few events have in our history, the crucial symbolic and psychological importance that buildings hold for us. As designers struggle to meet the challenge of rebuilding the World Trade Center site, they know that part of their mandate must be to create a design solution that is not only practical and aesthetically pleasing but one that is also psychologically healing for the individual and for America. Design training, however, has provided designers with few tools with which to understand and address the psychological aspect of design.

A recent design exercise, for example, underscored the blindness with which even architectural "greats" struggle to rethink the World Trade Center vision.[10] As one of fifteen famous architects asked to create ideas for the site, Peter Eisenman proposed the building of three office towers which would appear to be collapsing—buckling at the knees. If, in a moment of insanity, such buildings actually were to be built, they would enshrine and extend our trauma rather than heal the American psyche. How could designers come to propose such a disjuncture between people and place?

Only Daniel Libeskind enabled us to descend with grace and authenticity into the hell of this tragedy when he later proposed the preservation of the site's still-standing slurry walls. The archetypal rawness of these walls became the Rorschach image upon which we could all project not just the tragedy of 9/11, but the tragedies that are the rawest moments of our own lives. Perhaps Libeskind was uniquely able to capture the authenticity of this pain because, consciously or unconsciously, he could reach back to his own family's experience of descent into Holocaust hell. This personal history uniquely positioned him to understand both the deep impact of tragedy and the importance of emerging into a life of hope as symbolized by the spire he proposed for the site. The question remains, will the transcendent, healing promise of Libeskind's proposal survive the often conflicting visions and agendas of politicians, developers and planners who are likewise involved in the re-development process?

Meanwhile, too, with the advent of CAD, designers are becoming increasingly intoxicated with the potential of computer-aided design to expand their technological capabilities. While the capabilities offered by CAD are wonderful, the danger is that, eyes fixed on a computer screen, designers will become less and less attuned to the psychological and social dimension of the places they are designing. Design Psychology offers the opportunity to redress this imbalance.

With this in mind, push back from the computer as you begin to read about the subjective and autobiographical nature of Design Psychology. In fact, the purpose of this book is not to present a rigorous scientific study.[11] While many biographers can chronicle, comment on or give us insight into our lives, inevitably our autobiography can only have one author. Even when we attempt to write the book that is our environmental past,

> Except for a few medallions stamped with the likeness of our ancestors, our child-memory contains only worn coins. It is on the plane of the daydream and not on that of facts that childhood remains alive and poetically useful within us. Through this permanent childhood, we maintain the poetry of the past.[12]

I can make suggestions to my students, to architects, and to others about the meaning of their environmental stories and the implications of these stories when it comes to design. In the end, however, the truth and meaning of all our stories are forever a reality that each of us alone constructs.[13]

In the meantime, by deliberately writing this book in a way that weaves together story and theory, I have tried both to capture the poetic and subjective essence of Design Psychology and to speak to an audience that includes people/environment professionals as well as non-professionals. If I have succeeded, I hope that all will be inspired to read the poetry that is their space, in order to create some place that truly feels like home.

Below:
Office Tower Proposal by Peter Eisenman, Peter Eisenman Architects, Commissioned by *The New York Times*, September 2002 for the World Trade Center Site.

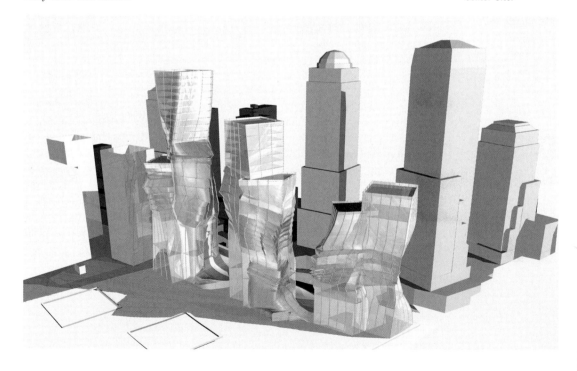

CHAPTER 1

The
Past

Opening the Treasure Chest

I have to move. I've rented this house for two years but now the landlady needs it for herself. I know what I want, at least I think I do: I'd like to buy a three bedroom house in this same neighborhood. I'd also like a place with a living room, a dining room, an eat-in kitchen and two bathrooms. A good size yard would be great. A fourth bedroom would really come in handy as a study or extra bedroom for visitors. I had a sun porch in my last house and it was wonderful. And I'd also like — Hang On! Am I being realistic?

The first step for anyone planning to move is to think and dream about what this next place will be like. We think about our most basic housing needs. We dream about our ideal home. We then try to balance fantasy and reality.

Objectively, I must think of my house as an adequate shelter for my family. I must also think of it as the biggest purchase I will ever make. As a result of this practical perspective ". . . the house has become increasingly similar to other products being bought and sold, used and discarded like a car or washing machine."[1] But the very idea of "discarding" a house in this way seems so cold-hearted. In fact, just thinking about my imaginary new home fills my head with images and emotions. I imagine myself and my family sitting by the fire in the cold winter, feelings of love and belonging created by the warmth.

Our basic need for shelter *must* be satisfied. Yet once we have achieved the security that a house provides, be it rented or owned, it is then possible to transform that house into a home. At this level the house becomes a setting for meaning; it becomes not only a physical structure but a symbol. But what exactly does it symbolize? Family? Hearth? Love? Belonging? Home has traditionally come to symbolize all of these things but above all, as Clare Cooper Marcus has suggested, "the house is a symbol of self."[2] She writes:

> It is the nature of man that he constantly seeks a rational explanation of the inexplicable, and so he struggles with the questions: What is self? Why here? Why now? In trying to comprehend this most basic of archetypes—self—to give it concrete substance . . . I believe, man . . . frequently selects the house, the basic protector of his internal environment (beyond skin and clothing) to represent or symbolize what is tantalizingly unrepresentable.[3]

How do we even begin to select our houses, these symbols to represent our true selfhoods? In discussing the house–self link, Cooper Marcus refers to the thinking of Carl Gustav Jung, one of the greatest psychologists of our times, who believed that timeless "archetypal" images, often revealed to us in dreams, provide clues about the path to psychic wholeness. In his autobiography, Jung discussed a series of house dreams which he had during his life in which house and self became synonymous. He built his house, the tower at Bollingen on the Zürichsee, as the manifestation of these dreams. Jung was uniquely able to describe the process of self-house growth:

> From the beginning I felt the Tower as in some way a place of maturation— a maternal womb or a maternal figure in which I could become what I was, what I am and will be. It gave me a feeling as if I were being reborn in stone. It is thus a concretisation of the individuation process . . . . During the building work of course, I never considered these matters . . . .. Only afterwards did I see how all the parts fitted together and that a meaningful form has resulted; a symbol of psychic wholeness.[4]

Still, most of us are not in the position to build our own homes. Instead we rely on architects to transform our dwellings and the psychic wholeness which they can represent into meaningful forms. Various architectural "isms" have suggested ways to create such meaning in architecture. The Greeks and Romans used symbols in architecture, often in the form of the sculptured human body, to express the eternal human values embodied in Classicism. Renaissance architecture also relied on human form to express its new Humanism. In the machine age such symbolism was discarded in favor of Modernism, an anti-ornament, functional machine aesthetic reflecting our rational, not spiritual being. Yet even in the machine age, the symbols that were erased from the landscape of our waking life visited us again at night in our dreaming, symbolic search for self.

In the wake of Modernism's failure to communicate with the public at large, Post-Modernism emerged as an attempt to create meaning in architecture. Despite its many variations,[5] all forms of Post-Modernism are linked in their reliance on symbolism as a way of expressing meaning in our culture. Yet while they may be preaching the same gospel, Post-Modernists are often doing so from churches that look very different from one another: they may agree on the pluralistic nature of their audience, but they may well disagree upon the type of symbolic expression that can best reach that audience.

For instance in the widely influential books *Learning from Las Vegas*[6] and *Complexity and Contradiction in Architecture*,[7] Robert Venturi and Denise Scott Brown also came to rethink the role of symbolism in architecture. They glorified the brash Las Vegas strip, and based their own popular, easily accessible architecture on such admiration. But their approach was widely criticized as a descent into the superficial, popular culture of Middle America. For many it represented a glorification of signs rather than symbols.

By way of contrast Michael Graves took a leading role in creating Post-Modern architecture that relied on his unique interpretation of classical form. Charles Jencks also stressed the vital need to strive towards symbolic architecture.[8] For him this meant using a wide range of symbolic motifs each having many "valences" or meanings. Still others rejected Post-Modernism, clinging to Modern architecture as an *overarching* symbol of modern society. More recently architects such as Frank Gehry dismantled conventional visual logic in favor of Deconstructiv*ism*.

Such philosophical debates surrounding architectural "isms" and the parade of styles continue to march in and out of the public limelight. Yet to many onlookers, the architectural marching bands seemed to be going around in circles. Left in the dust of architectural verbiage, the public gradually drifted away back . . . home.

The search for a new home is exciting yet also overwhelming. It is hard to know where even to begin.

If, as Bachelard, Jung, and Cooper Marcus have suggested, home and the process of human growth are intimately connected, perhaps one can best begin the process of Design Psychology, the search for self–place connection in the deepest sense, and meaning in architecture overall, by setting aside architecture's ongoing debates. Instead, as we engage in Design Psychology it is important to ask the questions "What do we mean by human growth?" and "In what ways is our sense of place connected to that growth?"

All human beings—everyone, everywhere and always—begin existence in homes constructed of the same material, of the same shape, size, light, sound, and temperature. We all begin life in the womb. Though we have no conscious memory of this, our earliest environment, we generally imagine our mother's womb to be a place of calm, of nurturing, of total safety and protection. Once we are born, however, we must learn to create our own places of safety and security, of nurturing and calm. How do we go about doing this?

Key thinkers have provided theories about the nature of child development including theories about intellectual, emotional, and social growth that are relevant in terms of environmental knowing. In the realm of *intellectual* growth, the theories of Jean Piaget have proved widely influential for environmental psychologists attempting to understand how the child's conception of the world develops. At birth, an infant has no words, no symbols with which to circumscribe the world. Instead, Piaget theorized that an infant's early world consists not of symbols but of basic impressions or "schemas"—the schema of a face, for example. He theorized that children "assimilate," or take in these schema, adding them into an already established storehouse of impressions. The child continues to gather and absorb this world of new data. Yet how does he or she cope with all of this information?

According to Piaget, the child does not simply pile up impressions. He believed that children enter into an active process of making sense of their world. They "accommodate" each new impression based on the set of impressions they already possess. Thus, for example, the child learns to distinguish between just "face" and his or her mother's face, and eventually he or she assimilates an ever increasing world of specific faces which become accommodated under the larger category of "face." In this way the child reaches an "equilibrium" between assimilation and accommodation. Thus, according to Piaget, children come to know and understand the outer world through a process of adaptation—the constant working of assimilation and accommodation.

> As an adult I can understand this process best when I think of my experience in a foreign country. During my first shopping expedition in England I was totally disoriented. Aisles and products were arranged very differently from what I was used to in America. The labeling of the products was equally unfamiliar. Eventually after visiting the market many times, I learned to assimilate this new reality (i.e. tomato paste in England comes in a tube not a can!) and gradually my mental image of this product was expanded as I accommodated this new information. Eventually what was previously strange became a familiar part of my shopping repertoire as I adapted to this new environment.

Similarly, the child is born from the womb into the foreign land that he comes to call home and must assimilate and accommodate as he adapts to this new environment around him. For the newborn, however, even the notion of "land" and outer world is foreign. The child must explore and learn what world is as he or she matures.

At what point does the child learn to do more than make sense of impressions? At what point does he or she become a symbol maker able to construct meaning in the outer world? Piaget identified distinct stages of intellectual development, sequential stepping stones to intellectual maturity. He believed that the child became a symbol maker between the ages of about two to seven years old. He theorized that children become able to think logically between the ages of seven to twelve and that by fifteen children were capable of higher order reasoning.[9] Although there has been much debate about Piaget's stage theory,[10] what seems indisputable to anyone who has observed children in intimate contact with the physical world is that there is a deeper involvement on the part of the child in that world, an involvement that has been gradually lost as the child becomes a socialized adult.[11]

One book that has proved widely influential for environmental psychologists, *The Ecology of the Imagination in Childhood*,[12] also stresses early phases of child development as especially relevant to the individual's developing sense of place. In this book, author Edith Cobb identified one stage of development which she called the "latency" period as especially significant. She considered this stage, from about ages five or six until about twelve, as a time when

> The child ... is poised ... halfway between inner and outer worlds .....
> Three- and four-dimensional realities possess the child's imagination and
> carry him into a deepening world image. He is, in fact, in love with the
> universe. That is to say he wants to possess the whole world as this theater
> of perception.[13]

If we again compare this experience to adult travel to a foreign country, we can understand why so often we feel a thrill when we encounter a place so new, so different, so unexplored. As in childhood, we again perceive the world around us as an entirety, as a sensory experience of unlabeled, unfamiliar sights, sounds and smells which we can absorb in an unedited way—not just as a series of signs *or* symbols.

Just as Bachelard felt that we are imbued with the poetic power of spaces, so Cobb believed that our non-verbal, childhood experience of place retained the same poetic, creative power.[14] With this idea in mind, Cobb amassed over three hundred volumes of autobiographical childhood memories of creative thinkers.[15] Through her study of those autobiographies she came to believe that creative thinkers, particularly, return to those magical, middle years of childhood "to renew the power and impulse to create at its very source, a source which they describe as the experience of emerging not only into the light of consciousness but into a living sense of a dynamic relationship with the outer world."[16] There is no mention of Cobb looking specifically at the autobiographies of architects. However, since architects inevitably wield such power over our physical world, an examination of their environmental autobiographies seems vitally relevant.

So, how does one go about examining the environmental histories of designers? The Design Psychology process provides a way for designers as well as non-designers systematically to explore their environmental autobiographies. In fact, the nine Design Psychology exercises embedded in these chapters helped Michael Graves, Charles Jencks, Andres Duany, and me explore our connection between our "self" and our sense of "intimate" place.

For example, a Favorite Childhood Place Visualizaton Exercise I did (see Exercise 4 at the end of this chapter),[17] helped me remember my favorite past environment, the woods across the street from my house where I spent hours every day as a child. For me, also, this was a magical place yet I had not thought about it in years, let alone written about it. However, when prompted, I was amazed by the clarity and detail of this memory:

> *I reach back and can remember "The Big Woods", the outdoor home*
> *away from home where all the children in the neighborhood played.*

Forty four years later I can still recall the smell of onion grass mixed with apple blossoms and winding paths that led from the blackberry stickers to the dark moist world of the tall pines. Susan, Lynne, Jay and I created life in this world in real and imagined ways: the fort made of found wood was my brother's domain, the stone house bordering the dirt road was clearly where the witch lived, a cardboard carton was a halfway house for tortoises, garden snakes, and other friends who passed with magic through our lives.

How can we come to forget places of such power? Certainly most of us can remember a variety of settings from our childhood including details of our home. Then, too, through memory's magnifying glass we can recall other places and things that vary in locale and scale including countries, regions, neighborhoods, houses, furniture, and even objects of special significance.

Back then we still could ride our bikes, play in the street, on lawns, play, gradually ride towards home. We were the only signs of life peopling our way to our (almost identical) car supported houses. Behind the bright pink door of my split-level island, I lay on the soft American carpet, den cushion under my head, watching TV and waiting for dinner.

Inevitably, our memory of and attachment to these places varies. Perhaps, though, we lose conscious memory of our most intimate childhood places as a result of what psychologist Ernest Schachtel called "early childhood amnesia."[18] The child grows into the symbol maker capable of more fully developed intellectual thought. Yet in the process, while the increasing ability to reason is acquired, the magical world of unlabeled sensory experience is lost and buried in a world of words.

Thus our experience of the environment can not be explained just as a process of shifting intellectual perceptions. Our sense of the world involves a psychic, *emotional* dynamic as well. Interestingly, Schachtel's theories draw together the worlds of intellectual and emotional knowing. Schachtel, particularly, conceived of a child's growth as a progression from "autocentric," or self-centered perception, sensations, and emotions[19] to an outward looking "allocentric perception" which

... always breaks through and transcends the confines of the labeled, the familiar and establishes a relation in which direct encounter with the object, itself, instead of with one or more of its labeled and familiar aspects takes place . . .. In the moments of all allocentric perception at its fullest we always are at the frontiers of our familiar world, breaking through the enclosing wall of explicit or implicit labels and encountering the inexhaustible other, which transcends all labels with which man tries to capture and tame it, so that he may use it and so its unfamiliarity will no longer disquiet him.[20]

This seems to echo the process of place knowing described by Bachelard, Cooper Marcus, and Cobb. Yet Schachtel further suggested that it is the security of the

Through memories' magnifying glass we can recall places and things that vary in locale and scale including countries, regions, neighborhoods, houses, furniture, and even objects of special significance.

mother's love that provides the background for such openness in the child. According to him, when that love is provided, the child is capable of tolerating uncertainty and newness in the environment. When such love is absent, an unchanging environment becomes a substitute source of security.[21]

Of course, as the father of psychoanalysis, Sigmund Freud also sought to retrieve and interpret childhood memories in order to help people grow into emotionally healthy adulthood. Yet Freud did not write specifically about people's relationship to the physical environment. In fact, Design Psychology as it is conceived here, while also probing our early childhood experience, is *not* psychoanalysis.

> *I keep dreaming that I am back in my childhood home. In these dreams,*
> *although my parents no longer live in this home, they still own it.*
> *Everything there looks exactly as it did when I was a child. In my dream*
> *I am relieved because I needn't buy a house now: I can simply move*
> *back to my old house. Then I realize that that house is too far away—*
> *that I have to find my own home. I wake up.*

My dream underscored the fact that change in home can symbolize personal change as well. On a superficial level the dream was about my house hunting attempts. On a deeper level, it was about my realization that my mother and father could no longer provide me with shelter. Instead I could only hope to build on the foundation of security they had provided. I had to establish my own *adult* home. In psychological terms, my unconscious was telling me that I "can't go home again."[22]

Clearly, our parents and our early experiences play a vital role in our lives. Sometimes, however, the role played by parents is not a positive one. Similarly, people's childhood experience of place is not always positive. In fact, when environmental psychologist Louise Chawla analyzed autobiographies in terms of environmental experience she was able to identify four significant forms of childhood place attachment including those identified below.[23]

FOUR FORMS OF CHILDHOOD PLACE ATTACHMENT

> ➤ *Affection*—the most common form of attachment associated with family, love, and security, creating a sense that "this is my place in the world"

> ➤ *Transcendence*—places remembered as an unforgettable living presence in themselves, exciting all five senses and inspiring exuberance, calm, or awe

> ➤ *Ambivalence*—when attachment is associated with pain and pleasure, i.e. a place stigmatized by society as a ghetto of poverty or racial inferiority thus a place where tenderness for home place is mixed with vulnerability and entrapment

➤ *Idealization*—where a place is invested with elaborate national, religious, or racial values and mentally inhabited this idealized place is an alternative to inadequate circumstances

Clearly, the "transcendent" experience of childhood place attachment referred to above is the experience Cobb discussed. For most people, however, environmental memories come laced with a mixture of emotions. "The Big Woods" was a place of transcendence for me. My house was a place of affection. It is harder for me to recall early childhood places of ambivalence or idealization, perhaps as a result of a different kind of idealization of place than that mentioned above.

Adults often view their early childhood environment and, in fact, their entire childhood, through rose-tinted spectacles—the childhood of a stereotypical ideal rather than a reality. For example, when I dig beyond my affectionate memories of home, I can also remember a house where the outer show of beautiful objects disguised domestic tensions behind the scenes—my father's illness, my brother's rebellion. All families have different dynamics of varying proportions which are reflected in home place. Indeed, we need only turn on the television to know that there are many children who live in houses of horror—homes in violence-torn zones or in settings of physical and/or sexual abuse where a mother's secure love may be a distant dream. Bachelard alludes to this experience when he writes, "Space that has been seized upon by the imagination cannot remain indifferent space. . . . The space of hatred and combat can only be studied in the context of impassioned subject matter and apocalyptic images."[24] In fact, when asking people to explore their environmental autobiographies, Clare Cooper Marcus has found that such exploration does sometimes trigger memories of painful family dynamics or of child abuse.[25] For adult survivors of these situations, especially, early childhood experience of place is recalled more painfully and must be explored more carefully.[26]

Interestingly, regardless of the overall positive or negative quality of people's early experience of place, whether indoor or outdoor spaces, adults' most frequently remembered *favorite* locales are similar in that they were environments controlled, manipulated or re-created in some way by them as children—places like my brother's fort where he reigned supreme.[27] Thus the meaning of such child-created places is profound as they represent our early attempts to create a place for ourselves in the world.

As adults we can continue to work to change or adapt our environment in a way that is positive for us. Yet in order to do so, we must first become aware of ways we have re-worked our past history of place—replicated or rejected it or undertaken some combination of the two. We can use this awareness to help us re-create the essence of our most satisfying childhood places. For others, however, awareness of the past can be a crucial step towards *rejecting* places that had a negative impact upon us.[28] We can consciously choose to create home places that no longer reverberate with echoes of our worst environmental experiences. Inevitably, however, as we attempt to make sense of our world and establish our place within it, we do so within the context of others. We come to know the world not just in an intellectual or emotional way but as part of our *social* development.

In his classic book *Childhood and Society* psychologist Erik Erikson suggested ways in which we grow in relationship to our social environment. Erikson postulated that there are "Eight Stages of Man,"[29] stages in which intellectual, emotional, and social growth are woven together not only as we progress through childhood but as we progress through adult life. For example Erikson's theories, like Schachtel's, stressed the need for the infant to establish an initial "basic trust" that the environment around them is predictable and stable. Once assured that this is so, the child may then feel secure to take "initiative," to explore the world and display "industry"—to plan, to construct, to make things and in this way begin positively to control the environment. Later, with adolescence, comes the need for positive self "identity." During this period young people are concerned with how they appear to others, not just to themselves. According to Erikson, once the person has become secure in their own identity, they are then capable of "intimacy," of loving someone else.

Gradually, as the healthy individual matures, the process of developing a loving relationship to other people and the world evolves. This perspective is different from the child's early infatuation with the universe. Now, according to Erikson, the mature adult can make a caring commitment to the world. They can choose "generativity"—to have their own children, or guide the next generation. In environmental terms, having confidently defined their own self in relation to the world, the adult is then able to help others go through the process of self/environment evolution. Until, finally, the mature adult, typically in old age, has reached the stage of "integrity." Erikson explains:

> Only in him who in some way has taken care of things and people and has adapted himself to the triumphs and disappointments adherent to being human . . . only in him may gradually ripen the fruit of these seven stages.[30]

According to Erikson, failure to define oneself positively in relation to the world at these various stages can result in feelings of "mistrust," "shame," "doubt," "guilt," "inferiority," "role confusion," "isolation," "stagnation," and "despair." This list of potential pitfalls seems staggering. In truth, few of us climb Erikson's steps to growth without stumbling, though, according to Erikson's theory, we can retrace our steps, resolve conflicts, and continue to climb again. Yet Erikson was a Freudian. Thus such re-tracing inevitably involved traditional psychoanalysis.

Since the time of Freud, Jung, and Erikson, a variety of other psychological perspectives have emerged that suggest different though likewise relevant paths to psychic wholeness. For example cognitive psychology, like environmental psychology, recognizes that there is a dynamic relationship between people and their environment. Rather than stressing the importance of the unconscious workings of our *inner* life, however, cognitive psychologists are concerned with the sense that we make of our *outer* world.[31] Just as we may receive messages from the unconscious, cognitive psychologists believe that we receive messages, clues, information about the meaning of our world from the people and places that surround us. In the same way that Freudians interpret unconscious symbolism, cognitive psychologists interpret the information we receive from this social–physical environment. They believe that the understanding we gain from such interpretation can help us to achieve healthy human growth.

Cognitive psychologists also believe that we receive our first information about the world within the context of the family experience. Thus cognitive psychologists likewise recognize the influence of others, most especially of our parents in shaping our notion of the world. In fact, in order to understand our own sense of the environment, we can look back at the "messages" handed down to us from others—from our parents, grandparents, great-grandparents and so on and thereby trace the origins of our own self and place identity.[32] Though rarely examined as separate entities, the environments that our ancestors experienced will certainly have influenced their own development and consequent environmental perspective and values. These perspectives, these values are often communicated to us, their symbolic meaning binding the pages upon which our own environmental stories are written.

When we think about exploring our past through Design Psychology, we need to think not only about recovering our *own* roots but the roots of our ancestors as well. In environmental terms, we not only possess environmental autobiographies but also environmental *genealogies*, environmental family trees. Embedded in the stories that our parents, grandparents, or even great-grandparents tell or told us about the "old days" are the environmental scenarios within which the drama of family histories have been played out.

With this in mind, using information from my family members as well as my own memories/impressions, I completed the Environmental Family Tree Exercise (see Exercise 1, below). This exercise enabled me to reconstruct my family's environmental genealogy and its relevance for me.[33] By its very nature such reconstruction is a mixture of fact and fiction. Inevitably, it is as much an *impression* of my experience and my family's environmental experience over time as it is a description of the reality of that experience.

My maternal grandmother lived to be a hundred and there were many times when she told the story of her mother, a highly educated woman who had been married off and forced to leave her sophisticated city life to join my great-grandfather, an uneducated shopkeeper in a poor rural hamlet. Despite their differences, my great-grandparents had thirteen children whom they raised in that small Hungarian village:

> Our house was made with several materials—the exterior walls were
> made with mud and straw—mud and straw shaped into bricks and
> dried until very hard. The inside walls were made smooth with mud.
> The floors also were made from mud and cleaned with smooth mud
> once a week. We had three rooms: a large living room/bedroom. One
> very large kitchen, consisting of bedroom/kitchen—this is the room we
> lived in winter and summer. Then we had a small room called the
> "oven." This had a big oven made of mud that my mother baked the
> most delicious bread and cakes in. At the far end of the house we kept
> livestock (no connection to the rest of the house). In the backyard was a

Embedded in the stories that our parents, grandparents or even great-grandparents tell or told us about the old days are the environmental scenarios within which the drama of family histories have been played out.

vegetable garden, and the front and side a flower garden. The village
population was about three hundred families, maybe less. There was a
church, all white, very pretty in the middle of the village.[34]

My family told me many stories throughout my childhood of hardship in Hungary but also of a close-knit and lively family. Eventually these great-grandparents and all their children emigrated to America to build a better life. As a first-generation American, my mother described her early childhood home as follows:

We lived in a house in Queens Village, New York. It was a two family
house. We lived on the second floor, the Schneider family lived on the
first floor. The house was a gray or beige stucco finish and there was one
identical to it next door with a common driveway between. The street
was residential with simple houses on both sides of the street. The best
thing about this house was that it was right next to the library where I
spent hours reading. Even when we lived in a plain house, we always
had beautiful things: Your grandmother always loved beautiful things.[35]

In the years that followed my maternal grandparents continued to "pull themselves up by their bootstraps," each time improving their environmental circumstances. At one point my grandfather, a down-to-earth intellectual/artist, wanted to simplify their lives and move from the city to a farm in the country. My grandmother had visions of grandeur: she had always dreamed about the cultured city life from which *her* mother had been "exiled." She certainly did not want to return to anything resembling the Hungarian village from which she had escaped. Instead, they acquired a stately old Long Island mansion which they turned into a cross between a rooming house and old age home. From early on I could remember this home of my grandparents:

Sad old men and ladies looking for the bathroom shuffle along on the
worn Chinese carpet. They find their way between a hodge podge of
mahogany chairs, tables, and sideboards. Beneath crystal chandeliers,
in front of velvet curtains a graceful peasant girl made of marble pours
water frozen in time.

Both of my paternal grandparents (Russian immigrants) had died by the time I was born. Their environmental legacy was the New Jersey paint and wallpaper business which my father inherited and ran for all my childhood years. These grandparents had lived above this store and my father was raised there.

Shortly after I was born my parents bought a split level suburban home near the family business and near three other families of aunts, uncles, and cousins. My mother began working part time in the store, giving advice in the wallpaper department, finally branching out to become an interior designer in her own right. Our home was a decorated showcase of my mother's talents. Eventually my father died and my mother remarried. Later on, my remaining grandmother, parent, aunts and uncles, great aunts and great uncles all moved to luxury retirement communities in Florida. In some cases they moved within blocks of each other

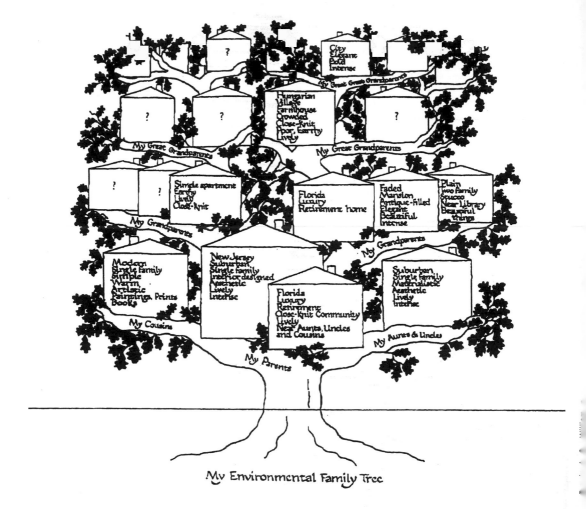

My Environmental Family Tree

so that they could all meet weekly, sometimes daily in each other's houses or go to their central clubhouse for lunch or dinner.

Environmental Family Tree.

On the one hand my family's story is very similar to that of other European immigrants who moved to the United States in the early 1900s and then worked hard to realize the American Dream. Yet on another level my family's story, indeed the story of any family, can be analyzed in environmental terms: what environmental choices did they make and why? In what way did these choices symbolize and affirm their selfhoods? What effect did this environmental legacy have upon the next generation?

Clearly, the important choices that my family made involved major moves including first emigrating to America and later migrating to Florida. Both of these changes were motivated by the desire to seek a more physically comfortable way of life, a reaction against the early family experience of poverty and hardship. In choosing to live near each other in the suburbs rather than the city or the country they reached a compromise: within the context of American suburban comfort they were able to re-create the feeling of the "family village," the positive core of their Hungarian legacy of place.

Within their homes the value of beauty and culture had been passed down from matriarch to matriarch: my great-grandmother yearned for and told stories about the sophisticated world of her childhood. My grandmother tried to recreate that environment in the sculptural objects, furniture, overall decor and finally the (faded) mansion she acquired. My mother earned a living by creating beautiful interiors for others.

Of course, choices were not always conscious. None of this past history was analyzed and interpreted in order to guide my family's environmental decision making. Yet the patterns existed in their choice of place, of houses, of furniture, and of special objects. Those patterns contained messages which had an effect from generation to generation. In my family those messages emphasized the importance of family, material comfort, education, and beauty. Aware of these messages, my family's core values, and their choices of place over time, I decided to analyze my own settlement pattern, the pattern of large scale places where I had lived, to see if this could guide my current place choice. To uncover my patterns of place choices, I continued the process of Design Psychology by doing the Environmental Time Line Exercise (see Exercise 2, below). I wrote down the names of large scale settings where I had lived in chronological order from birth to present. Then I indicated the ages at which I lived there:

Dwelling similar to the author's ancestors' home in Hungary.

Photograph by Balázs Molnár. Reprinted by permission.

My environmental time line:										
Place:	Jersey City, N.J.	Engle-wood, N.J.	Boston Mass.	Hart-ford, Conn.	New Bruns-wick, N.J.	Prince-ton, N.J.	New-castle, U.K.	York, U.K.	Bever-ley U.K.	Prince-ton, N.J.
Age: (years)	0–2	3–17	18–19	20–21	22–7	28–30	30–33	34–5	36–42	43–present

I then counted up the number of years I lived in each different *type* of place. It was sometimes difficult to distinguish between what I meant by a city, town, or suburb.[36] For example, Boston was definitely a city but would Englewood be considered a town or a suburb? I finally categorized each of the types of place in which I had lived by using the labels that seemed in line with *my* sense of each place, rather than any official definition.

Years lived in:
Large cities   9
Small cities/towns   7
Suburban towns   27

Clearly, I spent the majority of my life living in suburban towns. In fact, by far the longest time I spent in any one place was while growing up in Englewood, New Jersey, a suburban town on the outskirts of New York City.

> *No suburban isolation here: instead an open door routine of cousins*
> *visiting cousins (it seemed like everyday). We played, running from*
> *sprawling, unfenced lawn to lawn, back doors flung open with*
> *neighborhood kids sucked into the path of our happy tornado.*

Perhaps I was too comfortable here: the first time I lived in a city, when I went to university in Boston, I felt overwhelmed and adrift without the feeling of family, neighborliness, and community I had known in Englewood.

By far the most unusual aspect of my place history was the fact that I repeated the pattern of my ancestors by emigrating to another country. I moved to England for twelve years after meeting my future husband who was British.

> *Beverley was every American's fantasy of the ideal English town. It was*
> *a world lived on the streets, not in cars. I could walk my children to*
> *school every day then stroll back, chat with friends, stroll on to buy my*
> *fresh-baked bread.*

Obviously, I was reproducing the experience of neighborhood I had known as a child, but what other qualities of home place was I choosing to replicate or reject in establishing an adult home place? In order to examine this question I felt I needed to look more closely at the qualities of my large scale childhood home place. Bachelard suggested a way of doing this:

> . . . each one of us, then, should speak of his roadside benches; each one of us should make a surveyor's map of his lost fields and meadows . . .. Thus we cover the universe with drawings we have lived. These drawings need not be exact. They need only be tonalized on the mode of our inner space.[37]

Environmental psychologists have long been intrigued by the idea of such a "mental map," the imperfect image of a place that we carry in our minds. These maps reveal much about our notion of the places we experience. With this in mind I completed the next Mental Map Exercise (see Exercise 3, below). I drew a map of Englewood as I remembered it—almost as if I were drawing the map for someone who had never been there and wanted to visit it. I added as much detail as I could remember in order for me to recall the character, not just the size of the setting in which I had lived.

I needed some way to begin to analyze this map. To accomplish this, I referred to *The Image of the City*, a book that has become a classic for environmental psychologists. In this book, city planner Kevin Lynch used people's mental maps to identify a city's essence. He found that when creating mental maps, people were consistently giving examples of what he identified as five key elements of city form, including:[38]

➤ **Paths**—which provide access from one part of the city to another i.e. pedestrian or car byways;

➤ **Edges**—those parts of the city that serve as boundaries—riverfronts, waterfront, roads on the edge of a town;

➤ **Landmarks**—simply defined physical objects i.e. buildings, parks, statues, often used to help people find their way around a city or tell people where to go;

➤ **Nodes**—points in the city that serve as major transitions from one activity to another i.e. railway stations, bus, airlines or subway terminals;

➤ **Districts**—relatively large areas which are recognized as having some common character.

Although Englewood was not a city, I could still use Lynch's vocabulary to identify the same elements in my map. Then I was able to analyze the impact Englewood's form had upon me.

My high school sticks out in my mind as an Englewood landmark. Built in English Gothic style, it was a beautiful building with leaded glass windows and a noble tower. The school was in the middle of a park-like setting with a huge pond and stream nearby. The building and its green surrounds stood out even more because it contrasted so greatly with our adjacent homogenous neighborhood district of 1950s style homes. Another strong feature that made Englewood special was that you were always aware that it was on the edge of New York City. In fifteen minutes you could drive up the main street past the affluent houses of the "hill" district and drive across the bridge to New York City.

As an adult it is amazing for me to realize that the places where I chose to live all had towered landmarks (not an everyday architectural feature in America). Even the university I chose to attend was Gothic in style with a main tower as its centerpiece. I remember knowing little about that university when I applied there, only that I liked the feel of the place. Did I choose this university for its tower?!

The towns I chose to live in as an adult also were all on the outskirts of larger cities, as was the case with Englewood. However these "adult" towns had visually interesting architectural districts quite unlike that of my homogenized childhood neighborhood. Thus when it came to large scale settings, I could see how I had reworked—replicated or rejected—certain images of home place. In fact, certain features (the Gothic tower in this case) may even have come to symbolize my archetypal notion of home. In this sense such early imprinting seemed further testimony to the profound influence that childhood places have upon us.

Looking back at my environmental autobiography, I could see how my small and large scale sense of home had developed as a result of my intellectual, emotional, and social experience of place. After years of living in a foreign land, I also had come to see how much our experience of place is influenced by *culture* as well. Of course I could look back at my environmental family tree and see that my *family* possessed its own culture, its own set of treasured values reflected in the environments they created. In his book *House, Form and Culture*, architect Amos Rapoport went further by suggesting that whole cultures have structures that are reflected in their environment—their house or settlement patterns.[39] Thus he suggested that there is an overall experience of enculturation, of the passing on of environmental values not just within families but also within a society.[40] For Rapoport the environment is

> . . . a series of relationships between things and things, things and people, and people and people. These relationships are orderly, i.e., they have a pattern and a structure—the environment is *not* a random assemblage of things and people any more than a culture is a random assemblage of behaviors and beliefs.[41]

Thus Rapoport's ideas about dwelling and settlement have become important for environmental psychologists, as he, too, challenged the traditional idea of *physical determinism* that has underpinned much of architectural education. For him the idea that climate and the need for shelter, materials and technology, and site[42] determine the form of a house seems too narrow and simplistic. Instead he suggested that both environment and culture are guided by *choices* people make. When making these choices people rely on "certain values, norms, criteria, and

I could see how I had reworked—replicated or rejected—certain images of home place.

Photograph by the author.

Author's high school, Dwight Morrow High School, Englewood, New Jersey

Princeton High School, Princeton, New Jersey

Photograph by Mitchell Funk.

assumptions" all of which reflect the cultural core of a group. Rapoport suggests that core elements of a group might include such things as religion, family structure, food habits, and social identity.[43]

> Over the years the beautiful church towers of Beverley echoed a familiar
> form yet gradually they towered over me and, as a Jewish person, I
> imagined myself an outsider in an otherwise Christian town.

Beverley's cultural core as symbolized in its architecture and my own cultural identity felt vastly different. I felt out of place there. In the end, although I loved Beverley, my roots were clearly in the United States. Having divorced, I had decided to move back to America, but *where* in America? I did not want to live in the Fort Lauderdale area near the rest of my extended family because I didn't like the conspicuous consumption that remains part of that suburban Florida culture. Instead I chose to move to the more traditional town of Princeton, New Jersey where friends of twenty to thirty years standing also lived. Still, Princeton, an idyllic suburban community by many people's standards, is a very expensive place to *buy* a house. Rationally, consciously it seemed like a bad decision for a single parent on one income to make. Yet having explored my environmental autobiography up to this point, I could see that the messages I had received from early childhood onward contributed to make me feel that this was the right decision.

The University towers, the village green, with Tudored landmarks all around—sometimes I think I'm still in England. As I walk on, the town's four bagel stores and Princeton's train station with signs pointing to nearby New York or Philadelphia remind me that I'm nearer home.

Looking back at my early childhood experience of place, my environmental family tree and my own place pattern so far, I could understand why the desire to live in Princeton was especially compelling: here I felt I could return to New Jersey suburban life that formed the bulk of my childhood years. I could re-create the vital core of my family's environmental genealogy by living in a place that had a community feeling in the midst of the best educational opportunities that the town's renowned university had to offer. It was also a place where I could be physically comfortable. However, that comfort was not packaged in the banal suburbia of my childhood. Instead it had the feeling of the old world architecture and European culture I had found so appealing in the U.K. It resonated as the home place my great grandmother had yearned for. It was a place where I could pass down the best of my environmental legacy to my children. Yet the pressure was on. I had only a few months to find a house.

Assuming I could find a house to buy, what type of *dwelling* would reflect my sense of home? As Rapoport has rightly pointed out, we no longer live in a primitive or pre-industrial society where we, ourselves, build our own buildings symbolizing who we are as an individual or group. Instead we find that due to "greater complexity of problems and greater specialization—the design of buildings and settlements is increasingly the concern of professional designers."[44] What Rapoport is essentially describing is an institutionalization of the building process, where, at best, the dweller participates in decision making through design/build intermediaries. Choices, decisions about the form of the house are made with the *designer* retaining substantial power to translate dweller's needs and values.[45] Yet, if in the end we live in a built world made manifest by architects, we must also look further at how *they* have translated "some place like home" and what that translation means for us.

Michael Graves

Photograph by William Taylor. Courtesy Michael Graves, Architect.

I traveled only a few blocks to interview Michael Graves as his home and cheery, yellow, clapboard style office are also both in Princeton. When I opened the door to his firm, I was greeted by Loki—not his receptionist but his son's big black Labrador, who quickly settled down by the reception room's central fireplace. Graves' assistant cordially ushered me into the office library. Graves was running late so I had time to ponder the impressive scale models and books of this internationally acclaimed architect which now surrounded me.

In many ways, the career of Michael Graves has been a journey through architectural "isms." In his early years, Graves was the quintessential Modernist known for his Modern "white" houses. A member of the "New York Five" (Graves, Eisenman, Meier, Gwathmey, and Hejduk), all were committed to reviving the Le Corbusian style which typified Modernism.[46] Yet Graves' now famous Portland Building shocked the architectural establishment. That office complex, as well as his Humana Building (both completed in the early 1980s), were recognized as quintessential symbols of Post-Modernism. Studying the scale models of each, I could see how their playful style, their colorful facades could be heralded as such a radical departure from cool, rational Modernism and from Graves' own previous work. Yet when I perused *Graves' Residence*,[47] the book about his Princeton home, my impression was not simply of a Post-Modern dwelling but of one that harked back to Classicism. In fact, the library bookshelves seemed largely filled with books about classical art and architecture.

Modernism, Post-Modernism, Post-Modern Classicism—changing styles, changing forms, changing use of symbols—all mark the career of the architect but in what way do they symbolize Michael Graves, the man? Graves has played a major role in reshaping the nature of architecture in the late twentieth century,[48] yet what private face lies behind the public one? To what extent has Graves' environmental story laid the actual foundation for his very public choice of styles and his own choice of home?

Suddenly Michael Graves entered the library, polite and apologetic for being late. A fit looking man in his early sixties, Graves was casually though impeccably dressed, presenting an informal yet sophisticated demeanor. Rather than being overwhelmed by the Graves persona, I found myself at ease with his soft-spoken tone. He offered me a cup of coffee and we soon settled in to begin the session.

I first asked Graves why he wanted to be interviewed. He replied that he had been intrigued by my interest in the personal aspect of architecture which seemed a little different. I explained that the sessions *would* be different from typical interviews that focused on his famous buildings, his style, etc. Instead, I explained, we were to embark upon an exploration that I hoped would be as meaningful for him as for me. That exploration would look at his environmental past, its impact on his environmental present, its implications for his environmental future. We began by exploring Graves' environmental family tree.

Although we both had gravitated to the same town, Graves' environmental roots were completely different from mine. His ancestors had come to America generations ago. The first Graves was a Presbyterian minister. His mother came from Scotch Irish stock. Some ancestors settled in Massachusetts, some went South and others went to the Midwest. Graves' branch settled in Indiana. Thus his earliest impressions of his environmental genealogy are of a Midwestern landscape:

> I remember driving with my mother once a month from our Indianapolis
> suburb to my maternal grandmother's house in rural Indiana. It was
> sixty miles away. We'd go through the city, go through the country
> roads. It was like going to Martha's Vineyard—you change your attitude.
> It had the sense of a very continuous life away from Indianapolis, a
> really rural life.

At the end of the journey was his grandmother's "wonderful" creaky old Carpenter Gothic house:

> It was an extremely pleasant house—made pleasant by my grandmother.
> There was a pump in the kitchen and dark, floral wallpaper. Always
> waiting for us was the huge Thanksgiving-style dinner my grandmother
> prepared. I can remember my grandmother telling us stories, cooking.
> It was all very loving. The stories were all about her family and they
> were all true, though we didn't know that until we grew up.

With great nostalgia and an air of vulnerability, Graves described these scenes of "gathering and conviviality," his grandmother's very loving "wrap around us" as

she regularly told them the stories about the lives of their relatives in America in the late 1880s.

By way of contrast, his paternal grandfather lived in an Indiana suburb in a more pretentious Tudor house on a quarter-acre lot:

The house was entirely different from my grandmother's house. My grandfather had a chauffeur. His job was to take care of the cars and the lawn as well. It was also his job to take the grandchildren to ride horses on Saturday mornings. That was something that pulled us together but it was more ritual than it was love. My grandfather was divorced and we were never close to his new wife.

Graves described the Indianapolis suburbs *he* grew up in as similar to any other suburb in America. All three houses he lived in there were on small plots of land with front and sides "compromised" by neighbors but with a private back garden. Graves remembers this stage of his childhood and that garden with a mixture of idealization and sardonic affection:

> *I was a pretty normal kid. When I got home from practices (football,*
> *etc.) often there was still daylight. I would go out and water the roses.*
> *I could walk out through the back door into this stupid little garden:*
> *we had a victory garden in those days. I got interested in that kind*
> *of activity—cycles of the year, watching things grow.*

His memories of his life within his home were more ambivalent. His mother also told stories as part of their family scene. Graves candidly explained that his father, an alcoholic, was gone much of the time and not a presence in the house.

Graves was forthcoming, articulate, and insightful in describing his environmental history. In an attempt to dig deeper into his early childhood memory of place, I then suggested that he embark upon the Favorite Childhood Place Visualization Exercise.[49] I asked him to close his eyes as I read him my visualization script. Graves was friendly yet firm and formal in explaining that he felt uncomfortable and did not want to shut his eyes. Instead he told me about a summer camp with interesting character but that was not really a favorite environment. However, eyes open, Graves could remember a favorite, transcendent world, the world of the Indiana stockyards where his grandfather, father and uncle all worked.

As a boy, Graves went to the stockyards with his father and became completely enamored with this place:

> *An exaggerated building with great elevated passageways all made of*
> *wood which crisscrossed in the air, more like Piranesi, though I didn't*
> *know that at the time. It was not just the passageways, but that you*
> *looked **down** on the animals in their pens. Also attached to the*
> *stockyards was a wooden bar in a kind of Western movie style—all*
> *wood. There was a character to it that I've never seen since. I went back*
> *as a grown-up but it's been demolished.*

> *For my own development, I would like to see how it influenced me.*
> *I talk about character a lot. I wasn't so aware of it when I was in*
> *school. Now I'm more aware of what that experience meant: it was*
> *dramatic. This was an exaggerated building. For me it was the*
> *recognition of the importance of character. It affected how I later*
> *came to regard Modernity—particularly its lack of breadth.*

> *Understand that I'm from a place in the Midwest without much culture,*
> *without much building. The library, the church were real buildings*
> *but they were so ordinary that you wouldn't think twice about them.*
> *The profundity of the stockyards was a result of its contrast compared*
> *to my house, school, shopping center, etc.*

Michael Graves as a Child in the Suburbs of Indianapolis.

Moving on from this vivid childhood memory, I asked Graves to complete his environmental time line:

Michael Graves' environmental time line						
Place	*Indianapolis*	*Cincinnati*	*Boston*	*New York City*	*Rome*	*Princeton*
Age (years)	0–18	18–24	24–26	26–27	27–29	29– present

Overall, Graves had spent over fifty years living in the suburbs compared to approximately nine years living in cities. As Graves' time line grew, however, the real differences that emerged were between the ordinary Midwestern landscape he left behind and the new, rich environmental experiences to which he was exposed. These new experiences of place could not have been in greater contrast to the landscape of his youth. Graves remembered the first six years he spent in architecture school in Cincinnati:

> *The experiences I had there early on were very broadening for a kid from Indianapolis. I saw everything from the way people live in the city to the suburbs. I didn't even know that people lived that way. I was in architecture school but didn't even know living patterns! I didn't even know who Frank Lloyd Wright was!*

Graves went from there on to Harvard University in Cambridge, Massachusetts to get his master's degree. He reflected on the contrast:

> *Life in Indianapolis was very easy for me, non-threatening. I didn't know any other life. It was very easy on my bicycle, on the streets with places to play in the "burbs" . . . This was swell but it had biases in that we didn't go to theater, exhibitions, galleries. We didn't travel. We weren't deprived. We just didn't do those things. Out of my class of thirty-six at Harvard, I was the only one who had never been to Europe!*

Graves acknowledged:

> *I often think if I had gone directly to Rome . . . it would have been a mistake. It was good to go from Cincinnati to Cambridge, then to New York, then to Rome. They were stepping stones to bigger, wider cultures. If it had happened more directly, there might have been a rupture in the experience.*

Perhaps Graves' biggest cultural transformation occurred at age twenty-seven when he went to Rome in the early 1960s to spend two years at the American Academy, an experience which was to have "a huge influence like something I could never imagine":

> *I first arrived in Rome in the evening and friends drove me around in a Volkswagen to all the great monuments—St. Peters, the Coliseum, etc. To see these things that you only looked at in books for years in minutes! You weren't back in the suburbs but you were almost there— you were almost in a rural setting. I was back to my roots again, but living in a big courtyard house designed by Stanford White.*

> *We had a marvelously huge studio which became our living room, workspace and entertainment space. The courtyard was extraordinarily pleasant and quiet . . .. I did an architectural design competition while I was there. I was still very much a Modernist. Modernism was still steeped in moralism—"you must do this!" I only realized when I got back here that I was going outside the bounds of Modernism in terms of color, etc. The divergence came about through reflections of my experience of Rome, the historical influence. There were also other*

influences that had to do with the domestic setting: meals at the
Academy with painters, sculptors, architects, landscape architects,
all fellows—that was an extraordinary experience. I got a short course
about all those disciplines. We were still kids. It was a very rich
experience. Enough of us did like each other that talk was always
easy. I've retained many of those friendships today.

Graves described this experience as a return to his roots yet he was in Rome not the Midwest! The roots he referred to were not literal ones. His home in Italy seemed to combine the best of suburban and city life as did his journeys from Indianapolis to his grandmother's warm home. The scene he remembered appeared a scene of total conviviality, a re-creation of the times in his grandmother's house which he had recalled so affectionately. Yet the stories told in the Rome courtyard were not wrapped in his grandmother's shawl but in the aura of art and culture that had been so lacking in Indianapolis. Graves clearly acknowledged his own development while in Rome. He was able to let go of Modernism's "moralism" and let color replace whiteness. In Rome, culture and conviviality joined hands for Graves on both a personal and an architectural level.

When Graves graduated from Harvard, he always thought that he would go back to Indianapolis, "because I knew the practices there, I thought I'd have better opportunities there and because my family was there. I never dreamed I'd get the [Rome] prize." Instead, upon his return from Rome, Graves applied to teach in all the architecture schools within commuting distance of New York City. He was offered a job at Princeton University and he has been Princeton-based ever since. Looking back he could see that in choosing Princeton, he chose to live in a suburban setting similar to the Indiana suburbs where he had spent the majority of his early life. However, this suburb offered the educational and cultural opportunities that Indiana lacked:

Although I only planned to be in Princeton for a short time teaching at
the university, my wife got pregnant and I decided to stay and build my
practice here. I liked it O.K. but thirty years ago it was a different place.
The university wasn't co-ed. Nor was it as popular as it is today. Since
then, the explosion of everything in the immediate area has brought a
kind of roundness to the town's life which is quite satisfying. It's a
university town, a commercial center with a variety of people. There's
something to be said for that. . . . Princeton is like a small, contained
city but avoiding all the negatives of a big city. It's a good base. In some
ways it's like Verona, rather insular yet manageable, though Princeton
has greater choices.

It was time to drive around the corner to see Graves' residence which I had heard and read so much about. As we were leaving, Graves made sure to say, "I enjoyed this. This was fun." He had obviously welcomed the chance to reminisce. Reminiscence of past environments was soon to become reflection on present and future environments. What I was soon to see was not just a symbol of Post-Modern Neoclassic domestic architecture but a place like home that revealed so much more.

Charles Jencks

Photograph by the author.

I had planned my trip to Charles Jencks' Cape Cod summer house carefully, leaving plenty of time to follow his directions meticulously. After an eight-hour drive north from Princeton, I turned off the highway to the Cape's local road and finally turned off again to go the last few miles to his house. I was soon lost in an unbelievable labyrinth of dirt roads that meandered in all different directions. I continued to "bear right" as he had suggested. I drove through what seemed an almost enchanted forest of oak and scrub pine. Hidden in this wild landscape I would suddenly come across one house and then another.

I had no idea what the house of this prolific architectural theorist would actually look like. He had virtually coined the phrase "Post-Modernism." Would his summer house be an amazing Post-Modern residence like his London Thematic House? A stylized, wooden, meaning-filled dwelling like his Los Angeles Symbolic House? A re-creation of a traditional Scottish castle? A new Jencksian vision not yet shared with the architectural world?

I seemed to be driving endlessly. I turned around and twice started again to try to find my way. Each time I got lost. I was getting anxious and upset: I was going to be very late. I kept going towards the ocean as Jencks suggested, "Until you can't go any further." At last I came to a dead end, to what looked like the simplest beach house "box" it was possible to imagine. After the high drama of his other residences and of my journey, it seemed impossible that this was the home of one of the world's most influential architectural critics.

I looked up and there, unmistakably, was Charles Jencks, tall and lean, bounding down the steps to greet me warmly, full of concern that I had become lost. In his mid-fifties, Jencks was casually dressed in shorts and a short-sleeved shirt. We entered this plain bungalow and settled in the equally simple living room/dining room/kitchen area. It was a relief to sit in this sun-filled room and look out over the ocean through the back windows.

Our discussions continued over that afternoon and the next two days. His environmental story led us down innumerable, rich, sometimes overgrown paths. Inevitably they all meandered back to this warm home.

Charles Jencks' American roots go back to the 1640s, when his ancestors came from England to settle in the Eastern portion of the United States. He began his story by describing his mother's side of the family:

> She came from a very feisty family, the Pearls, who emigrated from England to New England and made their living casting bells. I imagine, they were mostly farming types who led rugged lives and were often very poor . . ..

He motioned me to an old black and white photograph hanging on the wall in the hallway:

> I'll show you this picture of one of their houses. Actually it's in a museum of family homesteads, the Pearl Homestead. I believe it's 17th or 18th century.
>
> My mother, daughter of a professor, Dr. Raymond Pearl, was poor enough as a child to worry about the Depression . . ... Her father was an amazing character, who adopted the big picture of reality, the wide-screen view . . .. He was quite a famous biologist who wrote ten or more books. One of his best friends was H.L. Mencken, the polymath and journalist from Baltimore, and he and Mencken, being independent spirits, set up a still during Prohibition. When my mother came home from school their house would be giving off aromas of alcohol and could be smelled several blocks away causing her acute embarrussment.
>
> They had a "Thursday Night Club" (or some such evening ritual) where they'd invite other creative people to discuss current affairs. It was quite a literary/cultural/free-thinking club. But the house my parents lived in was probably a more conventional house in Rowland Park, a Baltimore suburb. I lived there up to the age of two so I don't remember a thing about it. My mother's father, who always wanted a male heir and was thus pleased when I came along, died when I was one.

We sat back down and Jencks began to describe a very different environmental family tree on his father's side:

> The relevant part that I remember was my grandmother, my father's mother, Eleanor Platt Jencks. She lived in this house, Number 1 Mount

Vernon Place in Baltimore, which was the number one house in that area that was looked over by a beautiful classical monument, a huge memorial column. It was really grand—now it's an Oriental museum connected to the Walters Art Gallery. My father was brought up there and I only went there to visit.

It was like an 1840s' Florentine palazzo but done in brick—Baltimore style. It had been upgraded by several families before my grandfather bought it. He was an upstanding citizen and lawyer involved in finance and property. He was twenty to thirty years older than his wife and died of a heart attack, brought on by overworking on civic affairs, when my father was eleven. This was a great sadness and obvious trauma for my father, as he told me once when we visited his summer childhood house in New Hampshire.

My father always called his way of life and morals the "Mt. Vernon Place Upbringing". That's how he referred to it—its style, its high-minded values and it meant, for instance, he was brought up never to be alone with a woman in a room. Can you imagine? He was brought up with a sense of noblesse oblige. For instance, when the Baltimore fire occurred, my grandfather hired the New York City fire department to come down to help put it out. That kind of obligation, or at least the story of it, was deep in our family. If you have the money—do it! There was no compromise. The house clearly symbolized that upbringing for him and for us.

Architecturally the interior of the house was re-designed by my great uncle who was a well-known American architect named Charles Platt. He brought up my father when his father died and influenced my father and the Mt. Vernon Place house. Platt was something of a creative Revivalist who worked in the Classical tradition, an artist and painter who believed that art was the most important thing. First he went to Paris and became an etcher or engraver; then he went to Italy and studied Italian gardens and became a landscape architect. He was so good at these things that people said "Would you design a house to go with your garden?" Thus he became an architect to the old establishment in this country. He was even given one of the biggest jobs Frank Lloyd Wright had—the MacCormack House—I say to my chagrin. Yet he wasn't a nasty or competitive man, but extremely nice and decent.

And so he formed my father's character and gave him a sense that you could be a gentleman and an artist and not compromise. The morality of not compromising with taste was strong in my father, an aristocratic value that was imbued in us. My father had integrity he got from Uncle Charles, and that's presumably why I was named Charles. But I do know my father was very affected by him.

Charles Jencks' Cape
Cod Shack (bungalow)
by the Ocean, Truro,
1977.

*As far as the house was concerned, Platt brought in the high style, the
Italian style, even a Ghirlandaio painting. For instance, one of the
rooms, the library, was a "Room of Caesars." The house had a sweeping
staircase, a wide marble staircase in front of you as you entered, and it
was surmounted by a dome made by Tiffany . . .. I can remember being
very small sitting in the big, red high-back chairs in the dining room.
It had all sorts of mysteries when I was young, as if it were haunted:
imagine this huge mansion and only one old woman there. It felt like
thirty rooms and only one inhabitant. Everything was under cloths or
sheets, so it was a bit scary.*

It seemed as if Jencks enjoyed sharing his family's environmental history with
me although he kept cautioning, "I don't think any of this will be helpful to you."
Soon his sister, Penelope Jencks, a sculptor in her own right, entered the room.
She, too, had a warm, welcoming and unpretentious manner. By then Jencks had
begun to speak about the house in Westport, Connecticut, where he moved from
Baltimore at age two and a half. He remembered the inside of the studio as having
a "grand atmosphere" with a turn of the century American Renaissance quality:
"wonderful Spanish portraits," "a mantelpiece from Italy." Yet on the outside this
studio and the main house were New England clapboard, saltbox. Jencks started
to draw a picture of the house. He remembered the garage underneath the studio

and the stone walls. Penelope helped him fill in the details, remembering a corn-field, for instance. Jencks laughed, "Oh Right! I haven't thought about this place in thirty years." Their collaborative efforts to remember continued, but soon Penelope stopped and perceptively said to me: "What you are interested in is not so much the *reality* of these places but Charles' *memory* of them." I nodded in agreement and she graciously exited, inviting me to call her if I had any further questions that needed clarifying.

In fact, Jencks had very little more to say about the Connecticut house and rapidly moved on:

> *Maybe I should just tell you that the most important house for me*
> *growing up is the house that my sister lives in across on the bayside*
> *here, the Bay House. I came there when I was a week old and have*
> *spent nearly every summer here, so my memories really are of the Cape.*
> *The house was built by my uncle, another architect, Francis Jencks.*
> *Uncle Francis was also influenced by Charles Platt and his kind of*
> *understated architecture. It's a shingle style house—a very simple plan.*

Jencks laughed, "unlike my architecture!" He continued:

> *It has all those noble aspects which Charles Platt had talked about: that*
> *a building and a garden should look like they had always been there.*
> *That was their aesthetic and it meant sobriety, gravitas and*
> *understatement. A new building should be part of history, and reveal*
> *the continuity of the place. They were against any kind of ostentation,*
> *so the house is inconspicuous except in the way it surveys the*
> *landscape and bay. You know you can't even say it's classical. It's a*
> *New England Cape Cod house, but it's done so well you might think it's*
> *an original. Yet it's not a reproduction of anything, but rather an*
> *original using the vernacular. That's where I grew up and have the*
> *fondest memories.*

Jencks had been speaking throughout with enthusiasm and with an increasing affection for all of these memories. All of a sudden he stopped, "This *is* a great subject you're into, it's always a pleasure to think about one's past." He continued:

> *The reason that my connections to my sister's Bay House are so strong*
> *is quite obvious. Summer was always a time of liberation from the*
> *work-a-day world—an enchanted, three months of freedom. I was*
> *there every June to September from the time I was one week old.*
> *The shingle-style house was finished the week before I was born—*
> *June, 1939. I lived there every summer for the first sixteen to seventeen*
> *years of my life. So that was really where my home was, psychologically.*

Jencks suggested I stop there on my way back to see how enchanting it really is.

> *When my parents had it there were very few scrub pines and none that*
> *blocked the spectacular view. They hadn't grown, so you could look out*

Jencks' family tree was a fascinating mixture of opposites: on the one hand, the wealth and opulence of his grandmother's home and the aristocratic ethos that it symbolized. On the other hand, the commitment to understatement and modesty of his father's Cape Cod house.

Sitting Room Interior—
Mount Vernon Place.

at the whole bay which came around to the left and right, in a fifty-mile semi-circle. Idyllic, spectacular, the ideal contrast of nature and culture. It was as if the whole Cape was invented for our house, and nature was protected as far as you could see. No other houses were visible. We had a kind of psychological relationship to the place which was very personal and that seemed to be permanent.

The house was simple and understated on the inside. It had framed panels on the walls for paintings. Plain floor boards of nice wood Everything was done with good materials but, as I say, there was virtually no ornament and virtually no "architecture." Just space, light, windows, and the right decisions. Everything was done for orientation, for views: how does the building face the landscape, the sun, the view? How does it work? There was a studio as well as the house and they were, like a Morandi still life, sculptural objects on a landscape: how do they relate together? They're definitely in dialogue; subtly, not brutally placed. They're positioned with respect to each other and the road. So you could say, if you want, that it had a classical relationship to the country in a way that an Italian villa does. Charles Platt brought the Italian Renaissance to America and he designed gardens that you approach through the house as its culmination. The funny thing is—apropos your interview—Michael Graves, more than me, is in the Platt tradition. He's also very attentive to the relationships between landscape and building.

In fact, we always entered the house through the back door, because Americans always enter through the kitchen. But then you went through to the "salon" and—Wham—the most beautiful view in Cape Cod! It's stunning because there is both heroic nature and scrub pine. It was the **modest** *nature that really captivated me as a five-year old because I was interested in playing around the house, with cars and little toys. Digging into the side of a hill—endless play for hours at a time, for summer after summer, playing games around the house. I wasn't interested in architecture. You know that famous remark of Walter Benjamin that architecture is "often experienced inattentively." I was just* **there***.*

Jencks stopped again to say what an interesting subject this was. He, like Michael Graves, obviously enjoyed the chance to reminisce, to remember these people and places he had not thought about for a long time.

Jencks' family tree was a fascinating mixture of opposites: on the one hand the wealth and opulence of his grandmother's city home and the aristocratic ethos that it symbolized. On the other hand, the commitment to understatement and modesty of his father's Cape house overlooking the bay. In between these extremes was the Westport house which drew from both traditions: modest on the outside, aristocratic in a few parts on the inside. But how had this environmental genealogy affected Jencks? In order to try to determine this, I asked Jencks to draw a time line of settings he had lived in throughout his life.

Charles Jencks' environmental time line					
Place	*Rowland Park, Baltimore*	*Westport, Conn.*	*N. Andover, MA.*	*Cambridge, MA.*	*London, U.K.*
Age (years)	$0–2^1/_2$	$2^1/_2–11$	11–17	17–25	25– present

Adding up years spent in each type of place, it was clear that Jencks had only spent his infancy in suburbia. The rest of his childhood and adolescence he passed in what was then the countryside of Westport and the rural setting of his boarding school in North Andover, Massachusetts. Interestingly, however, for the next thirty years he chose to live in cities, a totally different large scale setting from that of his childhood. Of course, not included here was his time spent on the Cape which, he was quick to point out, was a constant throughout. I wondered why he had chosen the city instead of the country. Jencks said practically nothing about his time in boarding school. I wondered if this experience had influenced him and asked Jencks about those years.

*The school was in a very beautiful, isolated, small area by a lake, but
for us students transported from miles away and then isolated, it
became something of a gulag. It had only three hundred people, a
monastery for rich boys. Isolation is not good for a community. It feeds
rumors, provinciality and petty despots. The architecture was New
England Repro. It was not open, an open community like Harvard.*

His memories of North Andover contained none of the affection or idealization
that his other place-memories embodied. More than ambivalence, his description
of this "closed" environment was full of loathing, and the change from there to
Harvard was a relief. Jencks gave practical reasons for moving to city environments including proximity to schools, jobs, etc. Overall he added, "I love city life
and its cosmopolitan advantages. I could live in London and not feel oppressed.
After all, as Johnson famously said, 'If you're tired of London, you're tired of
life!'"

Interestingly, Jencks had included only London in his time line, not his other
current residences on the Cape, in Los Angeles or in Scotland. I asked him which
one he really considered home, expecting him to say London. To my surprise he
commented:

*Psychologically I always think of the Cape Cod Bay House as my home.
Since I live in both places, the city and the country, I'm a typical,
hybrid Post-Modern person. No nationality—but bi-national, bi-costal,
bi-everything. I'm not either American, or English, or Scots, but
generally Anglo-Saxon.*

Jencks too, then, had come full circle to the British cultural core of his earliest
ancestors. With homes in England and America, he was in the unique and lucky
position of being able to bridge the distance between his Old and New Worlds.

Our time was up for that day. Jencks had to dash off. Before he did so, however,
he urged me again to drive by his sister's Bay House. He drew me a small map to
help me find my way.

I followed the labyrinthine road again and finally reached the house. Jencks
was right. It, too, was the simplest, gray, shingle Cape Cod dwelling imaginable.
Set back from the road, surrounded by green, overlooking the bay, the house was
in a world of its own. I knocked on the door. No one was there. I walked around
the back and came upon the equally simple studio. I put my face right up to the
window and then drew back again, startled. Inside, dominating the room was the
enormous sculptural bust of Eleanor Roosevelt, obviously a work in progress. For
a moment, in the dim light, I thought it was a bust of Caesar . . ..[50]

Andres Duany

When traveling at 65mph on a superhighway in the Florida sunshine, I always pretend that I am in a convertible, feeling that the world is a place of pure energy and possibility. My tropical adrenalin rush was even more pronounced on this February day, since I was on my way to visit Andres Duany, the current darling of the international planning world. Despite my giddiness, I tried to pay careful attention not only to the directions to Duany's Coral Gables home, but to the route along the way.

Duany and his wife, Elizabeth Plater-Zyberk, are both champions of the New Urbanism—the planning movement revolutionizing the layout and design of American towns and cities in an effort to create walkable, people-centered communities. Naturally, I was curious to see if this couple was actually living their dream. Was their home a dwelling on a small lot, set on a thoughtfully landscaped street with sidewalks leading to nearby shops and services?

Exiting the highway, I drove down a main road. The ficus trees and lush palms framing the roadside felt suburban yet the "7–11" store and *something* about the road felt urban, too. At first I sensed that I was in a middle-class neighborhood. As I drove on, though, it felt like I had crossed an almost invisible demarcation line from a middle-class area to one of upper-class enclaves—with Duany/Plater-Zyberk's street right at the dividing line. I deliberately drove past the turnoff to their street. I was early and wanted to further explore the neighborhood.

Any hopes of finding a nearby town center, a place to get a cup of coffee, diminished as I drove on.[51] Lawns were getting bigger, walls hiding larger homes loomed higher. A few minutes from Duany's street, I finally reached a graceful roundabout. Seeing only an exclusive, gated community there, I went full circle and headed back to the trusty "7–11." As I parked among the pick-up trucks, I saw and heard the first signs of local street life: the melody of Spanish-speaking customers and cashiers, reminding me that Miami was, after all, "Little Havana."

I arrived at Duany's home right on time. This simple, modest stucco dwelling displayed none of the stereotypical symbols of traditional neighborhood design. Although set on a relatively small lot and of classical feel, the home had no back alley parking, no white picket fence to walk around, no front gate to open, no front porch to pause upon before I knocked. Still, given the great success and democratic values of the Duany/Plater-Zyberk team, it was impressive that the couple had chosen to live in an aesthetically pleasing yet approachable home.

Andres Duany himself answered the door. His strong and welcoming handshake seemed to match his solid frame. It was Saturday and he was casually dressed as if to be comfortable without trying to impress. This put me at ease and I imaged a genuineness about him. His handsome, dark coloring created an aura of intensity that did not feel like nervousness but rather an intensity of energy and intelligence.

I only had a moment to divine more from this first impression of Duany before the whirlwind that was his household enveloped us. The phone was ringing. His dachshund was yapping around us. To the left was a lovely courtyard filled with tropical plants and the lean, attractive woman I presumed was Elizabeth Plater-Zyberk, talking intensely to a person seated next to her.

Duany ushered me into a simple, white dining room with a wood-beamed ceiling. The room was filled with a large, solid, Arts and Crafts style dining room table and chairs. Duany invited me to sit and I was about to introduce the concept of Design Psychology, when he was called away for a phone conference about revising Georgia's entire planning code.

He returned apologetic, speaking in an animated way to a colleague from England who was walking next to him. He introduced me to this house guest, the head of the new Institute for Traditional Architecture, who joined us briefly and then excused himself, returning to the general hubbub that was Duany's household.

Soon I began leading Duany through the Environmental Family Tree Exercise. Although his ancestors were originally from Spain, Duany's roots were firmly planted in Cuba. On his mother's side, Duany's great-grandfather had immigrated from Spain where his son (Duany's maternal grandfather) became a country doctor. His maternal grandmother was the great-granddaughter of a plantation owner, a hero who died in the first Cuban War of Independence in 1870. As a result of the defeat in the war, she had grown up in modest circumstances in an American bungalow that had been bought as a prefabricated kit from Mobile, Alabama. When she was married, her house was a "delightful French plantation house on the top of a hill" which Duany knew very well, as it had become a family weekend gathering place. The second house (in the city) of these grandparents, however, was modernist—"absolutely modernist"—according to Duany, a combination medical laboratory and residence with curving walls, horizontal windows and the parts "very nicely separated from each other."

Duany's ancestors on his father's side had been in Cuba since the 17th century, becoming wealthy within the Spanish empire. Duany explained that sophistication entered his family with his father's father, a cosmopolitan man who studied

Residence of Andres
Duany and Elizabeth
Plater-Zyberk.

in Paris. This grandfather also built a wonderful plantation house when he returned to Cuba, but his own father had later rented it out and built a modernist house. Duany obviously loved the original classical homes of his grandparents and detested their later modernist houses. He explained:

> In my mind both of these modernist houses were pretty awful, while the grandparents had marvelous houses. Both of which, by the way, were colonnaded around. One had light French metal columns. The other was heavier neoclassical. I think of myself as disappointed in having grown up in a modernist house.

According to Duany, his parents "believed in Modernism" and when they moved to Barcelona after the Castro revolution, they moved to a modernist apartment. Duany continued:

> My mother still has Danish silverware so extreme in its design that it hardly picked up food properly. Furniture that basically you couldn't use. Three-legged chairs that when you stood up, they fell backwards and their backs broke . . .. That kind of thing.

It was not that Duany was opposed to simplicity. In fact, as we sat talking around his dining room table, Duany explained:

> This room, for example, is very close to my ideal. It has a big table in it and books. Everything else is extraneous. The "room of the table." The word "simple" excites me.

As soon as he had finished talking with relish about this simple space, Duany remembered:

> [What] I forgot to say was [that] in the summer in Spain we'd sometimes rent a peasant house on the Mediterranean. I developed an admiration for the simplicity of the table in the middle of the room as the sole

furniture. Peasants don't have living rooms. They have the all-purpose
table. I thought it was really marvelous.

Thus Duany's environmental genealogy encompassed more than just the extreme contrast between the classical and modernist homes of his grandparents. In fact, rather than simply refering to the grand, classical houses of his upper-class ancestry, Duany seemed equally influenced by the more modest homes of his past. He recalled:

My grandfather built yet another country house where the family
actually used to gather on weekends [not in the plantation house where
they lived] and it had a plan very similar to this house but tropical. It
had a room probably very similar in shape to this room although it was
thatched. I'd forgotten that house completely actually but that's where I
*was most of the time. I would **look** at the other one on the hill but I was*
in the T shaped thatched house. I can draw it perfectly.

Similarly, Duany could trace back to his youth the cacophony of people and activity that I had already experienced in his Coral Gables home. In Cuba it had been a cultural tradition to have the house open to guests at all times. Thus the homes of his youth were always full of people. There were visitors several times a day. Duany turned around and pointed to the outbuilding across the patio, explaining that many people had lived in that outbuilding during the last 20 years. As his grandmother entered to offer us a cold drink, Duany explained that the first floor bedroom of his home is where she now lives. He described her contribution to his household:

I love having my grandmother here even when her friends visit. They sit
around here; my mother and three or four at a time. I get a great deal of
comfort—not so much in participating but in hearing them chatter. This
whole little hubbub. I am perfectly happy when they are all chattering
away and I am doing what I want to do. I think that must have been
something in my childhood—people, constantly conversing. The house full
of people talking and drinking coffee. Not so much meals—not people
coming over for parties or coming over for dinner—just people dropping by.

Similarly, Duany could remember with great nostalgia the stimulation of life on the streets during his youth in Barcelona. During those Franco years, the country was poor. Duany's family lived in a nice apartment but there was no tradition of hanging around in it. They were in the streets. The city was perfectly safe then. Even when Duany was thirteen or so and really had the run of the city. From his perspective, "It liberated the parents because we could take care of ourselves— They didn't have to drive us around." Duany described how

I used to spend every summer in cafes, hours every day. Doing everything in
cafes, reading, talking. You would always be out in public life. I miss that. I
would walk out of the apartment three to four times a day. Today if there
were a cafe nearby, I would just sit there and do my work. In fact, I'm quite
use to working in hubbub. I can't work when it's peaceful. I get nervous.

Andres Duany's
Paternal Grandparents'
House Built in 1907,
Now the Russian
Consulate in Vista
Alegre, Cuba.

House and Laboratory
of Andres Duany's
Maternal Grandfather,
Dr. A.M. Santos.

In Barcelona and in the villages where we spent the summer in the peasant houses, lunch, dinner and after dinner, too, was out of the house, which is what you can't do here.

It seemed clear that the importance Duany placed on the social life of spaces, on the human and walkable quality of neighborhood streets, had come from his own youthful experiences. Still, these experiences were in Europe and Cuba, not in America. Duany recognized, in fact, that he only "approximately" lives now what he and his wife practice. It was problematic for him that his house is a 15 minute walk from the town center instead of a 5 minute walk. He recognized that

We walk for exercise, but without the purpose that walking gives when a community is properly designed. If we had a town center near the house, it would be perfect.

Perhaps Duany had chosen to live in his present location because of his house rather than his neighborhood. Perhaps Duany had chosen his present dwelling because of the similarities between it and the homes of his youth which he remembered so fondly. Nevertheless Duany considered the most positive aspect of his family tree the fact that he had never lived in a conventional suburbia, an environment he described as "brutal":

> . . . The experience of driving to them is brutal . . . but once you enter these suburban houses which the American developers do so very well and Crate and Barrel furnishes—they are cocoons. People have large L-shaped leather couches with big TV sets, soft lighting, great stereo systems and video tapes and pretty good frozen food. They basically cocoon into these areas and emerge only sporadically for tasks, and when they' re young, to mixer-like environments, like extended college parties . . .. I think it's a privilege not to have been exposed to that.

Certainly such places could not have been in greater contrast to the European and Cuban environments Duany had experienced.

As this Environmental Family Tree Exercise was drawing to a close, Duany retrieved a family photo album. Going backward in time, he showed me the "wonderful" Gothic Yale buildings of his college years, his family's apartment in Spain, the modernist Cuban house, and finally indicated, "Here's the thatched roof house. It was a T-shaped building—just like this house. That's where we used to hang around on weekends with the family."

"So when you saw this and bought this house, did you associate this room with that house?" I asked.

> I loved it immediately, so it must have been familiar.

I probed further about any connections between homes of Duany's early experience of place and his present home as we began the Environmental Time Line Exercise:

"Thinking about the setting you live in now, do you feel you've chosen to live in a setting that is similar or different from the setting you experienced as a child?"

> This house is an excellent private realm from my point of view. Other houses are too big. But this is not the best public realm—when I step outside there's no comparison to Santiago, Barcelona, Paris; the public realm is very inferior. I make a distinction [between the public and private realm] because you couldn't find a house like this in Barcelona, for example. I'm asking too much, but it would be wonderful to achieve the balance.

> This house has a courtyard and I'm actually fanatic about courtyards. The privacy of the backyard is one of the things that, increasingly, we try to achieve in our towns—to force builders to build extreme privacy into their backyards. One of our projects, Windsor, achieves it. I think it's one way to achieve higher density. The reason people want big lots is it's the only method they know to achieve privacy—by increasing quantity, rather than by typology. Another way is by type with a house

that shoves itself to the edges and clears a space in the middle. I like absolute privacy in the yard and then stepping out the front door to a real public life. I think that contrast, that immediate contrast—between community and privacy is the New Urbanist ideal.

I know of certain English villages, for example, where the high street is only one building deep. You get a very intense paved urbanity on the street side and the backyard gives to the country. There are sometimes chickens back there. That's an ideal—the intensification of environments. I've lived in such places in my mind—and I'm drawn to them.

"So, why do you think that's so compelling to you?"

It could be because, as an urbanist, I think it permits both the ideal of community and of privacy that can actually achieve high density. Such conceptions have the advantages of high density—without the absence of private open space.

"Right, but I guess as you described that, it just seems like the Spanish court-yard houses that I know. There it seems to make a lot of sense."

Yeah, they're Hispanic also. I have never lived in one, but they were around me. In Santiago, for example. Well actually, to tell you the truth—this is interesting. My grandmother and grandfather lived in a perfect courtyard house when I was a child and I would visit them. I remember it! Before they moved to the house with the modernist laboratory. Well before that they had a courtyard house, a "patio" house, exactly as I'm [describing it]—present to the downtown and then a wonderful treed courtyard inside.

"So, actually rather than it being separate from your experience—"

It's actually part of my experience, absolutely.

Duany called into the next room to his grandmother to ask what year they lived in the laboratorio.
"And you could remember the 'patio'?", I asked.

Yes, I remember the "patio."

"What do you remember?"

Well, just like photographs—the surrounding columns, the trees in it—— the mango tree. It was destroyed later. It was sold to a printer, who then covered the "patio" to make a factory, so I never actually saw it after I was three years old.

"But you said you remember it."

I think that I could draw it.

Duany began to draw.

"So what have you got here?"

You enter through here and this is called the "zaguan." Bedrooms were on this side, the kitchen was here, there was a "traspatio"—a service patio in the back. I think there was a big mango tree there. This is the rest—the living room, all with really tall ceilings.

"Don't you think it's completely incredible that you remember this from when you were three?"

Yes, but not only that—I've also designed houses exactly like this. Yeah, it's incredible. I remember, remember my uncle Charles sleeping there, and I remember the dark wood, and I remember this open kitchen there. I remember and then it was gone. They moved out in '53 and it was gone.

"So when you design houses exactly like this, is that conscious?"

No. Well, of the "patio," in general, yes.

It seemed fascinating that we could trace the appeal of Duany's present court-yard house and those he designs all the way back in time to a simple home of his grandfather. As Duany completed the next "Mental Map Exercise," it also became apparent that his environmental genealogy influenced not only his sense of dwelling but of large scale place as well.

The memorable setting of his youth that Duany began to sketch was the layout of the Vista Alegre portion of Santiago de Cuba, a place in which he had lived up to the age of ten. At the center of his drawing was an oval ("very distinct") with three diagonal streets radiating off the oval. He then drew an avenue that joined the other end of the oval to the old city which contained a square and his "very big Jesuit school." Also included in the drawing was San Juan Hill, a place he was "very conscious of" as it was a national park—a place where the great battle of Teddy Roosevelt had taken place and the scene of much fighting during the 1956–58 revolution. Finally, also, Duany sketched the location of his childhood home and that of "Grandfather One and Grandfather Two." Duany recalled:

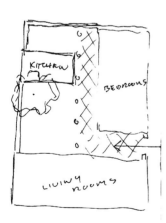

Sketch by Andres Duany of the
Courtyard of his Grandfather's House.

I was very conscious that my grandfather had laid out this part of the city—that I lived in this other part that had been laid out by my father—by my family. My father had done this part—the suburban curvilinear part in the '50s and my grandfather who'd been in Paris, laid out this City Beautiful part around 1900. They were both developers.

The oval was memorable. That was my grandfather's particular idea and he called it, for marketing purposes, a carrefour. Which of course it is not, as a carrefour means just a simple intersection in French, but he thought it sounded elegant. Everyone in Santiago called it "El Carrefour." He abused the terminology for marketing purposes.

"I can't help but notice that a dominant circle is down the road from you."

Yeah, I love that circle. I just had it measured, in fact, last week. I had to know what its dimension is. . . . I sent out two from our office and said, "Don't have yourselves killed." I have the drawings that were done last Friday.

"Why did you do that?"

Because I know that's the way a circle should work and the modern traffic engineers we work with won't draw them that way. They make them too small. So I had to demonstrate to them empirically. We've had several circles built their way in our new towns and they're always wrong. So I finally concluded that they don't know what they're talking about. This one [near me] has tremendous traffic capacity and is very easy to use. The new ones they design are very hard to use.

This is what I do. I'm a town planner—so were my father and grandfather. I grew up with this. They were developers, but they did their own urban design.

I suggested that Duany go deeper into his memory by doing the Favorite Childhood Place Visualization. Quite willing to continue, Duany declared to his family that he was creating a quiet zone for the next hour and closed the kitchen door. Soon he could recall in great sensory detail one of the triangles just off the oval of his mental map of Santiago:

It was designed as a park, but it was walled—it had a low stone wall— and at one time it was a zoo . . . and I remember seeing it as a zoo. What I smelled were the parrots.

It was a gravelly place. It was full of ficus trees inside—like the trees here, like they have here in Coral Gables. The ficus are the trees that have the roots that come down from the branches. I think the vision of these walls is what was memorable—even if they were low—that it was a walled park. Now, of course, in retrospect, in my memory it's been crossed with a lot of things—I've sort of bred it with the Coral Gables style stone walls and then the gravel is like Paris parks: maybe it was [like that], maybe it wasn't. I don't know. . . . My imagination probably made the walls higher . . . so the place was more secret, was more enclosed.

By the way, the one thing that I can never forget is that next to this . . . triangular park was my grandfather's modernist house. I remember that at that place . . . is where Fidel Castro spoke after the revolution—the only time that I ever saw him live, speaking. He was actually at the point of the triangle speaking to the people standing in the oval—and I'll never forget that. It was very memorable.

We paused momentarily, and then I asked, "Has any of this form of the large scale setting from your childhood gone into your plan for Seaside, for example?"

". . . My grandmother and grandfather lived in a perfect courtyard house when I was a child and I would visit them. I remember it! . . . I've also designed houses exactly like this."
Andres Duany

I think the interest in town planning developed naturally, probably has to do with dining room conversation, y'know over the table with Father. By the way, I arrived at this conclusion relatively recently, five to ten years ago. When my father would speak about development and, as a good son I would, of course, not be interested.

Duany laughed and continued:

But I think a lot like him now . . . I sound like him to myself. The criticisms I give developers . . . are the kind of criticisms my father would have done.

"Which is what?"

They waste a lot of money . . . that they don't really understand—not what's best for people, that's too arrogant—but what people really want.

"So are you working to change that?"

I'm fascinated by—changing the big picture, the whole thing—I mean I just can't get interested in changing one or another developer's point of view. I want to change the entire model. I think that we've figured out how to do it already and we're now beginning to get commissioned to do it. Like that call I took about writing the model code for the state of Georgia.

That's what we've been doing for twenty years: something quite similar to what my father and grandfather did, but ours is really more sophisticated. We've gone back to really sophisticated sources. After all, my father and grandfather were provincials. My father's was the Levittown in Santiago de Cuba, not the Chicago; my grandfather's was not in Paris—he had memories of Paris. We now have direct access to the most brilliant people and so we're operating at a more sophisticated level—our proposed neighborhood structure, for example, is much more sophisticated than my father's . . . and grandfather's.

Right now, I've been writing a model code that could be national—a whole new code. We're thinking it through from the beginning. It's tiring . . . it isn't just work. There's so many implications to everything involved with code writing. The way you have to play a game many moves ahead.

Glancing at his watch, Duany explained that there was a meeting he had to dash out to now—a meeting with Cuban architects who had left Castro's Cuba but who were still concerned about the preservation of Havana's fine old architecture. He suggested that I might like to come and sit in on the discussion although it would be mostly in Spanish. Fairly sure that I could keep up with the Spanish, I said, "Let's go!"

Within minutes I no longer had to *pretend* I was in the convertible doing 65mph into the Florida sunshine, I *was* in Andres Duany's silver Porche, top down, speeding toward the meeting with his Cuban colleagues. Duany explained that cars were his main indulgence. Given his energy and charisma, the luxury sports car seemed to fit with his own brand of tropical adrenalin. The combination of wind and racing engine made it difficult to hear, but I tried to listen intently to Duany's enthusiastic vision for preserving Cuban cities.

He believed that most Latin American cities were still in good physical condition as late as the 1960s but have been ruined over the past forty years. Yet Cuba's isolation meant that its infrastructure and unique architecture had merely been neglected rather than bulldozed. In the future, however, as Castro's life and regime approached a natural end, change—the opening up of the economy—seemed possible. Duany saw this as an opportunity to do things differently:

> You have this whole . . . magical situation—being able to do it right . . .
> and here I am, a Cuban planner who knows exactly how to deal with North
> American developers. I can work effectively to protect the city. We know
> the developers here, who are the ones poised to ruin it. What we're trying
> to do is write codes that are accepted by the Cuban government
> legislatively and then here, in principle, by the developers. So even if they
> don't talk to each other, at least they are working with the same templates.

We rounded a corner, parked and were warmly greeted by a small group of designers and artists, most of whom were relatively recent immigrants, who had been in the U.S. for five, ten or fifteen years. Among them was the meeting's host, according to Duany, "one of the fine old architects of Cuba," now paralyzed and wheelchair bound.

As the group began its discussions, I could not understand all the Spanish terminology. However, I could read through the draft charter the group had developed which set forth a list of principles to preserve the essence of Cuban architecture. Above all, it was easy to feel the passion and dedication these professionals felt for their homeland. After we left the meeting, Duany spoke with relish about Havana:

> First of all, it's a really fascinating city . . .. I can't tell you how interesting
> it is . . .. It's incredible—to see a city like that, of that quality, not ruined.
> It's of the quality of Washington. I mean, even San Francisco
> architecturally is not much compared to Havana. The quality is incredible.
>
> I wish that's all I had to do. That would be really a pleasure . . . but I have
> to slip it in between everything else.

Our discussions had come to a natural end for the afternoon. I would return the next day. I looked forward to learning more about ways Duany's Design Psychology was woven into his vision for changing both the world of planning and design on a national—and international—level.

Design Psychology Exercises:
The Past

You want to buy a house.

You want to redecorate.

You want to design a garden, a school, a workplace, a park, a city.

You look to newspapers, to magazines, to books, to designers, to mentors.

*And then you can look to . . . YOU, just **you** and the accumulation of all you are and all you have been and all you have the power to become . . .*

The following Design Psychology exercises are meant to help you explore your deepest sense of home and place—past, present, and future. Ideally, these exercises should be completed:

> ➤ in conjunction with reading this entire book;

> ➤ in the past, present, future sequence presented here;

> ➤ over a period of time rather than at one sitting in order to allow time for reflection between exercises.

In all cases, the exercises are suggested for use as a springboard, as catalysts for further discussion and contemplation about the relationship between one's self and place. In particular, the exercises are meant to encourage self–place growth, not to assist in delving into the emotional complexities of people's non-environmental lives. They are not intended as any form of therapy though, in fact, any discussion involving personal growth always has the potential to strike a very personal note.

With this in mind, those entering into the personal aspect of the Design Psychology process should participate only on the level at which they feel comfortable. Participants may also seek to discuss questions or issues raised by the exercises with environment/psychology professionals able to guide any conversation within the limits of that professional's own expertise, skills, and sensitivity. Overall my hope is that readers will use these exercises to become more conscious of the meaning the environment holds for them and that they will encourage all more consciously to envision and create homes and other places that express a fulfilling self–place bond.

DESIGN PSYCHOLOGY EXERCISES: THE PAST

Exercise 1   Environmental Family Tree

Embedded in the stories that our parents, grandparents or even great-grandparents told us about the "old days" are the environmental scenarios within which the drama of family histories have been played out. Though rarely examined as separate entities, the environments that our ancestors experienced will certainly have influenced their own development and environmental perspective and values. These perspectives, theses values may be communicated to us, forming our own environmental attitude and values: they represent our environmental family tree.

Your Environmental Family Tree

Drawing by Sue Williamson.

Environmental Family Tree.

Fill in this blank Environmental Family Tree by using nouns or adjectives to describe the large scale places or homes of your ancestors. These do not need to be places you have experienced; they can just be places you have heard about. The homes and places you describe can be environments of your grandparents, aunts, uncles, cousins or even friends who had a major impact on you/your family. There is no right or wrong "answer" to this exercise: you may write inside or outside the boxes. Simply do this exercise at a level that feels comfortable to you.

Reflections:

1. In what way(s), if any, did your family's environmental experiences differ from generation to generation?

2. In what way(s), if any, did the environmental experiences stay the same from generation to generation?

3. In what way(s), if any, do you think your environmental genealogy has influenced your own environmental perspective and values?

4. In what way(s), if any, do you think that influence has been positive or negative?

5. What sense of home do you want to pass down to future generations as part of your legacy of place?

6. Do you have any further reflections on how your environmental family tree may have influenced you?

Exercise 2   Environmental Time Line

Create a time line of large scale settings you have lived in from birth to present.

Example

My Environmental Time Line:

Place:	Jersey City, N.J.	Engle-wood, N.J.	Boston MA.	Hart-ford, Conn.	New Bruns-wick, N.J.	Prince-ton, N.J.	New-castle, U.K.	York, U.K.	Bever-ley U.K.	Prince-ton, N.J.
Age: (years)	0–2	3–17	18–19	20–21	22–7	28–30	30–33	34–5	36–42	43–present

Create a time line giving the names of *settings* you lived in for six months or more. Indicate your age at each particular place.

Place:
_____

Ages:

1. Looking at your environmental time line, how many years have you lived in each of the following types of setting? (Use your own sense of these places to determine whether those places are a city, town, village etc.)

2. Overall, what type of setting did you live in the most under the age of eighteen? Did you like living in this type of setting? Why or why not?

3. What type of setting (city, town, suburb, village or countryside) did you live in for the greatest period of time as an adult? If so, why do you think you chose to live in that type of setting?

4. Is there a place(s) on the time line where you lived as a child or an adult that you feel had a major impact on you? If so, why do you think that place(s) had that impact?

5. Thinking about the setting you live in now, do you feel you have chosen to live in a setting that is in any way similar or different from the settings you experienced as a child: i.e. city? town? suburb? village? countryside?

6. Are you happy living in your current setting or would you choose to move again? Why or why not?

7. Do you have any further reflections on past, present or future choice of home setting?

Exercise 3   Mental map

Draw a map of *one* of the settings (city, town, suburb, village or country setting) that you lived in *before age eighteen* that was memorable for you. The map does not have to be perfect, exact or even accurate. Just draw this place as you remember experiencing it—almost as if you were drawing a map for someone who has never been to that place and wants to visit it. Add as much detail as you remember.

What you have just drawn is a "mental map," an image of the environment as experienced by you. Kevin Lynch analyzed people's mental maps and identified five key elements of city form that consistently appeared in those maps:

> *Paths*—which provide access from one part of the city to another i.e. pedestrian or car byways

> *Edges*—those parts of the city that serve as boundaries—riverfronts, waterfronts, roads on the edge of a town

> *Landmarks*—simply defined physical objects i.e. buildings, parks, statues, often used to help people find their way around a city or to tell people where to go

> *Nodes*—serve as points in the city where there are major transitions from one activity to another i.e. railway stations, bus, airline or subway terminals

> *Districts*—relatively large areas which are recognized as having some common character

Answer the following questions using Lynch's vocabulary to analyze your larger surroundings and to become more aware of those qualities of place that are especially pleasing or significant to you.

1. Thinking about your map, what, if anything, made this setting distinctive? Did it have paths, edges, landmarks or nodes that were particularly memorable for you? In what way(s) were they memorable?

2. As an adult do you feel that any settings you chose to live in during your life contained forms (paths, edges, landmarks, nodes, districts) similar to those that appeared in your mental map? Describe any similarities or differences.

3. Does the large scale setting where you presently reside repeat elements of city form from another significant place that you lived?

4. Which, if any, of the elements of your past settings would you want to replicate or reject when choosing a place to live in the future?

5. If a designer, do you think your own design work has replicated any of the character of these forms from your childhood settings?

6. Do you have any further reflections on any connections between your image of past, present, and future settings?

Exercise 4   Favorite Childhood Place Visualization

The purpose of this exercise is to help you recall a favorite place from the past that may have influenced your present sense of home and place. This exercise can be undertaken on either a self-guided basis or guided basis—with someone reading the script below to you. Whether done on a guided or self-guided basis, participants should complete this exercise only on the level at which they feel comfortable as early memories of place are pleasant for some yet sometimes painful for others.

Self-Guided Visualization

Find a quiet place by yourself where you can relax without distraction. Listen to your breathing. Close your eyes. Make sure you are comfortable. Relax.

Try to remember a favorite place from childhood, a country or city place, an inside or outside place. Try to recall this place in as much detail as possible including what you remember seeing, smelling, touching, hearing or even tasting there. See if you can remember anything you did there or any people who experienced this place with you. Above all, remember how you felt there or what meaning this place had for you.

Guided Visualization

The following script should be read to you slowly, with pauses as indicated to allow your imagination to work in between each separate sentence.

Relax. Listen to your breathing. Close your eyes. Make sure you are comfortable. Breathe easily . . .. Begin to imagine that you are resting comfortably on a carpet . . . that the carpet is really much smaller . . . your own special carpet . . . a moving one. Feel that you are sitting on it in the middle of a huge field. Feel the carpet become magical. Let it begin to float upwards, off the ground, into the sky, higher and higher, gently, safely . . .. Look down as you move over the tops of trees, of buildings . . .. See everything become smaller as you float higher . . .. Feel relaxed, peaceful . . . happy . . ..

Now try to remember another favorite place—perhaps a place you have not thought about in a long time. Some favorite place from childhood, a country or city place, an inside or outside place . . .. Decide that you want to go there and feel your carpet slowly move you through the clouds, further . . . and further until you can see the paths/roads leading to that place . . .. Float down further following above the path. Land softly in front of your favorite place. Step off your carpet and walk into your place.

What do you see there? . . . Look carefully all around . . .. Notice the colors . . . the shapes . . . the textures . . .. Look at the different things there . . .. Notice one small thing . . .. Walk towards it . . .. Pick it up if you want to. How does it feel? . . . Put it down . . .. Walk on to a comfortable spot and slowly sit down . . .. What do you hear there? Listen! . . . Remember the smells around you . . .. Feel relaxed . . . peaceful.

Now imagine getting up. Do anything in that place that you used to do there . . .. Say something to that person . . .. Have them answer . . .. Be alone again. Then, only if you want to, change something in that place as if with no effort— add something, take something away, or leave it all as it is, whatever feels right. . . .

Now look carefully around once more . . .. Walk back out of your place. Walk towards your carpet again . . .. Move carefully on to it.

When you are ready, have the carpet move again. Slowly begin to float up towards the sky. Higher and higher . . .. See your favorite place below you becoming smaller . . . smaller . . . smaller . . .. Move on through the sky. Reach out and touch a cloud. Move through it. Look down and see the buildings below again. Trees, cars . . .. See this place . . .. This room . . .. Float slowly down . . .. When you are ready, open your eyes.

After you have completed the self-guided or guided visualization, answer the following questions:

1. Were you able to remember such a place from childhood? If so, reflect on what you remembered. Take a few minutes to draw or write about the favorite place you visualized. There is no right or wrong to this exercise. Include whatever helps you re-create the quality of that place: the shapes, color, textures, objects, people, etc. that you remembered. Above all, reflect on the meaning of that place for you and why you chose that place to remember.

Drawing/reflections:

2. Think about any ways that past favorite environment resembles some environment in your present life. Are the feelings you experience in this present place similar to any feelings you had in your favorite place from the past? Draw/write about this present place.

Drawings/reflections:

3. If you are a designer, are there environments you have designed that repeat the qualities of this favorite past environment? If so, in what way(s)?

4. Are there elements of this past environment which you have not incorporated in your home or in your designs but which you would like to incorporate?

5. Any further reflections on the influence of this past favorite place upon your present and/or future sense of home and place.

CHAPTER 2

The
Present

Resounding Echoes

My realtor [estate agent] has shown me at least twenty-five houses and none of them has come close to what I want. She's started to do a weekly computer search and sends me the description and photograph of any house that looks promising. I've amassed a virtual collection of split levels, condominiums, and ranches! How do I begin to look beyond this 2-D paper to find a 3-D home that feels well-rounded and whole?

In adulthood, as we enter into the actual and not just the poetic search for home, we can continue to use Design Psychology to guide us in that search. Our book of remembrances of places past need not be simply left on the shelf of childhood memory. Our place–self connection endures and grows beyond childhood. Thus we can read the chapters already written about our past and then *read on* as our self-place story continues to unfold in the present.

In doing so, it is helpful to look again at theory in order to understand the nature of adult growth. There are innumerable psychological theories postulating models of healthy adult growth. However, the work of the renowned humanistic psychologist Abraham Maslow has proved particularly rewarding for many who probe the self–place connection within the realm of Design Psychology.[1]

For Maslow the child's natural curiosity to find out more about the all-absorbing world around them changes as they grow into adulthood. He believed that the adult wants to know more about the *meaning* of the world beyond its physical reality. As a humanistic psychologist Maslow believed that it is possible for people to examine their deepest human values in order to realize their fullest potential. According to Maslow, we are all motivated to achieve this fulfilling, psychic wholeness in order to become what he called "self-actualized" human beings. Maslow's description of the self-actualized person's experience of the world sounds remarkably familiar:

> Self-actualized people have the wonderful capacity to appreciate, again and again, freshly and naively, the basic good of life, with awe, pleasure, wonder, and even ecstasy, however stale these experiences may have become to others . . . thus, for such a person, any sunset may be as beautiful as the first one, any flower may be of breath-taking loveliness, even after he has seen a million flowers.[2]

Such words seem to echo the transcendent connection to place referred to by Bachelard, Cobb, and Chawla. Yet how do we achieve this existential connection to place in adulthood?

Maslow's theory suggests that whether consciously or not, we are all motivated to become self-actualized individuals. He believed that this can only happen once we have satisfied a hierarchy of human needs. Maslow's classic hierarchy includes the following pyramid of needs which must be met in order to climb toward self-actualization.[3]

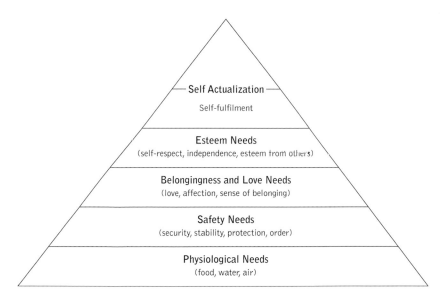

Needs at the bottom of this hierarchy must be met before the individual can progress toward the peak of self-actualization. Maslow included shelter at the very base of this pyramid. Thus he emphasized the vital role of the environment as part of the very foundation upon which future satisfaction is built.

Just as we can move up Maslow's hierarchy in personal terms, so, too, can we move up the hierarchy in terms of home/environment. With this in mind, Maslow's hierarchy can be adapted to create a pyramid of *housing* needs as follows:[4]

According to this model, "home as self-actualization" can be reached once other levels of housing needs have been satisfied including the need for:

➤ **Home as shelter**—home as a structure that meets our basic physical needs including our need for safety and protection;

➤ **Home as psychological satisfaction**—home as an arena that meets our need for self-expression, for sharing feelings of love and belonging;

➤ **Home as social satisfaction**—home as a place that meets our needs for privacy, independence and freedom as well as allowing us to achieve dignity as part of community;

➤ **Home as aesthetic satisfaction**—home as a setting for experiencing the pleasure of beauty.

Potential homeowners often refer to the need to buy a house in order to "get one's feet on the housing ladder," to buy a house that can then be sold for a profit in order to buy a more expensive house closer to one's "ideal home." Climbing the ladder of "home as self-actualization" does not necessarily involve homeownership or even the purchase of a single family dwelling. Home-self actualization may be achieved when owning a palatial mansion, renting an apartment, or staying at a commune! Home achieved in the fullest sense implies not only a satisfying of physical needs but of deeper existential needs as well.

How do we climb the rungs of this deeper home-self ladder? How do we achieve home as shelter, home as psychological, social, and aesthetic satisfaction?

> *The choice to move back to America after my divorce involved a giant*
> *leap of faith. I needed to find a job, to find a house, and to rebuild my*
> *life. I needed to conquer my fear that I wouldn't be able to provide basic*
> *shelter and security for my children, never mind provide them with*
> *feelings of love and belonging. To overcome this fear I imagined that the*
> *children and I were on a tiny sailboat crossing the Atlantic. There were*
> *many storms. I kept my hand firmly on the rudder. We landed safely on*
> *American shores. I began to build.*

My fears of homelessness were only temporary, but millions of homeless people live permanently without a roof over their heads. Their very basic need is for *home-as-shelter*. The contrast between those seeking housing and those able to establish house as home can be great. The aim of people on the bottom of the economic ladder can be simply to

> . . . Find a house or apartment that will provide safe shelter, in other words, adequate room for sleeping, relaxing, and eating and a haven from noise, odors, dirt and interpersonal violence and abuse . . .. Only in the advanced working class and in the middle class does one find a more elaborate conception of the house as a private domain that offers opportunities for recreation and expressive self-fulfillment and a stage for the display of affluence.[5]

The lack of freedom to carve out a true home place that symbolizes and affirms one's selfhood has emotional as well as physical consequences. Those living on the margins come to believe that ". . . the environment is threatening more than it is rewarding—that rewards reflect the infrequent working of good luck and that danger is endemic."[6] Thus perhaps most psychologically devastating for individuals in this position is the sense that they have no choices, that they are not able to affect the environment in any way: "their physical world is telling them they are inferior and bad just as effectively perhaps as do their human interactions."[7] Faced with this environmental assault on their self-esteem, it would seem impossible for anyone without permanent shelter to become a "whole" person.

In a sincere attempt to offer a solution to the environmental aspect of such crisis, in the 1960s architects and planners erased vast neighborhoods of substandard housing and replaced them with soulless high rises. Although full of good intentions, this policy led cities down the road to housing hell. Rationally, objectively, such urban renewal appeared to provide secure and safe housing. These houses, however, were never considered homes by those who lived there. Such modern high rise symbols of progress held no meaning for inhabitants who felt cast adrift from the past associations that had been embodied in their more traditional homes. Improved plumbing could not replace the network of friendships and communities that was disrupted and lost. Years later, the predominant image of such failed housing was the dynamiting of these abandoned buildings to make way for the construction of more people-centered environments.[8] Design professionals underestimated people's need to live in places where they feel not only physically safe but secure in their attachment to home.[9]

How could architects and planners go so wrong? Traditionally we have seen it as the architect's responsibility to create a shelter that is house but can also be home. However, the majority of architects who have built our dwellings have been trained to consider house as shelter and/or sculptural structure. Thus the deeper importance of the relationship between dweller and dwelling may be lost.

> *I've stopped in the middle of writing this chapter to view a house for sale around the corner. Described as a "delightfully different ranch in a picturesque setting," it seemed to meet all my requirements: it was in the price range I could afford, in my neighborhood, and had three bedrooms, a living room, kitchen/dining area and two bathrooms. I was delighted to find that the house backed on beautiful woods and a stream. In my mind's eye I could envision my children virtually living along the stream, exploring this "big woods" as I had done in Englewood.*
>
> *I visited the house for the second time during a torrential rainstorm. Water was leaking through a bedroom ceiling and seeping into the basement right on to the fuse box!*

House as shelter *is* of utmost importance and should by no means be disregarded. Instead, it should be seen as only one of a hierarchy of housing needs which people seek to satisfy. I was searching for a place that provided shelter and security while also meeting my need for *home as psychological satisfaction.* Unlike Jung, though, I was not in the position to *build* a home that nurtured physical security and psychic wholeness. Instead I simply hoped to select a house that was safe and secure *and* came as near as possible to reflecting my own self–place connection.

> *Frightened by the condition of this last house, I've reviewed my library of house descriptions to find something in better shape. I've made an appointment to see a three bedroom condominium. The condo complex is only three years old, so it should be in good condition. It also would be a relief not to have to worry about mowing the lawn, painting the outside of the house or having to continually fix things in an older property. But, can I really see myself living amidst a sea of mass produced housing so reminiscent of the homogenous neighborhood of my childhood? Is this really me?*

According to Cooper Marcus, such a reaction against mass housing is not unusual. She observes:

In the contemporary English-speaking world, a premium is put on originality, on having a house that is unique and somewhat different from the others on the street, for the inhabitants who identify with these houses are themselves struggling to maintain some sense of personal uniqueness in an increasingly conformist world.[10]

The condo was much as I imagined it. It had a bright, white open space living room and dining room complete with cathedral ceiling. Included was a fireplace, a dishwasher, three bathrooms and a whirlpool tub—an instant home with all the modern conveniences. Yet somehow it didn't feel like home. It seemed more like American "hotel modern" sending messages of a life of comfort and luxury prepackaged, as if stamped out of a mold—a mold that had nothing to do with my self-image.

If such a house did not fit my image of home and self, what type of house *would* allow for such self-expression? Should I re-create my early experience of dwelling and buy a split level reminiscent of my childhood home in Englewood? I went to see a split level for sale around the corner and felt like I was visiting a ghost. I could not go back to *this* home again, so filled with mixed memories, so synonymous with the conventional life which I had rejected. Reproducing my childhood home in every detail was not the answer.

My self-image seemed more unconventional, revolving around a life in the arts and of ideas rather than of material pursuits. Thinking back to Englewood again, I remembered a nearby neighborhood where many academics and artists lived. Set in a horseshoe type street, houses there had a straightforward, modern design. My favorite cousins lived there, too. I remembered loving not only the simplicity of their home's exterior but the simplicity of its interior with natural wood-beamed ceilings and huge expanses of glass. Yet these houses, too, were mass produced and suburban. Was there something about the *character* of these houses that reflected my own personality?

There has been little specific research on the connection between personality and place.[11] However Jung developed an entire theory of *Psychological Types.*[12] According to Jung, everyone has a unique personality type, although one personality can also include aspects of other types as well. Jung believed that different psychological types relied upon some combination of sensing or intuition and thinking or feeling in order to make sense of the world:[13]

Type		Characteristic
Sensing (S)	=	Practical
or		
Intuition (N)	=	Innovative
Thinking (T)	=	Objective
or		
Feeling (F)	=	Personal

Thus according to Jung, a person may be one of four different types including sensing plus thinking (ST), sensing plus feeling (SF), intuition plus feeling (NF) or intuition plus thinking (NT).

Considering Jung's theories in terms of environmental psychology raises the question, "Are some people more predisposed to certain environments depending upon their personality?" As I continued the process of Design Psychology, I did a variation of the Personality and Place Exercise (see Exercise 4 below) by taking a personality test based on Jung's personality type theory. I scored as a "sensing feeling" person with my *feeling* mode predominating. I could appreciate why the warmth of the wood of Englewood's artists' houses appealed to me.

Similarly, I scored as slightly more of what Jung called an extravert (E), a sociable, outward turning person rather than an introvert (I), a more private, inward turning person. There is some evidence that extraverts require a higher level of environmental stimulation than introverts.[14] Thus the extravert may be happiest in places where contact with people is available or encouraged. The introvert, on the other hand, tends to be more territorial and requires private places to work alone, read, meditate or simply be with few or no people.[15] If one were to draw the ideal houses for an extravert versus an introvert, such designs might reflect the nature of the extravert's need to open outward, the introvert's need to preserve and explore inward territory. As an extravert I could see why the Englewood "artists' " house had appealed to me: windows opening out on to the world, a round horseshoe setting that drew neighbors together.

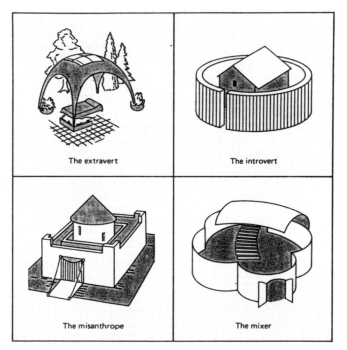

The extravert

The introvert

The misanthrope

The mixer

Reprinted by permission.

Four Designs to Suit Four Distinct Personalities

When assessing the degree to which we wish to open out to or withdraw from the world around us, we are not simply talking about the need for stimulation, we are also asking, "How connected do we want to be to those around us?" On a deep level this question resonates as part of the process we began at birth—the process of defining our relationship to the outer world. Early attachment, especially to mother, must eventually give way to healthy separation if one is to develop toward mature adulthood. As environmental psychologists Altman and Chemers suggest,

> A person who is successful at regulating openness/closedness not only comes to know where he or she begins and ends but also is able to develop a competence at controlling life events. If a person . . . is consistently more lonely and isolated than desired, or if a person cannot prevent intrusion . . . then it is hard to see how that person can have a clear sense of self.[16]

Thus when climbing the ladder to home as self-actualization, one must not only select a home that expresses our individuality, but one that allows for satisfying relationships with others. How can such *home as social satisfaction* be achieved? What *is* appropriate distance between self and others in environmental terms?

The very term *personal space* has become familiar for describing one's need to maintain appropriate distance. Personal space can be defined as "an invisible boundary surrounding us, into which others may not trespass. It moves with us, expanding and contracting according to the situation in which we find ourselves."[17]

In his now classic book, *The Hidden Dimension*, anthropologist Edward T. Hall identified four spatial zones that typify human interaction including *intimate distance* (0–$1\frac{1}{2}$ feet), *personal distance* ($1\frac{1}{2}$–4 feet), *social distance* (4–12 feet) and *public distance* (more than 12 feet).[18] In Hall's terms, appropriate distance meant expanding or contracting one's "space bubble" depending upon whether one was making very personal contact, interacting with close friends and everyday acquaintances or conducting informal or formal business.[19]

> *I've just gotten the details on a nearby house that sounds great. It has four bedrooms, a living room, dining room, kitchen, study and two bathrooms. If there is anything my family needs right now it's space. My daughter's tiny room has only enough space for her bed and dresser. My bedroom is doubling as a study with my books and notes for this manuscript piled up everywhere. We're falling over one another. A four bedroom house sounds like heaven!*

The need for people to maintain different degrees of spatial distance is made visible when people define *territory* inside and outside of the home. Territories, too, make a statement about our need to be both connected as well as separate from those around us.

Those of us who share a house with others face the issue: what is the place for me within these four walls versus the place for my roommate, spouse, sibling, partner, children and/or lodger? Even those who live alone make important decisions about sharing their home environment with the outside world: Do I want to live near people or keep more to my self? Will I encourage visitors? If so, where will I entertain them or put them up?

How do we establish appropriate boundaries between self and others within our dwellings? Just as there are different degrees of personal space, so there are various territories that can be established within a home. Researchers Sebba and Churchman have suggested that such territories can include, for example:[20]

1. *Individual space*—space, which belongs to each person alone, where privacy can be maintained, such as in a private study or workshop;

2. *Shared space*—space belonging to a sub-group within the family (i.e. parents or children) such as a playroom or parents' bedroom;

3. *Public space*—space belonging to all of those within the home and to outsiders as well, such as the living room or kitchen.

Interestingly, as with favorite childhood places, it has been suggested that the most satisfying homes allow for *control* of territory by the individuals who live there.[21] Of key importance may be that *all* of those sharing a house have the opportunity to establish private as well as shared and public spaces in a way that meets everyone's needs equally. Yet, especially in homes plagued by overcrowding, there may be no opportunity to choose private places. The implications of lack of privacy should not be overlooked for

> . . . every corner in a house, every angle in a room, every inch of secluded space in which we like to hide, or withdraw into ourselves, is a symbol of solitude for the imagination; that is to say, it is the germ of a room, or of a house.[22]

Inevitably, however, people's power to establish places for themselves within the home is reliant upon both human and design factors. Much depends both upon the dynamics of the people living within the home and the configuration of the home itself.[23]

> *I've just gone to see the four bedroom house for sale. It is in excellent condition, with lots of space. I have a gut feeling that this is the house for me.*

Continuing the process of Design Psychology, I completed the Environmental Sociogram Exercise (see Exercise 6 below). Thus I translated the floor plan of this house in my mind's eye to imagine how the space would allow for individual, shared and public space for my family. Floor plans are traditionally labeled functionally, yet such functional labels often have no bearing on the way home territory really is used by its inhabitants.

> *In terms of **individual space,** this would be a great house: the children could each have their own room upstairs. I could have my own bedroom*

downstairs. I love my kids and like to be with them, yet I also need time and space for myself.

*In terms of **shared space**, the kids could be on an "all-kids" floor. They are already fairly close and I hope that being together upstairs could help cement this bond. They could decide together how to use the open space in front of their rooms: an animal corner? a games corner? an art area?*

*In terms of **public space**, there is enough room to accommodate a variety of uses. The family room seems a nice open area for our cozy couch and TV—a place for us all to cuddle up together. The living room could then be the more formal room for visitors. The room adjacent to the living room has double doors: perfect as a study—door closed when concentrating, door open when just playing computer games together.*

Still I'm not sure where the real core of this house is—I'd miss having what I had in Beverley, a fireplace and eat-in kitchen with a table to gather around and story tell together.

The way that space is actually used must be negotiated between those sharing the home. While some dwellers may be trained designers, rarely have any of us received training about how to negotiate, together, ways to transform a house into a shared home.[24]

People often discuss and make decisions on a practical level about such basic issues as the function of individual rooms. However, the meaning and the vision we have for the entire home more often than not remain undiscussed and unexplored. Yet it is this meaning and vision that may drive the decisions that we make about our home environment. Often it is our individual environmental autobiographies that forge this meaning and vision. Clare Cooper Marcus explains:

Creating a home together may be one of the most taxing negotiations any couple has to make. Each person brings to the situation a history of environmontal experiences dating back to his or her first awareness of home in infancy and childhood. Each has—largely subconsciously—created a set of spatial and aesthetic preferences that will influence feelings about a range of issues about home including location, size, form, style decoration, furnishings, privacy, territory and use.[25]

Just as a house may be a symbol of self, so it also may be a symbol of the dynamics between the people that inhabit it.

Bill, a New Jersey architect, and I had been seeing each other for about a year. Each weekend he would come to Princeton or the children and I would go to stay in his house in Newark, N.J. As my house hunt became more focused, we began to discuss where our relationship was going and whether or not we wanted to live together—whether I should buy a house at all. He wanted me to move up to Newark.

I thought about his Newark house and could see that it really was a symbol of him and the relationship between us:

The house was classically handsome, an all white Greek Revival mansion built at the turn of the century. Passers-by regularly stopped their cars in front of the dwelling to admire its charisma and power. On the inside there was a generosity, sensitivity in every detail, a truth in materials that was astounding: carved mahogany moldings, original Tiffany windows, a huge stone fireplace. I loved just lying by the fire for hours and enjoying the depth of all this that surrounded me.

Overall, however, the house was dark. There were more rooms there than I was able to count or keep track of. My children loved running through those rooms bringing noise and light to the house. In return the house was big enough for each of them to have a palatial weekend bedroom and they imagined themselves the prince and princess there.

The children were always wary about exploring the third, attic floor—it seemed too remote and mysterious. Although I never admitted it, I too was scared to climb up those creaky winding steps. I went up there once, looking for Bill late one night. I got frightened and turned back. Perhaps in a few months I would go up there again in daylight, open that last bedroom door to have a good look in.

I loved Bill and so did my children but there were parts of him that were very complex, hard to understand, and which I was reluctant to explore. Some of the differences between us and between our differing perceptions of home emerged as he began to do the Design Psychology exercises.

Bill also had grown up in a middle class, split level, suburban New Jersey home. Surrounding him were not only leafy streets, but the impressive mansions of the town's wealthy inhabitants. What he enjoyed most was the (now developed) rural aspect of this suburbia. In fact his mental map of home place showed mostly green open space. There was a life, a character to that green space which Bill could still remember: he could recall the nearby horse farm and a lake which was a landmark amidst the green. The woods contained bears. A wall separated his "own" home territory near the woods from that of the bears.

Yet as his time line illustrated, although he had spent most of his childhood in the suburbs, he spent most of his adult life in the city. In explaining this choice, he spoke of his dislike of "the social rigidity of middle class suburbia." By way of contrast, he enjoyed living in the city because of the diversity of people and places there.

Digging deeper, we began to explore his *favorite* home places from his past. Bill's memories, however, were mostly negative memories of an unhappy childhood. Home for him was a place to be avoided, to escape from. Escape meant spending hours with a friendly, welcoming neighborhood family, and swimming in their backyard pool. His friends included not just the sons and daughters of the town's wealthy whites but the African American cooks from local downtown restaurants. These friends opened their back alley kitchen doors to give Bill what he needed most: kindness and food.

Like all of us, Bill reworked—replicated and/or rejected—his childhood experience of place to create an adult place that felt some place like home. He also chose to live in a mansion like those of his wealthy childhood neighbors. Yet *his* mansion is set in a largely African American city, not an "idyllic" white suburb. Nevertheless, the mansion is in the suburban section of Newark, one block away from a green open space park and lake reminiscent of his childhood environment. In his backyard Bill built a swimming pool, a place where the children and I (and many others whom he welcomed) spent endless happy hours. Surrounding this space he built a giant wall to mark this private backyard and defend it against the "city bears"—the noise and activity beyond his territory.

I could imagine us living in Bill's house. After all my grandparents, too, had ended up with such a mansion. But did I want to live in a city? I had already made so many friends in Princeton's small community. Newark was also a city in a constant state of crisis. I was struggling to bring shelter and security into my life and the lives of my children. Did I really want to move into an environment where issues of basic survival would surround us daily? Bill reminded me that pain and struggle, cruelty and violence exist not just on city streets but behind suburban doors.

. . . pain and struggle, cruelty and violence exist not just on city streets but behind suburban doors.

How do we establish healthy relationships not just within a dwelling but outside of it as well? Seeking to regain a sense of community, many cities replaced their doomed high rises of the 1960s with low scale housing designed on the principles of "defensible space" outlined by Oscar Newman in the 1970s.[26] Newman argued that strongly defined, semi-private spaces engendered feelings of "ownership" of territory thereby encouraging a sense of community and discouraging crime since such areas became "controlled" by residents.[27] Thus he suggested including semi-private spaces in the design of social housing: the designing of all spaces as if they appear to "belong" to someone.

Seeking their own solution, many other urbanites simply "took flight" from the city and moved to the suburbs imagining that they would find friendly, intimate, safe neighborhoods and communities there. Yet architect Christopher Alexander has also challenged this image, suggesting that increasingly in our society, in cities and suburbs, we have lost intimate contact—the vital, close contact between two people in which "they reveal themselves in all their weakness, without fear."[28] He lamented a growing introversion, what he called an "autonomy-withdrawal syndrome".[29] According to him, this syndrome is caused by the stress of our society and the lack of "association and cooperation" that characterized pre-industrialized society. Alexander believed that increasingly:

. . . when people get home, they want to get away from all the stress outside. People do not want to be perpetually exposed; they often want to be withdrawn. But withdrawal soon becomes a habit. People reach a point where they are permanently withdrawn, they lose the habit of showing themselves to others as they really are, and they become unable and unwilling to let other people into their own world.[30]

In his landmark book *A Pattern Language*,[31] Alexander suggested revolutionary new patterns of design that he felt could restore intimate contact between people. Such radical rethinking about the way we plan our cities and towns has inspired others such as the New Urbanists to offer alternative patterns of urban planning. Hailed as "the most important phenomenon to emerge in American architecture in the post-Cold War era,"[32] the New Urbanism is responsible for the spread of small town type developments throughout the United States. Hoping to restore our sense of contact and community, such developments are characterized by a high level of density, by shops, schools and recreation that are within walking distance and by porches, stoops and balconies which help "animate" the street.[33]

However, this approach has also been criticized by many as an artificial creation of community that does not really address long term issues of community building in the fullest sense.[34] Nevertheless, despite criticism, all such attempts to architecturally determine social relationships have been influential and contain practical wisdom. As with our life-long struggle to carve a place in the world, such healthy carving inevitably seems best achieved when people themselves take control of their environment. In Newark, for example, the work of the New Community Corporation, a community development agency, seemed to me to represent a more holistic example of the way the lives of people *and* their environments can improve together.

Guided by this ethos of self-determination, New Community Corporation does not simply rely on an outside developer to reconstruct Newark's *physical* community. They built their own housing, nurseries, old age homes, etc. They re-open and run supermarkets and stores previously shut down and abandoned by big national chains. They train and provide jobs for hundreds of people in the city of Newark. They build community in the widest possible sense.

When New Community was started thirty years ago by one parish priest, Father Bill Linder, there were only a few such neighborhood-based developments in existence. Now there are roughly two thousand such groups where, "Like farmers raising a neighbor's barn, people in impoverished areas throughout the country are uniting, applying for loans and grants, and supervising the building or renovation of their own development."[35]

Although I had come to love Newark and had total respect for Bill's contribution in building that community, I still felt more comfortable in the suburban setting of my childhood. Bill had considered moving to Princeton, but it reminded him too much of his unhappy childhood home. His life and sense of home were very much tied to Newark. The weeks were going by and I had to live somewhere! I made an offer on the four-bedroom house, but worried about what this would mean for the future of our relationship.

I drove by my potential home many times while waiting to see if my offer would be accepted. Each time the choice of this place felt right: the house was a very simple modern design, set in a horseshoe with many other houses encircling it. It had large windows all around. I could see inside to the wood-beamed ceilings as I drove by. The image of my favorite Englewood cousins' past home and my present image of self merged in this house.

"PAST" House of
Author's Cousins
Forty Years Ago.

Photograph by the author.

"PRESENT" House Envisioned by the
Author as her Future Residence.

Photograph by the author.

Michael Graves

Michael Graves politely escorted me to his black Mercedes. Loki, the dog, suddenly appeared again, followed us and jumped excitedly into the back seat. Although we drove around the corner, Graves' office and house are so close to one another we could easily have walked. Instead, we turned down an un-remarkable suburban street and made a sharp turn in between two nondescript houses on to a long, narrow driveway. As we approached what I saw was Italy in Princeton, a simple, warm terracotta building, a form in total contrast to the conventional houses that surrounded it.

We parked and Loki jumped out of the back seat to wait dutifully in the warm yet formal courtyard in front of Graves' residence. Graves rewarded her with affectionate pats and opened the front door. Once inside, the beauty and drama of this place did not disappoint. Graves had spent the last twenty years completing this home. It had the feel of a museum with beautiful objects all around. Much of the furniture was in the Biedermeier style—"restrained, inventive, Classical"[36]—which has become associated with the Graves' style. Furniture and objects seemed meticulously chosen and placed.

Graves asked me where I wanted to sit. I hesitated. I wanted to choose a place where we would be most comfortable but was not sure where that would be in this studied environment. I left the decision to him and he seated us in the break-fast room, a room previously described by him as done in "American convivial."[37]

I began by asking Graves what his reaction was when he first saw this building.

*Several things. It was a ruin. (There aren't any ruins in Princeton!) It had a Hadrian's Wall quality about it. It had a characteristic that was definitely **not** Princeton. It was a ruin, but not a Disneyfied version of a ruin. It had a certain integrity. It didn't seem to be styled. I found out later why that character came through: it was built by Italian masons. They built it as a Tuscan warehouse, a Tuscan **barn**. I say Tuscan because it had these characteristics of lots of surface, small windows. Its character was almost shocking to find in Princeton but something I already admired.*

In fact, the warehouse was originally built as a furniture repository for Princeton University. As such, the interior had forty-four rooms but none more than 10 feet long.

It also appealed because it was a sizeable, big building. Once the interior partitions were removed, the shell could be retrofitted very easily. It was large enough that I thought I might have an office in it as well as my residence.

I was surprised to find that at this earlier stage of his life, Graves had been struggling just to make ends meet:

I was thought of as a gifted, talented architect, but I couldn't pay my bills. It was hard getting commissions and I didn't make money in the practice. Part of the appeal of this place was that it was so large and cost only $30,000 to buy. At the beginning, I lived in the kitchen. It had no drawers, no cupboards—just boxes, a counter and some plywood shelves.

In the book *Graves' Residence*, he referred to the warehouse, saying, "It became the great issue of my life to get it finished." I asked him why this was so.

I couldn't even afford a kitchen! I thought something is wrong with this picture if I can't get the artistic side to pay for itself. I couldn't have managed any more negativity in my life—if my kids had gotten sick, or something like that I would have worried about how to pay for that. I wanted to get it right so I hired a financial person to help.

This proved a positive step in Graves' eyes. The security that he was able to establish via his business provided him with the resources to transform the warehouse from a makeshift shelter into a home.

Yet, just as he struggled to complete his architectural projects, so he also struggled to stabilize his personal life. Graves' first marriage to Gail ended in divorce even before he had purchased the warehouse. Graves then married Lucy and together they discovered this commercial building and started down the long road to turning domestic vision into reality. Sadly, the personal underpinning of this vision collapsed as Graves and Lucy also divorced.

Thus inevitably embedded in that transformation of his house as shelter was the personal, psychological transformation Graves would undergo in giving the house expression. In a 1983 interview with Charles Jencks, Graves spoke about the toll the stress of his work had taken on his personal life:

CJ: It makes being married to you difficult?

MG: It makes it impossible, you know; that's the greatest dilemma in my life. I want a family, I don't want to spend Christmas alone.

CJ: Apart from that there's the question of a change in approach, a change in style with a change in marriage and it strikes me that when you were married to Lucy, roughly between 1972 and 1977, there's a slight change in your architecture. With [Frank Lloyd] Wright you can see the influence of personal traumas, often in a very creative way. It's as if the change and growth in his architecture and personality is somehow connected with the change and growth in relation to women and the outside world. I'm not advocating polygamy; I'm trying to look for relationships between private life and public architecture."[38]

Thinking about this relationship, Jencks commented on the changes he had observed in Graves' architecture during the time of the architect's second marriage: "Slowly, tentatively, more conventional elements are introduced into his repertoire: the emphasis on the hearth, window and door, the molding used as a scaling device to divide up the wall, the voided keystone, the semantic use of colour. The painted murals take up these themes also."[39]

The greatest issue in Graves' life was finishing the warehouse; his greatest dilemma was wanting a family. The two visions seemed to be mutually incompatible. I wondered if Graves had been able to work through his own personal story to actualize both his home and his personal life.

We turned again to examine Graves' history to see if there were themes from the past that had continued to guide his growth in the present. I referred Graves back to his own environmental autobiography and asked him to comment on any ways his past environmental experiences were reflected in this present home:

The relationship of this house to the ground is something that is a discovery for me. It is something that I had in Indianapolis. I'm on the ground in both places. In New York I was on the twelfth floor. It's a big difference.

Graves went on to describe wistfully time spent in his present garden, seeming to yearn back to those times spent in the garden of his boyhood:

. . . I have so little time. Even this morning I thought: I went out at 8:00 a.m. and came back with some ivy to get it to grow vertically on the fence rather than fall over. I need to spend eight to ten hours a day doing that. I don't have eight to ten hours.

Photograph by Marek Bulaj. Courtesy Michael Graves, Architect.

Breakfast Room,
The Warehouse, Princeton, N.J.

This garden, like the one in Indianapolis, is easily reached through a back door. It is also relatively small, surrounded by the rest of suburbia. However, Graves' present garden is a simple yet elegant pebbled and grassed space which reminded me of what he described as "the many informal wine and pasta dinners enjoyed in roadside farmhouse gardens while touring Italy":

What happened in Rome since the Academy days still has an effect. I go to Rome every summer for a week. There are times when coming back from day trips it is still light out at seven or eight in the evening—there's a scheduled stop for dinner at a simple farmhouse with a stone gravel terrace with tables set with oil cloth with great bowls of pasta, bread, dogs running around and no bugs. People just sitting there eating and drinking and talking.

I can't help but be influenced by that. I come back and to some extent make part of that wonderful experience part of my life here: I can buy the best olive oil, the freshest tomatoes. I can have those moments. It doesn't come as naturally but it's important because it's richer in meaning.

Thus, his present home place reflected someone who was no longer the small town outsider at Harvard, someone who had never been to Europe but an urbane sophisticate. Yet when I asked him if *inside* he still thought of himself as a small town boy, he replied, "Yes." Where is that Indiana youth reflected in this Princeton home? I asked Graves to return to the theme of distinguishing character as typified by the Indiana stockyards which had so profoundly impressed him.

Garden Wall,
The Warehouse,
Princeton, New Jersey.

He had been drawn to the warehouse, like the stockyards, because it was an "oddity," because it had character.

I asked him if there were any similar conscious or unconscious connections between his past and the present environments he has designed. I mentioned, for example, the Great Room in the Denver Library with its great wooden vaulted ceiling, reminiscent, it seemed, of the stockyards. He agreed that it reflected the "indelible mark made by character." He explained:

> There's also a connection because it's in part wood and there's a curious abstracted structure in the middle meant to evoke the West. Part of the frame in the center is meant to be ambiguous. Whether I thought about it consciously or unconsciously I'm not that sure.

As I sat listening at the breakfast table, I looked up and was shocked and delighted by the narrow, dramatic high ceiling above our heads. Graves' words—"character," "oddity," "integrity"—suddenly seem to come together. Merging in my mind were images of the vaulted stockyards and this raised ceiling, images of the stockyard's narrow pens and of the warehouse's original forty-four narrow rooms. It was then that I could imagine the primal attraction this house had for Graves when he first encountered it. This warehouse *was* a Tuscan barn, whose original forty-four long thin rooms echoed the same form as those of the stockyards of his youth. The attraction, although not conscious, may have been irresistible to Graves, especially since that internal form was packaged and delivered in the ruin-like wrapping he had come to love so in Italy. In every way this house seemed to me to be a re-creation of that transcendent environment of his youth.

I suggested the connection between the stockyards and the warehouse to Graves. He looked shocked and replied, "It was my daughter who counted the rooms." Of course, who *counted* the rooms was totally inconsequential. The fact was they *existed* and represented a potential draw, an imprint, a schema of a profoundly experienced childhood environment.

Graves began to sketch a diagram of the interior layout and side internal passageway of the warehouse, explaining in a very businesslike, rational way how such an organization is just one possible internal arrangement of space. Suddenly he stopped, put his pencil down and looked at me saying, "The stockyards and this house *are* organized in the same way and there could be a connection."

So, what if there is a connection? Is there a profound meaning or message to be taken from this? One might speculate and say the stockyards, besides being a place of character, of exaggeration compared to the rest of Indianapolis, was also a place of men where Graves spent time with his otherwise absent father. In fact, Graves could recall his father's office in the stockyard's Exchange Building in vivid, sensory detail—remembering the sound of footsteps walking the wooden floors, for example. Thus it may have particular significance for him to re-create an echo of this place.

I decided to stop engaging in speculation and let Graves speak for himself about ways he felt the warehouse symbolized his own psychological expression, his own character. He referred back to the importance of character in general:

The Warehouse WAS a Tuscan barn, whose original 44 long thin rooms echoed the same form as those stockyards of Graves' youth.

Graves' Residence, The Warehouse, Princeton, New Jersey.

Indianapolis Stockyards (before demolition) of Michael Graves' Boyhood.

The interest in character, itself, is something I see as a distinguishing character of my work. If I were building a hotel in Egypt it doesn't look like a hotel in Ohio. It doesn't look like a hotel in Paris that I would do. Those things gain differences by virtue of the location, materials, the light and so on. It's not that I am just a regionalist because there is at the same time a kind of personality, **my** *personality lent to the work that is strong. Still, the characteristic of the place is an equal presence.*

. . . Paul Goldberger once wrote that I was the most original architect of our time. I, myself, don't value originality because I first value one's ability to use language that is the opposite of originality. My personal expression is within boundaries of that; that is part of the associative interest of the culture and variations on themes rather than changing themes. That personal expression is exaggeration. Someone recently called me a mannerist—by my definition a variation on language to call your attention to those principles or conventions that you may have gone to sleep on. Things that are taken for granted are pulled out and their values made extreme or heightened.

I administered the test based on Jungian personality types to Graves. The results indicate that his major traits include intuition and feeling with his feeling mode predominating. He also scored exactly halfway between introvert and extravert. This type of person often displays personal warmth. But, since they prefer intuition, their interest is not just in ways to be practical, but in ways to innovate. Fields they tend to be interested in include behavioral science, research, literature and art, and teaching.

I asked Graves if my interpretation and assessment correspond to the image he has of himself and he agrees that they do. He has continued to teach regularly at Princeton University despite his international success. Certainly where intuition is concerned, we agreed that the very fact that Graves bought the warehouse to begin with was testimony to his vision of a world of possibilities. But what about the feeling aspect of his personality, which came through so strongly on his personality test? I commented to him, "I see Italy, I see the stockyards here, but what you talked about in a very primal sense was that time with your grandmother, that conviviality. Where is that in this house?" He answered:

That's missing from this place. I had a girlfriend who, when my children visited on the weekend, would read to my son. That's one of the few times I can remember in this house that that kind of activity took place.

Our interview was finished for the day. Graves had been watching the clock, aware of the ongoing pressures of his international existence. As he cordially drove me back around to his office, he described his work commitments all around the world, a reality that he explained means he is forever jetting from place to place and hardly ever at home.

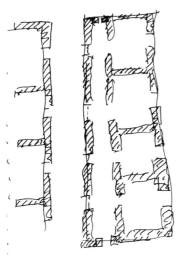

Graves' Sketch of Plan of "PRESENT" Warehouse Residence by way of comparison to "PAST" Stockyards of His Boyhood.

Stockyard Pens of Michael Graves' Boyhood. "PAST"

Western History Reading Room, Denver Central Library, Denver Colorado Designed by Michael Graves.

Charles
Jencks

Luckily when I returned to continue the interview with Jencks the next day, I did not get lost. After the last trip I was sure to concentrate on major landmarks. The labyrinth that previously had seemed so complex now appeared to have a logic, a direction and I quickly found my way to Jencks' Cape Cod bungalow.

Once again Jencks greeted me warmly, offering me a cold drink on such a hot day. It took a while for us to start. Jencks' teenage son and daughter and a house guest were coming and going, making their beach plans for the afternoon. Jencks was solicitous of them all, especially of his children, making sure their needs were met.

I began the interview by asking Jencks if he thought his environmental autobiography which we had discussed the previous day had influenced his present environments and values regarding place.

I think it did. I hadn't thought about the subject until you set this interview up, but I think there's some connection between past existential positions and present design. For instance I rejected the understated reticence and eternal timelessness of the classical tradition. My father liked Mies van der Rohe, but I disliked him, his aesthetic, his apolitical politics that led to his work for the Nazis. Mies' semi-spirituality was unworldly, distant from politics, society and the realities of economic life which are so important in architecture. I rejected this minimalism in favor of a rich multivalent aesthetic and ethic which deals with the problems of the city and the whole human comedy—the stuff of architecture. Also from my past is the deep subconscious valuing of privacy. I had the luxury of a private room, a private place for thinking and contemplation and one that the Cape landscape supported. Most of humanity doesn't have this freedom to be alone. I love Pascal's self-evident joke: "All the problems in the world come from people not being able to sit at home, alone in a room."

Because that was my background, I assumed that you could be alone in a room and think things out. I have that in architecture and for myself. I have this little retreat in the woods nearby, you'll see, I'll take you over there. In a sense I've designed the ultimate scholar's retreat in the woods and in that way continued my father's Bay House tradition. So it's important to give people isolation, as long as it's not enforced.

I asked Jencks if there were any other connections between his past and present environments.

The house of my grandparents at 1 Mount Vernon Place is typologically and historically like my Thematic House, both date from the 1840s. I've treated the London house on the street side in a very sober, rational way, and been a good contextualist . . .. As you go through the building to the private side it becomes more personal, so in that sense there is a definite conceptual continuity with my grandparents. There is also a somewhat related architectural language, a Freestyle Classicism. Other parallels? An interest in ornament and history, but that's where I distinguish my work and Post-Modernism from Revivalism. I'm not interested in either revivalism or traditionalism. I accept that the Modern Movement created a break with the past; but it's not a complete break. In sum, I couldn't live as my grandparents lived, I wouldn't approve of the style of life. Nor could I live the way my parents lived, nor could I live in their Cape Cod house.

I was listening to Jencks but, I commented, "When you described the sweeping staircase and dome at Mount Vernon Place, I kept seeing images of the sweeping staircase and dome you created in your Thematic House."[40]

So did I. There's a case where there is a strong, but perhaps fortuitous connection.

He began to elaborate:

In the mythology of my grandfather's house there was the staircase and dome that were so important and when I went back to Baltimore [to visit Mount Vernon Place] I thought I've also done this, but I thought rather simply, "Mine's better."

"In the mythology of my grandfather's house there was the staircase and dome that were *so* important and when I went back to Baltimore [to visit Mount Vernon Place] I thought I've done this . . ." Charles Jencks

Jencks laughed and continued:

I was aware of the Baltimore staircase and dome, but I wasn't aware of it as an influence. The conscious model was the staircase of Inigo Jones at the Queen's House in Greenwich. My wife, Maggie, and I visited the staircase and we wanted a spiral for other symbolic and functional reasons: to symbolize the sun and planets. That's where one should try to separate the fortuitous coincidence of form from unconscious intentions.

I asked Jencks what he thought was in his *conscious* mind. What did the Baltimore staircase symbolize?

A rhetorical flourish. A grand marble staircase that you could drive a car down, the life of a Hollywood musical: high kickers would come down it. It represented a grandiose opulent gesture in the 1900s. It was the most prominent sign in what is really a big, but modest, house. It's the old classic thing which Inigo Jones said, "Ye exterior of the house should be sober, rational and urban and not stand out, incite envy of the neighbors, but the interior should fly out licentiously and have a ball!" I'm misquoting, but the Inigo Jones' formulation was the typical aristocratic, English code: On the outside you're a gentleman like everyone else, but on the inside you're crazy and do what you want.

Jencks himself seemed quite rational on the outside and too full of energy and glee ever to be described as sober, though he was exceptionally polite in a very British way. He seemed crazy only in that most playful sense: Jencks had certainly done what he wanted to do in the Thematic House, meticulously developing the symbolic program for it. I wanted to know more about that symbolism, about his past and present sense of home. For example, was the library in his Thematic House in any way similar to the library in Mount Vernon Place? What was the mysterious "Room of Caesars?"

If my memory is right, as you entered the house you went into a big hallway with Corinthian pillars. Straight ahead and to the left was a library with these heads of Caesar, about ten sculptured heads in wood. They were really impressive and something that I now see, as you're doing this interview, that when I was later to create an architecture library in London—I wasn't conscious of a parallel before, but there is a similarity: the library as a kind of monument and focus with books as important items, as if sacred items.

Maybe the iconic gravity is a tradition in treating libraries: the library with Caesar's heads is an iconographic conceit with a history? It's not one I'm acquainted with. But the tie of Caesar and power to books is a

Exterior of Charles Jencks "PAST" grandparents' house, 1 Mt. Vernon Place.

Photograph by A. Aubrey Bodine. Reprinted by permission.

strange metaphor. You don't usually think of power and books together and at five years old it wasn't even in my pre-conscious mind, I didn't even know who Caesar was. I just responded to the rhetoric of the Room of Caesars and I saw all these busts.

The only room I remember strongly (and probably falsely) is the dining room with a big oak table and its huge red cardinal chairs with high backs, and a mantelpiece with an Italian painting over it.

I asked Jencks if there was a connection between the chairs of Mount Vernon Place and the heavy chairs featured in the Thematic House.

Exterior of Charles Jencks "PRESENT" London home, The Thematic House.

Photograph by Charles Jencks. Courtesy of Charles Jencks.

The chairs in the Thematic House were designed because Maggie's (my wife's) cousins were so big and they needed a big chair that they could fall back in. Maggie kept saying, "Bigger, bigger, bigger." A chair for me is a very important item of design. The chairs of my grandmother were impressive and have always remained in my mind as monumental things.

I looked around the Cape bungalow in which we were sitting. I could see absolutely *nothing* that could be considered monumental. In fact, Jencks explained to me that the bungalow was really a World War II barracks from North Carolina which was purchased for a dollar, brought by train to the Cape, and then

"THE PAST" Large Central Stair, 1 Mt. Vernon Place, Baltimore. "Grand manner, 19th century, with a Tiffany Dome and revivalist ornament—prefab signolic not symbolic architecture, a type I was criticizing." —Charles Jencks.

Photograph courtesy Charles Jencks.

hauled on to the dunes by horses. The structure was actually made of 16 foot prefabricated parts—which turned out to be "incredibly flexible" every time the house had to be moved back because of beach erosion.

The Thematic House and this bungalow could not have been more different. To me Jencks' London Thematic House was a re-working of his grandmother's house. Yet Jencks felt it was important to draw a distinction between a "fortuitous if interesting parallel" and an actual re-working of his grandmother's house.[41]

The bungalow reproduced his father's "bohemian artistic" values. His father, a concert pianist, had left the highly competitive performance circuit to compose music. He had just enough money not to worry about obtaining shelter and security. Jencks went on to talk further about the Thematic House:

"THE PRESENT" The "Cosmic Oval",
the Dome Designed by Charles Jencks
for his Thematic House.

Photograph by Charles Jencks. Courtesy of Charles Jencks.

*Every room [in the Thematic House] has ten meanings. That's why it is so difficult for you to do this interview. You can't ever get a simple reading if the determinants are so clearly plural. By definition there will never be an overriding reason to any **one** of my forms, because I consciously multi-coded them. Therefore you can't say, "This is caused by that."*

I was totally unconvinced by Jencks' claim that I could never understand the meaning of his Thematic House. Perhaps I could not understand the *intellectual* symbolism of his house but I could understand its *psychological* significance. I looked Jencks straight in the eye and replied, "I say, *WHY* has Charles Jencks done that? *Why* has he created a house where every room has ten meanings?" Jencks replied:

That has a lot to do with Coleridge. He's been uppermost throughout my life—Coleridge on the Imagination—was the title of a book by I.A. Richards that greatly influenced me. My work has always emphasized the multivalent, and I got that idea not through architecture but through literature, philosophy and the arts. Multivalence I developed to mean having many valences as in chemistry. There are many different kinds of bonds, or meanings that connect the concept to pluralism. So good design, I argued in Modern Movements *is multivalent. It's also the argument of Complexity Theory: the value of something is in its creative links. The more links, the more creative. A rather straight forward theory; the less links, the less creative. Signs have few links, or are just one-liners, whereas symbols are multivalent and have many links. That is the origin of multiple meanings in the Thematic House.*

I explained that I thought of symbolism in completely different terms—in psychological terms. His was certainly the *intellectual* rationale for the Thematic House, yet I believed there was an even deeper, symbolic rationale which suggested that the Thematic House symbolized Jencks' selfhood. Jencks and I began to explore this.

"You have this rich treasure of environments. You have these two different strains—your grandmother's house and then—"

The shack. High/low.

"Yes. Part of what I've been trying to make sense of is how you have come to terms with those two different parts. You referred to the Bay House as the house of your heart and a place of freedom during the summer time."

Not the architecture, the place. No question about it. [That place] is the center of my heart.

"And then you love Cape Cod and this simple barracks and connect it back to your father and your uncle."

Yes, right, but also the freedom, pleasure, and wildness of the place.

"So those values are still clearly central to you. When I thought about the Thematic House and where that is coming from, I thought: there is a lot of energy that you put into that house. Why? What has been the draw of that house because it is clearly a reproduction (in a totally different way) of your grandmother's house—when you look at the facade, the staircase, the Room of Caesars, the dome—all of those things."

These are fortuitous parallels, I agree.

"So why? What is the draw? This is what I think. (You can tell me if I'm totally off base.) When you described the Room of the Caesars with those books, I tried

"THE PAST" Spiral Staircase,
1 Mt. Vernon Place.

"THE
PRESENT"
The Spiral
"Solar Stair",
The Thematic
House.

to imagine you back at that age seeing that and all around you this room covered in sheets. To your father that must have been kind of creepy because it was his mother. To have your mother living like that . . ."

In a sepulchral atmosphere.

"Yes. It must have been unnerving."

Awful. He never said that.

But I bet it was."

I guess it was.

"But to you as a child it had a totally different aura."

Totally different: full of mystery. A past that was too magical to even think about!

"You related the Caesar busts to power. I think that was hitting the nail on the head: there were the books, the architecture, and the symbols of power all linked together. Perhaps the most compelling story you told me about that power was the one about your grandfather hiring the New York fire department to put out the Baltimore fire. When I think about you playing with the trucks and cars at the Bay House . . .. Well, when most children play like that, they *imagine* that they or their father would come around the corner with a fire truck and put out a fire. That would be the imaginary game. But your family did it in real life! You observed *untold, unfathomable* power! It must have left a tremendous impression."

It was clear that we were living a different kind of life compared to the life my father had been brought up in. I don't think I aspired to go back to his father's way of life at all. I don't deny that there are these parallelisms that you've seen and I've never thought about and that's of interest to me and to you. But I think of my life and choices as much more circumstantial. Maggie chose the London house not because of its particular qualities but because of the garden. Although on one level, on English terms, it's big. On American terms, it's not so grand and rather small. So far as I'm aware, I wasn't attempting to return to a situation of my father's father, of grandiosity or power.

"I don't think you were either. Let me just say, though, that part of what my book is about is that *everybody* thinks their reasons for choosing a certain home are circumstantial, but I don't think those reasons are just circumstantial."

Still, it *was* certainly hard to pick apart the fortuitous from the unconscious. Jencks and I began to try to explore which was which. For example, Jencks saw the choice of the Thematic House as circumstantial, explaining, "I didn't choose it. Maggie chose it."

"But you didn't say no."

As far as the architecture of the London house was concerned, I thought
it was really "sub"-Georgian, and I didn't really want to buy it.

"I don't think you even subconsciously thought: I'm going to re-create my grandmother's house as is. I really believe that the environmental experiences that children have at a very young age have a profound effect upon them and I think that the experience of your grandmother's house was more [to do with] trying to uncover the mystery of what was under those sheets. You re-did that house but in your *own* way. And what you uncovered from under those sheets is what's *really* in the Thematic House and what your book is about."

I believe that Jencks, himself, unknowingly had written about such a discovery process in his symbolic program for the Thematic House's Solar Stairway which also leads on to the roof of the library:

Above the head, through the sun wall, burst the sunrays—illuminating darkness and stupidity. The enlightenment of ideas breaks through the truth—peels it back layer after layer—showing surface, then insulation, then structure, so the decoration is The Truth revealed, both on the sun wall and in the dark sky. Its clouds are shown as black billows like the approaching night, while on the other side, the light of nine planets casts through evil a sharp beam that falls on the books. Thus Thought and imagination together crack open Truth to reveal Her hidden beauty. After which She is collected into the series of architectural books.[42]

For me, this was Jencks' "poetics of space" which, translated figuratively, meant: the truth of the power of the Library of Caesars is revealed. Yet this was *my* interpretation. Only Jencks could speak to his own experience.

At first Jencks looked shocked by what I was suggesting but then laughed,

I don't agree with you.

I tried to explain my interpretation further.

"You talk about symbolism, but I think the symbolic message to you was that there is a connection between words, architecture, and power. The one question I did not ask you is why you wanted to become an architect and architectural critic. To me it seems like the inevitable end point of those messages you got as a child. You started out as an English Literature major: the power of words. That power was embedded in the power of house as made manifest in the Library of Caesars. It was only logical that you would end up doing what you're doing. It was to the world's great good that this happened. I'm not saying that any of this is neurotic or crazy."

I profoundly disagree with you. I think, if I may say, mine is a
Post-Modern position on this: there are many ways to do a labrynthine
maze. You've taken me through one way, which I understand. But the
way I would describe how I became an architect or majored in English
Literature or any of that would be much more circumstantial. I would

say I was brought up subliminally, never explicitly to follow that path.
My uncle was an architect and I was named after an architect and we
lived in an architect-designed house.

Of course, it would have been only natural for Jencks to emulate Charles Platt, his father, his other uncle and any other role model adults who surrounded him. Still, as I explained to Jencks, "I don't think what you're saying and what I'm saying are mutually exclusive." I believe that Jencks modeled himself on his elders but the reality of those elders was made manifest in Mount Vernon Place as well as the other dwellings that were part of his environmental legacy. Jencks acknowledged,

They're not mutually exclusive.

Overall it seemed impossible for either Jencks or me to isolate the precise influence of his past. I remembered Bachelard's words, ". . . through the brilliance of an image, the distant past resounds with echoes, and it is hard to know at what depth these echoes will reverberate and die away."[43] In the end, only Jencks could finger the golden coins of his environmental memory in a way that was meaningful to *him*. Thus he continued:

My own history is so full of different things. I'd like to tell you about
other very strong experiences. (It's so nice that you're interested in all
this!) One thing I didn't mention is about my father's sister, Elizabeth
Wren, whose house is in the old town on School Street. I can remember
my first experience at about two here. Almost the first thing I remember
is being in a cot in a room with a four-poster bed. I remember looking
out and seeing the sewing machine and I didn't know if it was an
animal coming to get me or what. So I got really uptight.

The smell of the paint was so strong. The atmosphere was rather like
this ocean shack here. Very summery, full of lightness—pretty rather
than grave. So that was a very strong, wonderful experience—the smell
of those rooms was just SO nice. And it signaled for me the friendliness
of my aunt and my first cousin. The house exuded hominess and
comfort. In effect, in Westport and Cape Cod my father and mother
recreated that smell and that ambience of the home as a very strong,
friendly, warm place to be.

My aunt and uncle created a colorful flower garden surrounded by lilacs,
*and the smell of the lilacs and the flower beds was **so** overpowering at*
that age. I played in the flower garden until age five or six. So those
experiences were very strong. I don't know in what manner they have
been transformed, but let me say that all of this was completely
disregarded by my architectural training. In architectural school that is
the last thing you are trained to care about! Maggie obviously had her
own version of that and she wanted to give it to the Thematic House.

Returning to Jencks' comment on his architectural training, I explained: "Let me say that is exactly why I'm writing this book: because one's own environmental story is what I consider to be the missing part of architectural education. It is the core of the architect's sense of place. You can lay on all the architectural theory and courses that you want, but when it comes down to going through all those layers what continues to influence designers most profoundly is their own environmental story. My reason for interviewing you, Michael Graves and Andres Duany is to show how powerful that influence really is."

Still Jencks was insistent about the influence of others, and other buildings, on his environmental vision. Of special importance to him was the influence of his wife, Maggie, who had died the previous year. He looked around our ocean shack setting and poignantly explained:

> *The important thing throughout all of this was this house here where you sit. Every summer I came here with the children . . .. Maggie and I always came here. It has this incredible flexibility. So, in a kind of subliminal way, it's a Modernist "machine à habiter," but one which my wife Maggie loved for its modesty. She was much more of my great-uncle, Charles Platt's persuasion. She liked very modest things; her values from her father were against ostentation. She didn't like pretentious architecture and we used to have little arguments over symbolism.*

> *She had a terrific sensitivity of feeling, a highly developed feeling system, and was more attentive to this level than anyone else I've ever met. She could sense subtle differences that were extremely important, she never knew why—in people, situations, and environment. All of them. People responded to her positively because of that. Look at these multicolored blue couches with all the subtly related pillows. She created that warm mixture. This is a very dumb room, but her sensibility created the color harmonies. She created the ambience and I created the deep structure. In the London house she was also very good at functional and mood creation . . .. The house faces south and she thought of the window space overlooking the garden as a key place to gather before dinner.*

Jencks went on to describe how he and Maggie had discussed their different visions for the Thematic House, negotiated and reached decisions about its internal design. The master bedroom, particularly, had Maggie's imprint on it and Jencks considered this room one of the most successful in the house. Perhaps this successful give and take that typified their design process likewise typified their style together as a married couple. Maggie, as Jencks described her, certainly seemed the classic "sensing feeling" person. Yet what was Jencks' personality type?

I had him take the personality "type" test. His test taking approach was unique—he steadfastly refused to answer certain "either/or" questions when he felt neither of the alternatives applied to him. "Just choose the answer that *best* represents you," I suggested. He stuck to his guns. It seemed a point of integrity to him and he crossed out any question he felt might cause him to compromise his sense of the truth. Despite the eliminations, Jencks scored as a ENTJ, a clear extravert, an intuitive thinking person with the judgment mode (in this case the "thinking" mode) predominating. Such types may be summarized as follows:

> The basic driving force and need of ENTJs is to lead, and from an early age they can be observed taking over groups . . .. ENTJs have a strong urge to give structure where they are—to harness people to distant goals. Their empirical, objective, and extraverted thinking may be highly developed; if this is the case, they use classification, generalization, summarization, adduction of evidence and demonstration with ease . . . . Although ENTJs are tolerant of established procedures, they can abandon any procedure when it can be shown to be indifferent to the goal it seemingly serves . . . .

> ENTJs take charge of the home. When an ENTJ is present there will be little doubt as to who is in command. Because their work is so important to them, however, they can become increasingly absent, especially if male . . . . ENTJs expect a great deal of their mates, who need to possess a strong personality of their own, a well-developed autonomy, many and varied interests, and a healthy self-esteem.[44]

Could there be any doubt that Charles Jencks was a leader, certainly in the world of architecture? Using his highly developed sense of thinking, he was able to give definition to Post-Modernism, the movement that has since become internationally recognized. In doing so he demonstrated the ability to be the quintessential classifier. As for abandoning procedure—I had just observed his unique modus operandi in taking the personality test!

In terms of his choice of mate, his wife Maggie Keswick was also a person in her own right, who had published her own well-respected book about garden design. Jencks continued to describe Maggie as

> . . . Basically modest and unpretentious but she also had a high style existence. She was a peacock, a glamorous woman. She was yin and yang, as I am: we both liked high life and low life: high style urban, visible life, as well as getting away in the country.

I asked Jencks if he thought of himself as an ENTJ type.

> I suppose, being a male and an architect in this kind of world—logic, thinking, reason, control—these are male-type things.

> I must say that in the houses I've designed and lived in, I am aware that my wife's imprint was very strong in a way which I couldn't adequately deal with. She cared a lot about function and the relationship to the outside. As I grow older, and now that she's dead, I appreciate much more what she was saying. Being so design oriented and geometrically and theoretically oriented I've always put those issues first, and assumed the other things. But I underrated one's connection to nature. So, having just seen an Eisenman building two days ago in Cincinnati,

Garagia Rotonda, view of one inch dome, round void of sky, bed, and desk —a scholar's retreat.

I'm aware of its major fault—what Maggie would have said of it. It didn't have any connection to the outside. "Wonderful as a piece of design, but it is lacking in some connection to nature."

Yes, I recognize the personality profile, but the environment should be designed by more than one person. It's important that the environment is richer than a single position. I do think it's important for architecture to have structure, rigor, logic, theory—all of those things I may have contributed.

This seemed like a good time to visit Jencks' studio, which he was anxious to show me. This building also had been featured in his book *Toward Symbolic Architecture* and I was looking forward to viewing at first hand this structure which I had only seen in photographs. Thankfully we did not need to drive there but could just walk back over the dune and along a narrow footpath that led deep into the woods. As we walked, Jencks explained that this was the place where he came by himself to work. It also had served as a bedroom for him and his wife during the summers when his mother-in-law occupied the main bungalow bedroom.

I immediately recognized the blue "Garagia Rotunda." He had given the studio that name because it was ". . . the conjunction of two opposite building types: the lowliest, functional shed, most humble of covered spaces, and the highest symbolic building type, the heavenly dome or rotunda."[45] Interesting. The dome appears again.

As we approached, Jencks wanted me to appreciate the whole experience of this building and its surrounds: he encouraged me to walk on the carefully placed steps of wood, each 12 inches square. As we climbed the stairs to the minimalist outside porch he explained the importance of light and shadow. By way of example, he pointed to the most crucial component of the studio's design, the tiny, 1-inch (!) dome of sky that had been created in the porch's wood-canopied ceiling.

Jencks was still explaining the Post-Modernist thinking behind this structure as we prepared to enter the studio's main (and only) room. His explanation was similar to what I had already read about it:

> The combination of shingle vernacular and classical moldings; informal porches and Palladian plan; Medusa face and implicit face (on the back); prefabricated garage and sun-shade rotunda—all the dualities were meant to illustrate the double-coding of Post-Modernism. It had to be built by local builders, . . . to be accessible and regional, and yet contain refinements and allusions of an esoteric, personal nature. Above all it had to be multivalent, allow the variety of interpretation the breadth of reference and taste which I found in the work of Pre-Modernists such as Antonio Gaudi and Bernard Maybeck. But it also had to have a Free-Style Classical decorum, as well as their riotous expressiveness. So there were several contradictory theses, not one.[46]

I expected to see an equally rational, rigorous architectural interior. Yet when I entered, it was not so much what I saw (a simple space with a bed, two night tables with lamps, and a long table bordering the bottom of the bed), as what I felt. This felt like a place of complete romance, a love nest not a studio, a place of the heart not of the head. The light filtered softly on to the bed. The woods enclosed all around. This bed which had appeared so inconsequential in the photographs was clearly the central focus of this room.

"I rarely sleep here anymore", Jencks explained. He produced a simple director's chair and placed it by the long table at the foot of the bed saying, "This is where I sit every day to write." Behind this makeshift desk were two curtained spaces—one a bathroom and one a storage area which contained only a few books.

We sat on the porch in the sun for a long time and talked. I have no idea what we talked about. By this time I was no longer taping our interview. The mood of our conversation had changed. The pace had slowed. The words themselves had no meaning. I was just experiencing the transcendent sacredness of this place.

Andres Duany

This time when I knocked, it was Elizabeth Plater-Zyberk, Andres Duany's wife and partner, who answered the door. A thin, gracefully built woman with bright blue eyes, she seemed as fair as Duany was dark—his visual opposite. She greeted me in a friendly, yet business-like way and invited me in. I entered the house and exchanged pleasantries with this woman whom I had heard described as "brilliant," "rational," "utterly hard working," "cool and unflappable." At that moment she was simply holding her small dog which, she explained, they had rescued from a previous dire fate. The dog was calm in her arms. The house seemed quieter that Sunday. Duany soon appeared again ushering me into the dining-"room of the table."

I had been thinking a lot about the influence of Cuba upon Duany. I tried to imagine him standing in that park near his grandfather's house listening to Castro speaking charismatically to the crowd. Whether you agreed with Castro's politics or not, it was fascinating to think of the personal power he must have had to defy America. It must have been even more fascinating for Duany, a ten-year-old boy, who was living that revolutionary drama there and then. Had Duany, in fact, modeled his own revolutionary tactics in spreading the word about New Urbanism on the revolutionary tactics of Castro?

Duany acknowledged that as a child in Cuba in those years he had been in the position to observe Castro's rise to power. In fact, Duany gave me the reprint of an article that explained how he envisioned applying Castro-like tactics to influence the world of planning in America. Speaking to Yale School of Architecture students in 1987, he stated:

The big shock that we had when we graduated, nobody taught us this at Yale, was that even in suburbia, you are coded to within an inch of your life . . . . The building codes are incredible. It's almost impossible to do a hand rail with any real dignity now. It's beyond belief. Two things struck us: that the codes were very powerful and that people were prepared to be coded. They are used to being told everything. So instead of fighting the codes, why not take over "codes central" and write codes that do what you want them to do. We are not going to ever have an uncoded society any more, but why not take over the codes, instead of fighting them, instead of having them mangle your buildings. That was the first insight. We said "The key to reforming America is to get hold of the codes." We are not talking about making a little building. We are talking about thousands of acres, radically reforming America, just taking over. It would be revolutionary. By the way, in the Cuban Revolution, what Fidel Castro did was he captured the radio stations, instead of actually fighting the battles. He didn't even capture the radio stations; he bought the radio transmitters and since everybody had a radio, he broadcast the revolution, he broadcast the myth of the revolution and the revolution happened. The first modern revolution. What we are proposing is get hold of the radio transmitters of America, of the architectural radio transmitters and do it that way. Much more efficient, fewer casualties, fewer wasted hours, and so on . . ..[47]

Exactly how was Duany attempting to get hold of these "architectural radio transmitters?" By way of explanation, Duany pulled out the black TND pattern book which he and other prominent New Urbanists had created. I had seen the book but, until Duany reviewed it with me, had never quite grasped the extent to which this book of house plans actually presented a systematized method whereby these plans could be "plugged into" a larger "transmitter" of New Urbanist planning codes.

I was completely impressed by the highly developed logic that was embedded in this pattern book. A very practical handbook, it included residential plans for seven different market segments from starter homes to empty nester housing. Each plan also contained a code which linked these houses to their appropriate location in the urbanism of the neighborhood. Also included as part of the key was the area of the house, the lot size, the lot width, the climatic type, etc. In this way, when someone was looking for a particular type of house plan, for example, they could simply do a search of the criteria (the system was also available online) to see which house plans fit their stated requirements. They could then order the plans which would arrive the next day. Laying the book aside, Duany spoke passionately:

Do you know how frustrating it is when the only thing that some people think we do is picket fences? That all this is nostalgic stuff that doesn't operate in the real world? Actually we're eating up the real world.
*You know what happens when they really understand it? They say, "That's Fascism and it needs to be squashed." This is **empowering** to*

architects: instead of being some architects that sit around . . . doing
one house at a time, they can enter the plan industry that is responsible
for tens of thousands of houses a year.

In planning circles Duany has been nicknamed "The King." Did this unofficial title imply "The Master?" "The Indisputable Leader?" Was Duany a visionary revolutionary, a charismatic dictator, or both? I looked forward to completing the Personality and Place Exercise with Duany to find out more.

Meanwhile, however, the TND book reminded me of another systematized pattern book, Christopher Alexander's, *A Pattern Language*, widely regarded as a planning "bible" in its rigorous articulation of primal planning principles. Duany agreed that there was a connection, but felt,

> *"While Alexander always talks about the world as it **should** be, how*
> *houses **should** be produced . . .. I am dedicated to making it **happen**."*

I asked, "What was it that actually inspired you about Alexander?"

The Pattern Language *is really the most wonderful way to live.*
It's timeless and cross-cultural. It wasn't just idiosyncratic.

I kept probing, "So, what *was* it about Alexander's book?"

It's very systematic.

"Like the catechism?" I suggested.

Yes! It's structured like the Jesuit catechism, looking back. It's
systematic; from general to specific. It's also progressively
sophisticated—in each section restating of the same theme. This is
similar to what you do in the first grade. Then there is the more
elaborate statement which is the second grade catechism. Then there's
the technical argument. Everything interlocks and the world is
explained.

"So for you [with your Jesuit education] it was in the perfect form to write this book?"

Duany nodded in agreement and then went to retrieve Alexander's book. He brought it back and began showing me how the text was written.

Now look at this:

The street café provides a unique setting, special to cities: a place where people can sit lazily, legitimately, be on view and watch the world go by.[48]

It states it.

Then Duany pointed out further text:

The ingredients of a successful street café seem to be:

1. There is an established local clientele . . ..

2. In addition to the terrace which is open to the street, the café contains several other open spaces with games, fire, soft chairs, newspapers . . . .

3. The café serves simple food and drinks—some alcoholic drinks but it is not a bar . . ..[49]

Therefore:

Encourage local cafés to spring up in each neighborhood. Make them intimate places, with several rooms, open to a busy path, where people can sit with coffee or a drink and watch the world go by. Build the front of the café so that a set of tables stretch out of the café, right into the street.[50]

Duany continued drawing my attention to the structure of the book:

Here's another thing that's interesting. You see this. This shows whether it's dogma or not. The number of stars. Now that I think about all this . . ..

He then yelled over to the next room,

Liz, what is it when the Pope says something is "absolutely true?"

"Ex cathedra," she answered. Duany confirmed:

Ex cathedra . . .. Four stars confirm: this is unassailable. We know that this is the truth.

I indicated that I understood but then reflected, "So this book could be about veterinary medicine—written in that way, and it would have an instant appeal to you! What was it besides the *form* of the writing that was the essence of the appeal?"

It rang true. I had lived in enough places that had these elements that I could recognize that it was true—living in Santiago, in Paris, in Barcelona . . .. I can recognize such places.

"What was it beyond that, because those pictures . . .?"

*Emotionally, I **wanted** to live in these places. This is the world I **want** to live in. I can read this book and get into it like a novel. I can **imagine***

Houses with Porches and Balconies from *A Pattern Language.*

Courtyard of House at Windsor, Florida, Designed by Clemens Schaub According to New Urbanist Code.

what it is like . . . I love dreaming about living in places like this . . . .
If I had to go to jail, say, and could only have one book, there's no
question in my mind that this would be it. It would transport me to
more wonderful places than any other book I know.

"What are these places like that you dream about when you look at this book?"

Invariably vernacular. They include virtually no "high" architecture.
Places are organic, by which I mean they did not result from a single
design campaign, unlike high architecture which results from a single
design campaign.

Still not satisfied, I probed further, "When I asked you about his book you said, '*emotionally* I love it.' What was the book to you emotionally?"

It could be that we [Alexander and I] have the same sensibility.

"Which is what?"

A kind of peasant sensibility.

"What's so appealing about that?"

It could be possibly be that the house that my grandfather built was a
bohio at heart . . . one of the Cuban peasant houses . . . it could be that
when I would summer in Spain Balearic peasant houses . . . it could be
that this house of ours which we are now in is a kind of peasant house
with the single, simple table at the center of the main room.

Every time I see such places, I dream of spending time in them and I
feel strongly that if I were to deliver this, people would love it. That's
this sense of simple logic is universal.

Adding my own perspective on this, I commented: "I think there *are* these subjective experiences that we have out of which timeless lessons are learned. So the challenge is figuring out: of those subjective experiences that you have, which are timeless?" Duany continued:

For example, porches . . . they just make people drool with desire.
There's something emotional about them.

I agreed and added: "I think that's an example of something that makes perfect sense because, why does that resonate? Because it's about gathering and communal experience in a very human way. So even though you could say, 'well that was very personal for me,' it's that kind of experience that you can then extrapolate for other people as well.

"The ideal would be to extrapolate those primal, satisfying, and universal experiences and design them into other people's homes. The most positive outcome of these sessions would be to help make you conscious of which of your experiences are both personal *and* universal so you could include the essence of these experiences more consciously in your design process. As we've seen in the last two days, you are already doing that to some extent, unconsciously. Design Psychology just makes you more conscious—makes all these rich sources more readily accessible to you."

Still, as important as separating out the influence of Duany's environmental past was the importance of placing these experiences in the context of his personality and its influence on his design in the present. With this in mind, Duany completed the Personality and Place Exercise.

Like Charles Jencks, Duany scored as an ENTJ personality type: an extravert who relies on thinking and intuition, particularly thinking, although Duany came out with a strong "feeling" score as well. Perhaps it was no surprise that both of these men, leaders in the world of design, should possess a leadership personality type found in only 5 percent of the population.[51] I explained to Duany that ENTJs have a strong urge to provide structure wherever they are. He concurred:

Often in a new situation I become the leader in short order. And when I don't and I just sit there . . . finally, there's chaos and then I end up trying to pull it together for the group.

I continued by reading out the text relating to my description of ENTJs:

When in charge of an organization, ENTJs, more than any other type, desire, and generally have the ability, to visualize where the organization is going and seem to be able to communicate that vision to others. They are the natural organization builders and they cannot *not* lead. They find themselves in command and sometimes are mystified as to how this has happened. As administrators, ENTJs organize their units into a smooth functioning system, planning in advance, keeping both short term and long term objectives in mind . . .. ENTJs usually rise to the visions of responsibility and enjoy being executives. They are tireless in their devotion to their job and can easily block out other areas of life so they can work . . .. Inefficiency is especially rejected by ENTJs. . . .[52]

Yes, that's what I'm like these days.

"Repetition of error causes them to become impatient."

Yes.

I continue:

For the ENTJ, there must always be a reason for doing anything and people's feelings usually are not sufficient reason.[53]

Photograph courtesy Andres Duany.

"THE PAST" Chautilly House where Andres' Mother, Enid Santos was Born. Located in Small Village Outside of Santiago, Cuba. The House was Burned and Totally Destroyed During the Castro Revolution.

The most positive outcome of these sessions would be to help make you conscious of which of your experiences are both personal *and* universal. You could include the essence of these experiences more consciously in your design process.

Reprinted by permission.

Vernacular House with Porch and Balcony from *A Pattern Language*

Photograph by the author.

"THE PRESENT"
Houses with Porches
and Balconies at
Seaside, Florida

Right. Correct.

And, in conclusion,

ENTJs will support the policies of the organization and will expect others
to do so.[54]

*It's absolutely accurate . . .. Within an organization, I'm a good leader,
but I'm also a good soldier. So that I expect others to be good followers.
I expect others to do the same. When I recognize a leader like Leo Krier,
I'm his best disciple. But it has to be somebody who I think is a master.*

Duany went on to describe his early career at the prominent, signature-style
firm of Architectonica, where emphasis was on the design of individual buildings.
When Leon Krier, a prominent European designer, came to America in the late
1970s and gave one of his "brilliant" lectures, however, Duany felt Krier talked
them out of that "entire way of being." According to Duany, Krier made them
realize that it was the city and not the individual buildings that was important.
Duany described this as a "pivotal" experience that caused a very conscious
change. He referred to Krier as "still explicitly our master." Duany's willingness
to change professional directions may have been consistent with his own personality type for, ". . . although ENTJs are tolerant of established procedures, they can

Photograph courtesy Andres Duany

"THE PAST"
Local Peasant's
House Like the
One Andres Duany
Remembered from
his Childhood.

Photograph by Carlos Morales. Courtesy Andres Duany.

"THE PRESENT"
Dining Room of
Andres Duany's
and Elizabeth
Plater-Zyberk's
Residence.

abandon any procedure when it is shown to be indifferent to their goals. . . ."[55] While this modus operandi may work well for Duany, he laughingly explained,

> It drives people crazy . . . that I can switch quickly when I identify a more successful route.

I laughed too and asked why that was so. Duany replied:

> Because they're depending on me for stability. I bring them along eventually, but there's very few people that can switch quickly. They don't like the feeling. For example I run the first phases of our charrettes chaotically, on purpose, because I believe in both creative ferment at the beginning and productive discipline later. In the first three of four days of a charrette—I'm disruptive. I back any idea regardless of what it is. I try to bring anybody's idea, however apparently inane, to life. The latter days the charrette completely changes character. I become the boss and it's production mode because you also need to get work done. I do not believe that you can in a continuously disciplined way run a creative process.

Wanting to make sure I understood the working process Duany was describing, I asked, "So you start with the brainstorming bit which is creative chaos and then move into the discipline?"

> Yes, and some people yearn for the discipline . . .. They want to just get it done, so I have to be disruptive. I become a trusted leader by being the best listener. I focus on the inferences of what is said. I'm always reminding my own people:
>
> "Did you hear what he really meant when he said that? What he really meant is, 'No way that was gonna happen.'
>
> "But, he said he liked it."
>
> "Yeah, I know, but that is not what he means."
>
> I try to teach people to really be good listeners. It is empowering to them.

Duany returned to his "chaos theory":

> I'm interested in chaos. Our office of thirty-five people, for example, is a very horizontal organization—there's almost no hierarchy. And when it does organize itself, by negotiation of the concerned parties, Liz and I support it.

Duany's leadership style seemed to be one of great fluidity and responsiveness— of egalitarian values on the one hand, yet played out under his strong leadership on the other hand. In fact Duany himself, sincerely emphasized the importance of keeping the designer's ego in check in the face of a design world culture that perpetually gives birth to and then kills off its own superstar offspring. Duany explained:

> When I was at graduate school at Yale and I had the time to leaf through architecture magazines from its inception to its then current issue . . . I remember doing that for Architectural Forum, Architectural Review, Progressive Architecture, Architectural Record. It was fascinating. I saw reputations gradually made. Architects over the years would become the dominant figure then . . . they'd be thrown down and forgotten while still alive. Like death and life. They would still be working, but no one give a damn about them. I saw that happen time after time—I saw the classicist architects, the Deco architects then the various generations of modernist architects, then the post-modernist architects. At that time (1973) Paul Rudolph was at his lowest standing— but 20 years earlier he had been like a god. I see that happening still.

Duany continued to speak with passion about the appropriate place of architecture and planning in relation to the individual designer:

> . . . I think it's important that architecture be somewhat impersonal . . .. I'm completely uninterested in the personality of the architect, the inspiration of the architect, the biography of the architect, the ego of the architect. I'm much more interested in the principles involved in their work and if they are timeless principles.

> For example, if you were to ask me, "What do you think of this building?" and I would say, "I like it," you could say "I don't like it." Well . . . so what. I'm totally bored by that. It doesn't matter—it's just taste. Boring! On the other hand, a discussion on what the building does to the city . . . is interesting and because we would have a common language of judgment and also I have a right as a citizen to have an opinion about my city. That's an important discussion—what a building does to a city and it's a totally boring one to discuss whether you like it or not for aesthetic reasons. You could not get me to participate in that—it's a dead end . . .

> You cannot make a city . . . out of a collection of individual artistic expressions. I have an urbanist's rather than an artist's point of view . . .. For example, the architecture of Michael Graves—I love it—but it's exceedingly personal . . .. If he were to build within one of our towns, he would essentially steal the show . . . so we would confine him to civic buildings rather than private ones because it's alright for a civic building to be highly expressive in contrast to the buildings of the urban fabric that make the street and should be silent.

I think if Michael had to be an urban planner like we are, he would feel degraded. One of the ways I describe town planning is a quote from Bismarck: "Those who love laws and sausages shouldn't watch them being made."

I laughed and Duany went on:

. . . There's a dialectic between civic and private . . . . I think it is essential for a good architect to know the difference—to know when to be self-effacing and when to be . . . fully expressive. But, of course, most Modern architects don't know that. They don't understand the city. It isn't just that they design object buildings instead of spatially defined ones. I just don't think they have the faintest clue about urbanism. One of the things I appreciate about urbanism . . . is that it is substantially more objective than architecture—when it fails, it fails very evidently. You cannot cover up with theoretical pronouncements as with architecture.

It may seem that urbanism is more objective than architecture on the surface yet, to me, given our discussions, Duany's own planning theories and personal style also seemed subjectively (and to a large extent unconsciously) influenced by his own Design Psychology—his own childhood experience of place. Had not Barcelona's sidewalk cafés provided the model for the ideal weaving of the TND public and private realms? Wasn't that freedom of Barcelona streets the subconscious blueprint for the street life that Duany now espouses as crucial to the New Urbanism? Similarly, surely the recipe for the courtyard house set close up to the street including the extra ingredient of the live-work unit now so familiar in TND communities, was first stirred by the early magic of places like his grandfather's "laboratorio."

To suggest that these places may have been the early sources of Duany's inspiration is not to minimize his vision: every human being has his or her own psychodynamics. What seemed important here was simply to see how private experience had influenced the public theories of all the designers I was taking through the Design Psychology process in the hope that they would understand and analyze those experiences in a deeper, more conscious way in order to apply them most successfully to their current theories and practice.

For example, the idea of an animated street may be universally appealing yet much more achievable in Barcelona—in Europe where there is an extensive mass transit system which enables people to forsake the car and simply walk. In fact, New Urbanists have increasingly realized that the creation of mass transit options is crucial to the success of New Urbanist communities. Yet, given the difference of land scale and transport policies in Europe versus America, can Duany's walkable Barcelona/European experience be transplanted, or does it need to be further refined to fit the American context?

In those same Yale discussions, Duany had recognized the problem:

We do not expect that seamless kind of urban space that you find in Paris or in the Italian cities. I grant you, we think it is a superior space, it's just not an American space. We are not after this exquisite stuff, we are after the cultural reality.

Shifting gear, I questioned Duany further about ways his personality type might be related to the smaller scale world of his home. Here, too, his own dwelling and Arts and Crafts furniture appeared to hark back to the simple, vernacular peasant world as he reflected:

I like to think that this home has a certain austerity, a simplicity . . . that comes partially from the consistency in the furnishings and decor. Also very little is ornamental: a picture or photograph is done by somebody we know, because it is somebody we know—it means something. It's not there because it's pretty.

And of course this furniture is something that concerns me extraordinarily. It is timeless. I can't stand even the thought of fashion . . .. It takes so long to make buildings and communities, that to have them be out of style by the time they are finished (which happens continually) is very destructive. It's one of the most destructive tendencies in our culture today. So I yearn for timelessness in design. And the single most timeless design I have ever found in furniture is American Arts and Crafts. I think it straddles tradition and Modernism beautifully. It requires workmanship, but it's made by the machine.

I questioned him further, "In what ways do you think your house reflects anyone else's personality?"

Well, most areas were designed with Liz, and some, like the garden and kitchen, entirely by her. We agree on what's important. That is fairly astonishing because we're very different personalities.

That's different than our professional work together. We figured out early on that one or another of us should be the project manager. Which means that we can recommend and appeal. One or the other is the boss, so you don't actually escalate to having a genuine fight. In the end, it's one person's project. One of us will make the decision. We've never had to fight. We've never had to get to that point. We merely advocate.

"So," I asked, "how would you describe her personality and influence here in this house?" Duany pointed to the cover on a sofa across from us and replied:

Sometimes it's very simple. There are certain pieces that we have because she chose them. For example, that sofa there is in cloth from Guatemala: it never would have occurred to me to do that. She's looser, I think. There wasn't enough cloth of a singular pattern to cover all of the cushions. So it is made with three different cloths. Which is rather odd, but it was a great idea that I would not have had. Oh, and Liz will actually let things get old.

"Old in what way?"

Well, those rugs. I just replaced them on my own. They were absolutely in shreds. She will not throw anything away . . .. I think it has to do with the fact that her family was in Poland, in the war. They were displaced persons from 1939 to 1948. They came to this country. She was brought up with limits. On top of that, being from Philadelphia where old is definitely understood and preferred over new and shiny . . . in support of savvy gentility. It's done beautifully in Philadelphia.

So I'm the one that has to throw things out, paints things and so on. I throw away the plastic flowerpots and replace them with good ones. That kind of thing. That's how she's different. I think she accepts letting things age.

I thought it was interesting that both Duany and Plater-Zyberk were children of expatriate parents. Duany commented:

. . . Liz used to say that it was a problem having a European memory, although more recently she's more appreciative of it . . .. Both sets of parents have never been back. Both countries changed so much.

"So, if you had to guess what personality type she is, what do you think she would be?", I asked. Duany suggested:

I think she may be categorically different from me. People agree that we're different and thus complementary.

"So 'introverted,' 'sensing,' 'feeling?' Is that what she would be?"

Yeah. Extremely other-oriented, rather than abstract principle-oriented and she is extraordinarily effective, actually. Given any kind of formal job description, she would always get the job, not me.

I laughed and asked, "Why is that?"

I think people think that she's dependable and she won't cause problems— that she'll work things out. For example, she's extremely patient—really patient. Particularly in terms of finishing. She'll actually go through the work that is required to finish projects that could be endless.

For example, it's her garden, which is not a garden of principles. It's a garden of opportunity. Somebody gives us this or that plant, she finds a place to put it, as opposed to saying, as I would, "Well, wait a minute, what's the concept behind this?"

It was interesting that she takes charge of the garden given the description of ENTJ's "typical" mate, which I read out to Duany as I had to Jencks:

ENTJs take charge of the home. When an ENTJ is present, there will be little doubt as to who is in command. Because their work is so important to them however, they can become increasingly absent, especially males. Male or female, ENTJs expect a great deal of their mates, who need to present a strong personality of their own, a well developed economy, many and varied interests and a healthy self-esteem. A career wife, however, may not be appealing to a ENTJ man who is apt to view home and family as part of his professional background, a resource, and to add to his own career.[56]

Duany was quick to add:

That may be the case here.

In order to explore the dynamics of the Duany/Plater-Zyberk household, I asked Duany to complete the Environmental Sociogram Exercise. He drew his home's floor plan and indicated who "owned" the public, semi-private and private space, observing:

We think of each other as equals. Neither of us would want to take more space, but I take more.

In most things we do, one or the other is the boss. Someone has taken over putting the books away. I am the one who puts the kitchen in order (while not necessarily doing the dishes) while Liz takes care of finances, which she has a mind for.

There may be friction establishing roles at the beginning and finally someone just lets go and realizing that the other person is just doing a better job. We really don't like when the other rocks the boat so we don't get in the same boat.

Our session was over for the evening and Elizabeth Plater-Zyberk invited me into the kitchen to sit with them and have a drink. Their kitchen was as simple and unaffected as the rest of the house. The conversation was easy but interesting. Besides obvious intelligence, the characteristics they seem to share the most were sincerity and dedication. I felt admiration for their home, their work, and the personal and professional partnership they had created together.

Design Psychology Exercises: The Present

The soul unfolds
itself like a lotus
of countless
petals—Lao Tsu

Exercise 5   Personality and Place

The exercise which I administered to Michael Graves, Charles Jencks, and Andres Duany was the Keirsey Temperament Sorter which appears in *Please Understand Me: Character and Temperament Types* by David Keirsey and Marilyn Bates.[57] The following exercise represents a more general series of questions to help you probe any connections between your personality and your sense of place.

1. In what way(s), if any, do you think your personality is reflected in your present home? If you think your personality *is not* reflected in your home, *why* do you think this is so?

2. In what way(s), if any, do you think your home reflects anyone else's personality?

3. Overall, do you feel comfortable that your home reflects who you really are? If not, what changes would you make to your home so that it expresses who you are?

4. If you are a designer, are there any ways you think your personality is reflected in your design work?

5. Do you have any further reflections on any connections between your personality and your sense of place?

Exercise 6   Environmental Sociogram

If you share a house with someone, how is it functioning in terms of social space? Typically when we look at the floor plan of a home, we refer to the functional room labels on that plan to help us decipher the division of rooms (living room, dining room, kitchen, bedrooms, etc.) Instead, it is helpful to analyze the social dynamics of how these spaces are used by people.

Draw a rough floor plan of your house on a separate piece of paper. The plan does not have to be to scale or perfectly drawn. It need only be a plan indicating the relative sizes of rooms and their relationship to one another. Label the rooms in your house according to the following categories:[58]

> ➤ Individual space—space which belongs to each person alone, where privacy can be maintained as in a private study or workshop;

> ➤ Shared space—space belonging to a sub-group within the family (i.e. parents or children) such as a play room or parents' bedroom;

> ➤ Public space—space belonging to all those within the home.

Analyze the use of the different territories within your home by answering the following questions:

1. Does your house have an equal division of individual, shared and public spaces? If not, what type of space predominates and why?

2. Is the space use in your house equally divided between individuals? Does one person have more control over space than others? Does one group of people (i.e. parents? children?) have more control than any other group?

3. Is the division of control as you have described it above appropriate? What are the conflict areas, if any?

4. Overall, does the physical space in your home meet your social needs? If not, how could it be adapted to meet those needs?

5. Do you have any further reflections on ways you share your space?

CHAPTER 3

The
Future

The Poetry of Home

My bid on the house has been accepted. At last I'll have a home of my own. I'm trying NOT to get too excited about it yet because I still have the whole mortgage process to go through—an arduous and anxiety-ridden ordeal for so many potential homeowners. Assuming I do get a mortgage, will this house really be my ideal home?

Ascending closer now towards the peak of the self-actualized home, we can pause to hear Bachelard's words again:

> The dream house may be merely a dream ownership, the embodiment of everything that is considered convenient, comfortable, healthy, sound, desirable, by other people . . .. Maybe it is a good thing for us to keep a few dreams of a house that we shall live in later, always later, so much later in fact, that we shall not have time to achieve it. For a house that was final, one that stood in symmetrical relation to the house we were born in, would lead to thoughts—serious, sad thoughts—and not to dreams. It is better to live in a state of impermanence than in one of finality.[1]

In the search for "house as symbol of self," neither house nor self may remain constants and perhaps this is just as well. Clare Cooper Marcus also emphasized this point when she wrote about the search for a "place of the soul": "For some people, this place of soul nurturance may not be in the home at all; it may require spending time in another place or—over a life time—in varying soul-nourishing places, each appropriate to a particular stage of emotional development."[2]

Thus, it is important to see home not only in relation to the past and present, but as part of a life cycle that also includes a constantly changing future. In fact, it is estimated that, on average, an American will move at least fourteen times in his or her life; the British person at least eight times.[3] The place that feels like home today may not be your ideal place tomorrow.

Even beyond the internal, existential need for home, people's housing needs change depending upon their external situation including the composition of their household and their economic situation.[4] In fact, people may go through different stages of homeownership, each representing a different phase of life circumstances. For example, these phases can include the following stages:[5]

1. **Baseline stage**—an initial stage when housing choice may be made in relation to practical factors such as economics, contacts, and convenience rather than in comparison to a previous dwelling lived in as an adult.

2. **Stage of incremental change**—a period of "intermediate mobility" when people may move a number of times to resolve practical problems incrementally yet perhaps also in an effort to reach stage three below.

3. **Approximation of the ideal**—marks the acquisition of something near to the ideal home in the eyes of the individual or family. Even if this stage is not attained (which it frequently is not), it remains a goal to which dwellers aspire.

Thus as we search for the self-actualized home, we can reflect on the past, initiate change in the present, and anticipate as well as embrace the future.

When I finish this book, should I return to a conventional 9 to 5 job or continue to work from home? Luckily, this house I am about to buy does seem very flexible, offering me a number of different lifestyle options. If I choose to work from home, I can continue to work in the privacy of my study. If I decide to work full time, the extra bedroom could accommodate a full-time nanny. What about when the children are older and have left home and I'm retired? The master bedroom is downstairs so I can live here without needing to climb any stairs in my old age. Above all, will I still be living in my "new" home in the future? What will the purchase of this house mean for my relationship with Bill?

Given the current mobility of our society, the rapidly changing nature of the nuclear family, as well as unanticipated life crises, it is likely that increasingly our symbol of self may not be embodied in any *house* alone. In fact, when listening to people's environmental stories, Cooper Marcus found growing emphasis on special *objects* that move with people from house to house as key symbols of their identities.[6] Such cherished items often include, for example, pieces of furniture, visual art and photographs[7]—things valued for "past memories and associations, intrinsic qualities, style and utilitarian and personal values."[8]

In the family context, when special family objects have monetary value and are passed down to us, they become labeled family heirlooms. However, we can also inherit special objects that are psychological heirlooms. A framed photograph of a stern great-grandmother, an Art Deco vase painted in lively colors, and a rocking chair full of warmly rocked memories are also part of our environmental genealogies. In fact, objects handed down from one generation to another weave together the lives, the souls of people throughout the years as part of our environmental genealogies.

In this context we can read these artifacts for clues about our past familial world, much as archeologists would unlock the mysteries of civilizations by studying the riches of long-buried tombs. When we display our inherited artifacts in our homes along with any newly acquired objects and furniture, we draw together essences of our past and present worlds. When we bequeath all to the next generation, we contribute to their environmental genealogies. Thus we continue the weaving of generation to generation.

In this sense special objects can function in different ways. They provide us with insight and meaning. They give us stability and continuity in our otherwise changing world. "Surrounded by our things, we are rooted in and visually continuous with our pasts . . .. Things are our ballast."[9]

With this in mind, I continued the Design Psychology process by doing the Special Objects Inventory Exercise (see Exercise 7 below) to determine which things I wanted to bring with me to my new home. In my case this was easy. I had already gone through such a selection process when I moved back from England to America: I could only afford to return to the USA with those items that were most precious to me—my books, my paintings, objects or furniture collected from different countries, and photographs of my children's early years.

Many of the things which I have acquired have a non-Western quality to them. My cousin has very kindly given me the well-remembered Chinese rug salvaged from my grandmother's now demolished mansion. I have a beautiful framed Peshawar painting, a gift from my mother after visiting my brother in India. My black lacquer Chinese chest could hold all of our photo albums from England.

I am especially touched to have received a welcome back present from my favorite Englewood cousins: a kimono that my father bought while in Korea fifty years ago, the only possession I now have that belonged to him. It's something I'd like to hang in a special, prominent place. Yet, would this house done in "international eclectic" seem too contrived? I laugh: in many ways my story and my family's story has been an around the world journey. Why not celebrate that?

When I imagined these objects and furniture in my new home, I realized I wanted them to surround me, not only because of their emotional significance, but because I considered them *beautiful*. I loved the striking black and red *color* of my kimono, the *texture and pattern* in my Peshawar painting, and the delicate *shapes and lines* carved into my Chinese cabinet. In seeking home as self-actualization, no house could feel complete to me unless it met my need for *aesthetic* satisfaction.

Similarly, *House Beautiful, Better Homes and Gardens, Beautiful Home*—and the huge number of home decorating magazines available on any newsstand—are testimony to the importance others also attach to creating a home that is a setting for the enjoyment of beauty. Thus home as self-actualization must meet not only our most basic need for shelter and security, for psychological and social growth, it must also satisfy our basic *aesthetic* need.

Maslow pointed out that the need for beauty ". . . is found in every culture and in every age as far back as the cavemen."[10] He believed that certain people in particular have a basic aesthetic need and that they literally become sick when surrounded by ugliness and become well when their environment is beautiful.[11] Yet what constitutes beauty? Certainly this is an age-old question. One cannot hope to formulate the quintessential definition of beauty. Since Plato's time questions of aesthetics—of the good, the true, the beautiful, of taste and style—have been formulated and reformulated.[12] Yet it may be helpful to review certain schools of thought about what is beautiful, aesthetic, or artistic when thinking about beauty in the environment, in architecture, and when creating some place like home.

Most architects have been trained to think of architecture as an art form encompassing such basic aesthetic principles as mass, shape, color, texture, balance, and rhythm. Understood in this light, architecture is conceived as sculpture writ large and separate from its social, historical, economic, and psychological contexts. Thus, those responsible for designing our world come to understand beauty in relation to traditional aesthetic principles in art and architecture.

Yet, most environmental designers also recognize that their art form exists not simply in Platonic isolation, it exists too within a social and cultural context. Architecture, especially, remains our most public of art forms. Thus notions of "beautiful" architecture, of "beautiful" environments, are relative and dependent upon the public's notion of beauty. Of course, there is not simply one "public," one homogeneous mass of people all with the same sense of taste or style. We live in a society with many publics, many people with varying aesthetic preferences. This being the case, how can designers hope to create environments that fulfill each individual's need for aesthetic satisfaction?

In an attempt to come to grips with this question many designers have found the ideas of urban sociologist Herbert Gans especially useful. In his book *Popular Culture and High Culture: An Analysis and Evaluation of Taste*, Gans provided an important social/cultural perspective on notions of beauty, taste, and style. He theorized that there is a "taste structure" that results from the social and economic hierarchy in society with everyone affected by that hierarchy. Within American society, Gans identified what he called five "publics"/"cultures" that form the basis of the hierarchy including:[13]

➤ **High Culture** creators and critics whose emphasis is on *construction* of a work of art. They think they provide the "proper" culture for the rest of society often in the form of radical, iconoclastic expression.

➤ **Upper Middle Culture** upper middle class professionals who are not concerned with form but borrow from and alter high culture. Their fashionable photograph-filled art books may be casually though purposefully displayed to signal their sophistication.

➤ **Lower Middle Culture** America's dominant taste culture—teachers, accountants, etc. who value traditional morals and values. The art they prefer is romantic and representational.

➤ **Low Culture** skilled and semi-skilled factory and service workers. They reject culture and are not interested in abstract ideas or abstract art, for instance. They prefer ornateness or what Gans calls lavish, contemporary "Hollywood Modern."

➤ **Quasi Folk Culture** poor, unskilled workers not catered to by the mass media, ignored by society at large. They find expression in church or in street festivals for instance.

➤ **Fringe Cultures** youth, black and ethnic American cultures rely on a variety of alternative traditions and expressions

Although these categories may seem to pigeon hole or stereotype various groups, this was not Gans' intention. Gans did not make a value judgment about the worth of any of these groups in relation to taste culture. Instead he insisted that people were entitled to choose the taste culture they prefer, whether "high" or "low" culture.[14] Gans argued for a policy of *subcultural programming*, the provision of mass media programs, for instance, that express the aesthetic standards of all taste cultures. He saw this approach as a means of encouraging cultural diversity. Thus he made the case for *cultural democracy and cultural pluralism*.[15]

Thinking about Gans' theory, I could see that my own notion of beauty was shaped not only by my appreciation of such elements as color, texture, pattern, line, and shape but by other influences as well. To find out more about those influences, I completed the next Design Psychology Homestyle Exercise (see Exercise 8 below). In doing it, I was able to see that my personal taste was a composite of aesthetic as well as social and cultural influences.

For example, my family's cultural mobility particularly had affected me. As first generation Americans, my parents became upwardly mobile, wanting "taste culture of greater sophistication and higher status" compared to the folk and quasi-folk culture of *their* parents.[16] Thus my parents' upper middle class culture combined middle class conspicuous consumption with ersatz high art.

Following in their footsteps, I could see that my taste was also predominantly upper middle class. I had rejected all-out conspicuous consumption, yet my house was filled with home furnishings from trendy main street shops. Still, I had spent much of my adult years working in the world of the arts. Thus a favorite brick with the imprint of a fish on it was one of many decorative clues suggesting my connection to high culture.[17] When I was a Jewish Hungarian American living in England, I was certainly part of a fringe culture: no wonder my friends were amazed when I painted our front room paprika pink![18]

Similarly, architects and designers may recognize that their personal taste is a composite of different influences. Although trained in the tradition of "high art," they may be from middle class or working class backgrounds and cultures representing "lower" taste cultures. Such conflicts are supposedly "resolved" when design students are taught to reject "low class" culture as "bad" taste. Once converted, designers may rail against attempts to pander to popular taste. Wrestling with similar conflicts, dwellers may cling to familiar or traditional taste patterns or, alternatively, reject taste they actually feel comfortable with in order to appear more fashionable.

Is it possible to resolve such taste and culture conflicts? Charles Jencks sees the pluralism embodied in Gans' taste cultures as "an opportunity not a threat."[19] He points to James Stirling's Stuttgart Gallery and Robert Venturi's work at the National Gallery in London as examples of buildings which juxtapose high-tech and traditional languages without compromising either.[20]

Similarly Gans' thinking has been a touchstone for architect Denise Scott Brown. For her the challenge in civic architecture lies in finding out what taste cultures *share* and in this way appealing to many tastes and classes.[21] However, does such an approach simply run the risk of creating architecture that appeals to a banal common denominator?

Interestingly, Gans also believed that certain works appeal to all publics/taste cultures and thus prove exceptionally successful. He pointed to the success of performers Charlie Chaplin and Marilyn Monroe as examples of this phenomenon. For instance, Chaplin appealed to those belonging to lower cultures because he was a "slapstick comic and clown." For those belonging to higher cultures he was "a satirical critic of society."[22] Both performers could assume these dual high/low roles because they used their uniquely creative imaginations to communicate profound, universal truths in ways that were far from banal.

Can the same universal appeal be translated into fully satisfying architecture and home place? Chaplin and Monroe were not only able to cross social and cultural chasms, they were able to speak to everyone's common psychological world—to our shared experience of sadness and joy, success and failure. In this same way, works of art can appeal to us not only for reasons of pure aesthetics or for social/cultural reasons but because of their psychological significance. Renowned art theorist Herbert Read believed that art was able to communicate such universal human experience because "the technique of the artist is in some ways a means of breaking down the barriers between individual egos, uniting them all in some collective ego . . .."[23] Similarly, when discussing meaning in the

Photograph courtesy of Charles Jencks

visual arts, art historian Erwin Panofsky believed that such meaning existed on three levels:[24]

James Sterlings'
New Staatsgallerie,
Addition, Stuttgart,
1977–84.

> **pre-iconography** where objects and events are represented by lines, colors and volumes which make up the world of identifiable motifs, i.e. form;

> **iconography** where form has descriptive and interpretative meaning, subject matter, motifs which can be read and transmitted in relation to their literary hence cultural context;

> **iconology** where further meaning lies beneath pre-iconography and iconography—in the form of a "synthetic intuition," a meaning conditioned by personal psychology and "*Weltanschauung*," "a comprehensive conception or image of the universe and of man's relation to it."[25]

Panofsky concluded that ". . . we must bear in mind that the neatly differentiated categories . . . which seem to indicate three independent spheres of meaning, refer in reality to aspects of one phenomenon, namely, the work of art as a whole."[26]

As with Panofsky's theory about meaning in art, my contention is that fully satisfying design is a result of the combination of aesthetic form, and cultural/social *as well as* psychological significance. Panofsky provided art historians with a way of thinking about the visual arts that went beyond the mere search for form. In the same way, those searching for the meaning of place and home must look beyond architecture as sculpture or even architecture as social/cultural communication. Meaning in architecture must also encompass "synthetic intuition" and "*Weltanschauung*"—personal psychology and a wider existential sense of our place in the world.

Ideally, when these separate spheres of meaning come together, one has reached the pinnacle of "place as self-actualization." Having reached this peak, the individual is able profoundly to experience and express their vital bond with place. Although echoing it, this bond is no longer an infant's or child's perfect fusion with the world. It is an adult's recognition that they have a separate special identity, an identity which is at once individual and communal—an identity that can be expressed in the creation of place.

In the world of architecture Frank Lloyd Wright was one of those rare designers who was able to combine aesthetic sensibility, social/cultural language, and a personal yet at the same time *universal* sense of place. The source of his expression of meaning in architecture can be traced right back to his childhood roots. Wright himself provided a clue that suggests how directly he translated his environmental past into his future building work. In his autobiography he recalled *his* early experience:

And there was a small boy's mind fixed upon that spring-water stream flowing over the soft mud-bottom as it passed below the house. And whenever he could get into that stream, his was "recreation" in building dams of sticks and stones across it, sailing his shoes along the banks, wading and playing in it tirelessly whether he might or might not. Fascination for a child . . . running water![27]

Surely, his childhood fascination with running water was translated in his later architecture in the form of . . . Fallingwater! This famous house proved to be a universal example of successful architecture because it so creatively combined architectural principles with his personal (and our universal) experience of transcendent place. Bachelard celebrates such experience:

And so far from indulging in prolixity of expression, or losing oneself in the detail of light and shade, one feels that one is in the presence of an "essential" impression seeking expression; in short, in line with what our authors call a "psychological transcendent."[28]

Wright built Fallingwater in his later years. Was he able to create such satisfying residential architecture because he had reached Erikson's "eighth stage of integrity," Maslow's peak of self-actualization? Maslow concluded, for instance, that "It is only in the evolved and mature human being, in the self-actualizing, fully functioning person that truth, goodness, and beauty are so highly correlated that for all practical purposes they may be said to fuse into a unity."[29] Was Wright

a "transcender" in Maslow's sense? It is hard to say. However, while Wright did not consciously follow through or apply the (formalized) principles of Design Psychology, he seems to have engaged with the process intuitively; his own autobiography reveals a degree of self-reflection and striving toward growth that he hoped was visible in his architecture. For Wright the vision of "ideal" home was

Frank Lloyd Wright's Fallingwater, Connelsville, Pennsylvania.

> To thus make a human dwelling-place a complete work of art, in itself expressive and beautiful, intimately related to modern life and fit to live in, lending itself more freely and suitably to the individual needs of the dwellers as itself an harmonious entity, fitting in color, pattern and nature the utilities and be really an expression of them in character—this is the tall modern American opportunity in Architecture. True basis of a true Culture . . .. Surely we have here the higher ideal of unity as a more intimate working out of the expression of one's life in one's environment.[30]

To what extent would my new home be an intimate expression of my life? I still considered myself to be working *toward* psychological, social, and aesthetic satisfaction. Completing the Home-as-Self-Actualization Exercise (see Exercise 9 below) helped me assess the degree to which I felt I might achieve such satisfaction in my new home.

In terms of choosing Princeton as my home *setting*, I would certainly feel that I had chosen a stable, secure place to live. I felt my need for social growth could be achieved as my new home was both around the corner from old friends and part of a new circle of neighbors. Overall Princeton was a very physically attractive place, thus my need for an aesthetic setting could be satisfied.

In terms of *house*, I would also feel a greater security in a home of my own as opposed to rented accommodation. The house had enough space to provide us with both privacy and community. Yet what about aesthetic pleasure within the home, as well as overall psychological satisfaction?

Visions continue to form in my mind's eye as I imagine how I will transform the house to make it ours. The house is a pale green on the outside, shall I use a lot of green on the inside? I realize that I will be able to look out from the many large windows to the pond in the back and the wonderful trees that hug the house—cherry, apple and Japanese maples. It is not so much the green facade of the house I feel I should harmonize with but the beauty of the natural landscaping. There seems a calmness and simplicity about the house—an inside/outside oneness reminiscent of Japanese houses which would be consistent with the non-Western feel I hope to create on the inside. Most of all I'd look forward to replicating the house's simplicity, calmness, oneness in my own life.

Michael
Graves

When I arrived to complete the final portion of my interview, Michael Graves seemed preoccupied. He excused himself while he searched through his mail for the latest issue of *Newsweek*. Evidently it contained a photograph of him and architect Philip Johnson at Johnson's ninetieth birthday party. At last he found the picture, read the caption and showed it to me. There was no doubt about it, Graves was a prominent public figure. He had achieved esteem in the eyes of others, but had he created a world in which he could experience self-esteem, love, and belonging?

I showed Graves my adaptation of Maslow's hierarchy of needs and asked him to what extent he thought he had "self-actualized" home in the warehouse. He agreed that he had achieved home as shelter yet he acknowledged honestly and insightfully that he had not achieved home as a place for full psychological and social growth, as a place for sharing love and domestic community.

I have this thought that my daughter, who is a super mom, is showing me and my former wife how it should have been done . . . I have this sense that she is putting it back and trying to get it right on her own terms.

In a funny way I'm trying to do a similar kind of thing—although my father lived away a great part of the time. The domestic idea that was embodied in the house was missing. I'm doing it with the house though

living alone. Maybe that's what I'm doing as an architect—I'm trying to
*get it right now on my own terms with a **house** rather than a wife and*
children because the wife is gone and the children are grown and that
opportunity is somehow lost.

I have dated younger women and those women would probably have
wanted children. In a funny way I wouldn't mind starting over and trying
to get it right. That probably won't happen but nevertheless it's an
option. I think the house is a way of producing a stage for that to
happen. It can't replace it. I'm not equating personal life with house life.

Still Graves emphasized:

The sense of gathering and conviviality is something I always engaged
in a room. I wouldn't have known this without my grandmother. My
living room doesn't function like this—symbolically or functionally. I do
have two very comfortable chairs I can sit in and light a fire and the
reading stacks are right next to it. Sometimes I have parties, a sense of
conviviality and domestic gathering. If I had a child now the first thing
I'd do is move the couch out: I couldn't have Biedermeier here.

Graves cautioned against false expressions of warmth:

*One gets trapped by values and characteristics that **represent** warmth—*
cozy chairs. What I find more interesting is inviting someone in for a
drink or cheese and having a conversation.

His house still felt like a showcase, a museum, a monument to Graves' landmark style. I asked Graves what sense of home he wanted to pass down to future
generations as part of his legacy.

I don't believe in that. Peter Eisenman lives in Greenwich Village. He
sits on two Chesterfield couches around the fireplace. He has a butcher
block table—a middle class setting. His architecture is the opposite. He
says to me, "Michael, you always want my art to reflect my life!"

Graves obviously admired the close sense of family Eisenman had achieved in
his life, yet Graves felt he needed to be less prescriptive with his own children.
Nevertheless he acknowledged:

My art does reflect my life. The older I get, the place I choose to be, the
more it approaches my architecture. I take this domestic sense into an
office building. You take domestic life with you, the same issues of
posture, privacy, surround—there's a lot of crossover to the domestic
sense of the workplace.

I remembered the hearth as the centerpiece to Graves' office reception area and also remembered a conversation between him and Charles Jencks about the significance of hearth:

CJ: Another parallel with Wright's work is the emphasis on the hearth. You've emphasized the fireplace by surrounding it with paintings of figures, caryatids, and angels.

MG: That's true. I've used the hearth as one of the places where the ritual of gathering can take place—with water, fire and other natural elements. The architect has a chance to play here with ideas of myth and ritual of the culture. Wright would place an inglenook to either side of a fireplace, and centre it in the room, whereas Le Corbusier would put it, almost, in the corner. He was asking us to be the New Twentieth-Century Man, as if we didn't need the hearth any more . . ..

CJ: What are you trying to express in the paintings next to the hearth?

MG: The ritual of fire, the life of the occupants all coming together, the gathering of the family: it can be around a fire, or table, or window, or whatever is the most potent element in the room.

Living Room of the Warehouse Including Hearth and Biedermeier Furniture.

CJ: But your women seem to be offering something to the fire, in an almost religious sense.

MG: They're goddesses of the fire, both encouraging and dousing the flames.[31]

Jencks comments, finally:

A certain sad irony seems to accompany some of these wistful and beautiful altars. They seem to be stelae to a lost centre, to the family life and its sacred permanence that cannot be obtained in our society. The drawings of these icons have a melancholic air, the blues and terra-cottas and wispy outlines convey a lost dream."[32]

Yet that terracotta of the warehouse exterior remains a warm, feeling color and I was interested to discover that the exterior of the warehouse was not originally earth colored. The terracotta surfacing had been added later. Such warehouse/Graves transformations appeared to be ongoing. Graves seemed to be continuing to seek domestic and architectural fulfillment. He was sure to emphasize:

The domesticized life is important to me . . . I'm pushing the house towards an ideal that is not Utopian but is a domestic ideal for me. The green wall of the garden represents enclosure, containing a family, I suppose, or containing a life, canceling out other lives, maintaining a level of privacy, getting rid of those values that are prosaic.

To what degree *had* Graves' domestic sense *fully* crossed over into the workplace? Did his great architecture, in fact, mirror his domestic sense, a sensibility with roots firmly planted in childhood which had since grown and changed?

When I reviewed his architectural projects, certain motifs seemed consistently to appear. Was it just coincidence that the beautiful, Graves-designed San Juan Capistrano Library also consisted of a series of processional halls leading to spaces with raised ceilings and wooden strut work reminiscent of the Indianapolis stockyards? Similarly, the exterior wooden fencing capping Graves' Venice, California Library seemed largely decorative yet bore an astounding resemblance to the stockyard fencing of Graves' childhood.

I also recalled reading a description of the Portland Building:

The base of the building is covered in green ceramic tile; the main body is cream-colored with large areas of terra cotta; and the penthouse is blue. According to Graves, the colors were chosen for their associations; green for the garden, terra cotta for the earth, and blue for the sky.[33]

Given our conversation, I interpreted this as the green echo of the garden of Graves' youth, the terracotta warmth of Italy as the feeling aspect of Graves' personality. Above all, the introduction of color in contrast to the cityscape seems once again to refer us back to the more pervasive connection here—the indelible mark made upon Graves in his youth by buildings of character. It is this notion of character that remains the consistent and central thread in all of his work, regardless of the specific form that character takes. Clearly, it has been just as essential to Graves to nurture his architectural vision as it was for him to tend his victory garden.

While he had gained international esteem, however, Graves expressed particular disappointment that his talent had never been allowed expression closer to home: although he had long been a faculty member at the School of Architecture at Princeton University, he had never been given a major commission at the University.

> Princeton isn't big enough to make it a major location for one's buildings. Princeton University doesn't allow faculty members to practice on campus. That would be a wonderful thing if you could build, teach and work in the same place. To live in Princeton for thirty-five years and not be able to build here—that's too bad. You could also say almost none of us got to practice in New York City. At the same time it's hard to point to New York City and say it's a city of great buildings. Something, somewhere, the restrictions, or time or whatever has not allowed the extraordinary to occur there.

> If you think about the great architects associated with cities—John Nash, Brunelleschi—they had a certain mobility but they were associated with a place. Almost none of us are. We are all running around the world doing projects in Tokyo, in Manila, in Cairo. It's really quite mad. People think it's glamorous but it's not.

Graves went on to describe the complete hassle involved in negotiating the New York City traffic calling his most recent sojourn "a dreadful experience . . . . Living here is an avoidance of all that waste of time . . . I didn't realize that when I moved to Princeton." Yet in analyzing his home setting as a place that provided aesthetic pleasure Graves expressed dissatisfaction:

> If you were to replay your life, you might live in a place where there is culture to look at—in Rome, Paris or London as opposed to Tokyo, which is a steel and glass disaster. You could say that Princeton is anything but a disaster but it's very limited in what you can look at. The University is pleasant enough. You have **good** buildings but not **great** buildings.

> You might say—"You had your chance. Why didn't you live in Rome?" I'm not Italian. My work is a kind of family. Italy isn't building and I want to build.

I asked Graves if he would consider moving again.

> I won't move again. I may not always be at the University, but Princeton is still a good base.

The Warehouse Before Addition of Terra Cotta Surfacing

The Warehouse After Addition of Terra Cotta Surfacing

The Original Stockyard
Pens from Michael
Graves' Childhood.

Exterior of Los Angeles Public Library, Abbot Kinney Memorial Branch, Venice California Originally Designed by Michael Graves.

Gallery, San Juan Capistrano Regional
Library Designed by Michael Graves.

The Portland Building, Portland, Oregon
(View From Fifth Avenue) Designed by Michael Graves.

The Portland
Building—I
interpreted this as
the green echo of
the garden of
Graves' youth, the
terracotta warmth
of Italy as the
feeling aspect of
Graves' personality.
Above all, the
introduction of
color in contrast to
the cityscape seems
once again to refer
us back to the
more pervasive
connection here—
the indelible mark
made upon Graves
in his youth by
buildings of
character.

Instead, in terms of home as self-actualization, Graves clearly derived his greatest aesthetic pleasure from his actual house and from the special objects contained within it. When I asked Graves to complete the Homestyle Exercise, he clearly identified himself as a member of "high culture," characterizing his parents as coming from "lower middle culture." Thus especially meaningful to him were objects he placed in the "Grand Tour" category. His inkwells, for example, are little Temples of Vesta, miniature pieces of architecture yet with a practical function as well. Graves explained,

They emphasize the importance of travel for me. It was a very big deal
for me to travel in, around and out of Rome.

Graves also categorized his paintings and drawings as special to him because he himself draws and paints.

I don't collect avidly but if I see something in a gallery or antique shop
in Italy or France, I might acquire it. I see something once every two
years or so. The drawings start to have a range of subject matter:
landscapes, animals, historic scenes . . ..

As if to pre-empt my next question, Graves pointed to the livestock in the old Indiana stockyard photograph I had brought with me and quickly added that he did not think it had to do with the stockyards, merely that he liked to populate landscapes. No connection had even occurred to me, but I thought it was an interesting possibility. Was he sure there was no connection between his landscape paintings and his memories of Indiana?

*It **might** have to do with the stockyards. The stockyards haven't been an*
overriding interest for me for years and years. My ability to draw came
from my childhood more than the subject matter.

Other special objects included his Greek and Etruscan pots. They appealed to him both in terms of pure aesthetics (their relief—the problem of drawing, painting and depicting space) yet also as examples of

How art can express culture and how culture cared for the domestic
qualities of life. Those pots were used at the table. Their past is part of the
cycle of life from birth to death and since I design table-top objects . . ..

Graves also stressed the importance of furniture as special objects. He saw his Biedermeier as possessing a purely aesthetic, architectural quality yet also expressing the culture from which it was derived.

When asked if there were any other special objects he would like to include in his home that reflected who he was, Graves mentioned paintings by David or Ingres, ". . . if I could afford them." Interestingly, however, when I asked Graves to imagine what single object he would save if his house caught fire, he replied:

> *I have a little picture album. It has my parents' pictures in it. I might*
> *grab that because it reaches into the past. It connects.*

Moving from the past to the future, I asked Graves about new possibilities where his sense of home was concerned. In terms of the warehouse, he reflected:

> *There are lots of things I'd like to do with it. Not only finish what was*
> *started but to build more. What would the building be like if I added a*
> *major structure, added a symposium space? Visiting critics could live here*
> *during their 6 to 12 weeks in Princeton. The things that I've collected, the*
> *things that are here, perhaps, would give pleasure to other people.*

Consciously or not, this environmental legacy that Graves envisioned seemed a combination of the legacy of his Indiana grandmother and of his American Academy in Rome experience, Princeton style. Would Graves simply be content to re-create that sense of informal conviviality for others after his lifetime, or could he also re-create it *now* for himself?

Graves spoke about possible plans to build a villa in Egypt, a place to go "to eat well and play golf . . . to be far away from everything that would be a distraction." Though he added that he was uncertain whether he would really like that. In a similar vein, Graves mentioned projected plans for an apartment in Florida, a place to play golf in the winter "that's just for *me*." It would be a place where, despite his responsibilities, he could say, "This Saturday is *mine*." He envisioned that such a place would not have the Biedermeier. Instead, it would be "lighter, zippier—someplace I can sit down in a bathing suit."

As our interview came to a close, I walked slowly back out of Michael Graves' stunning house. It was certainly easy to see why this residence has been endlessly photographed and filmed and why it enters our minds as a model for others attempting to create some place like home. Still, the Graves residence and the overall Graves style which it typifies seemed to say as much about one individual man as about a master designer. This ideal home, remained quintessentially Graves' home, an amalgam of visual and emotional imagery drawn from his own environmental story—a story which continues to be written.

Note

As this book goes to press, a new and unfortuate chaper to Michael Grave's life story has been written: Graves contracted a spinal cord infection in February 2003 which left him paralyzed from the waist down. It is uncertain whether he will ever walk again. As such, Grave's office is adapting his home for wheelchair access, while also retaining the warehouse's character and elegance.

Vase From the Collection
of Michael Graves,
The Warehouse, Princeton,
New Jersey.

Charles
Jencks

Jencks paused before we embarked upon our final interview session. He found it impossible to believe that I could really get to the bottom of his environmental sources in only six hours. I agreed with him. It *was* impossible to truly explore the riches of anyone's treasure chest of place in such a brief time period. In fact, I believe the meaning of home and place is something that can continue to be explored throughout one's life.

With this in mind, the main purpose of this last session with Charles Jencks simply would be to enable him to reflect on all that we had said so far about his self-environment. We began by looking at Maslow's hierarchy. To what extent did he feel he had self-actualized home?

I've never had any problem with "shelter and security." I've been given a "sense of love and belonging" by my wife and friends. "Self-expression?" Yes. "Self-esteem?" Partly. But I've had a continuous cross-fire of attacks from the Modernists and Prince Charles followers and others who dislike Post-Modernism. So, I don't get esteem all the time, nor have I sought it. "English people"—I don't fit into a niche where they can put me, but I have a lot of English friends that have gotten used to me. I'm not particularly well thought of in England, but I've always had people in the home that have loved me. So it's a home. As for "social growth"—I've always had plenty of privacy and community. "Aesthetic pleasure?" Too much! I love my studio as a place for

aesthetic pleasure. I love to look at the play of light and shadow. This
bungalow gives me low culture aesthetic pleasure because it's funky.
High culture studio, low culture here. In London, again, every room is
designed so you get aesthetic overkill. One of the problems in designing
the Thematic House is I designed too much.

I was curious about the source of Jencks' high/low dual aesthetic preferences.
He commented on the difference between previous generations:

There was a shift in taste cultures and living standards between my
father and grandmother.

As a member of the next generation I wondered how Jencks had been able to
reconcile these great differences. The messages he had received from his father,
the "artist and gentleman" was "don't compromise one's opinions, taste, values,
and judgment." Yet Jencks challenged this perspective:

I don't think that's the proper place of either the artist or the gentleman
because compromise is also important as is engagement with a
*heterogeneous society. Of course, I believe in **part** of the aristocratic*
tradition—that there are trans-human standards which are hard to
grasp. But it's also important to grasp the nature of society and
compromise and worldliness. So I don't accept the elitist half of the
*aristocratic equation. I **do** accept that we are **not** the measure of all*
*things. It's rather like the church which is full of **both** compromise **and***
other-worldliness.

Yet how had Jencks translated this world of opposites into some place that
seemed like home for him? Jencks had mentioned his family's shift in taste
cultures. I knew he had also been influenced by Herbert Gans' theory of class and
culture. Jencks had used Gans' theory to argue the case for pluralism in a 1994
Guardian article.[34] Thus I suggested to him that he is operating through two very
different symbolic worlds. The world of his grandmother and Mount Vernon Place
and the world of his father as made manifest in this bungalow and the Bay House.
What Gans' theory did for him in a nice way—part of why the ideas of taste
cultures were so appealing—is that it reconciled opposites, the pluralism that he
was experiencing in his life in environmental terms. I hypothesized that the
consequence of this for Jencks on the public level was that he had become a great
advocate of pluralism, but that was partly because he had come to believe in it
privately.
Jencks nodded

I agree with you, particularly what you said about trying to reconcile
those different tastes.

Yet Jencks was still quick to insist that the main reason he had created the Thematic House was to illustrate his theories of Post-Modernism:

> I did the London house as a [piece of] polemic because in 1979, when we bought it, Post-Modern architecture partly existed because of my naming it. Already you could see it was having its problems of ornament and ersatz. There was so much bad Post-Modernism caused (my argument was) by Robert Venturi's false understanding of what a symbol is. So I did my building as a polemic against his "Decorated Shed," to say symbolism is not about sticking signs on a building. In fact, such commercial and unthinking collage usually destroys a building. Symbolism is something that cuts across all levels of meaning. A sign, like a stop sign or a traffic sign, has **one** meaning whereas symbolism has connotations which are unfathomable. It is fundamentally **not** a one-liner. So I disagreed with Venturi. I knew he was wrong and his mistake was dangerous. Of course, his influence and creativity are not altogether bad. I don't deny that one has to take on commercial tasks and Route 66. He did inventively: more power to him. It's just that he, like a lot of revolutionaries, mistakes a small for a big truth.

> So you have to understand that the Thematic House is my attempt to ground ornament, polychromy, expression, form, all the rest of it—all the things that Post-Modernists were running away with in a kind of drunken orgy of building. I sought to ground form in symbolism . . .. The only way you can influence people is to persuade them that there's more **power** to what you're doing, more power out of doing what you think is good. Symbolism is a way of giving order and **meaning** to what was out-of-control expression.

Wanting to know more about the *psychological* meaning place held for Jencks, I engaged him in the Favorite Childhood Place Visualization Exercise. Jencks was quite willing to follow my directions and close his eyes.

> I imagined a meadow in Boundbrook Island on Cape Cod just before you get to my sister's house. This place is now overgrown with trees but it used to have trees just at the end. It was a very peaceful place, with a velvet soft ground of a peculiar grass. It was one of my favorite spots, but I don't know why. Maybe because it was so peaceful, because the grass was so inviting—you thought it would make a perfect outdoor bed.

> The second place I imagined as a favorite haunt was on the walk to the Bay where we used to go down to the beach all the time as a family—my mother, father and sister. It was a little wooded area with pseudo-acacia trees. Again, it had that very soft grass underneath and was a very cool place. It has it's own microclimate, so it's always a respite, an oasis, on

*a hot walk. In there were grape vines and some old remains of two
houses. But the brick is still there and I imagined picking up a brick
when I went through this exercise. It is a magical place—but a very
modest place. I walked with Maggie several times through it. I imagined
being with her. It's a sanctuary, an Arcadian place.*

I asked Jencks if this favorite place from the past reminded him of any place
in the present.

*Well, I've created this garden in Scotland. I hadn't thought until you
mentioned it, but in a kind of far-fetched analogy, it's not unlike what I
call the area of paradise or death, the place where I'm constructing a
kind of wild, anarchic growth in a garden which is otherwise tended. I
had difficulty in doing this because the gardener's proclivity is to tend
and clean up dead trees. But I'm also interested in places that are
riotous, primeval, and uncontrolled. If you can get a wild sanctuary
right, it's sometimes more magical than a designed one. I hadn't thought
until now, but it has a ruin and where I'm designing this part of the
garden are the old ruins of a castle which was vandalized. So, in fact,
there are stones lying around like those tiny bricks in a jungle, in a kind
of overgrowth.*

Jencks stopped speaking for a moment and then, with a laugh of recognition,
continued:

*In a sense both spaces have these old trees that are dying. Dying trees
can be really poignant and always stand out in a garden, though not
in the forest. So, as it happens, the image is one I am now trying to
re-create.*

*Suppose there is a parallel that I am now seeing? I hadn't thought until
now that I'm trying to re-create anything except to create a vast
symbolic program that the garden has. "Paradise and Hell" are pretty
much the program there and I decided this with Maggie before she died.
Death and resurrection were an important aspect of the garden here
because things die and then new growth sprouts up in superabundance.
So it's a very good symbol . . .. The famous quote around which the
Poussin painting was created—Et in Arcadia Ego—: "Death is even in
arcadia." I'm very conscious of this. I lived with a dying wife for two
years and I will put a monument in there to her [and I have put her
statue there]. It's something that's on my mind.*

When Jencks spoke of death and resurrection, of the time spent with his dying
wife, I sensed no self-pity. The creation of the garden and the idea of a monument
seemed a very fitting use of place to symbolize this passing phase of his life.
Jencks continued:

The garden is what Maggie and I have been working on for the last five or six years. In a sense it's a culmination of my life, because if you look at my work as an architect, I've often written about something and then tried to carry through the ideas at the same time. I started with the book, Adhocism *and I shared my adhoc work with my first wife. My next polemical book was on Post-Modernism and the Cape studio was constructed to illustrate post-modern theories of double coding. The third polemical book, was on the Thematic House (also called the Cosmic House) which developed and tested ideas of symbolism. The book I've just written,* The Architecture of the Jumping Universe, *is on cosmogenesis, science and the universe and that's what's been influencing the design of the garden in Scotland. So the four periods of my life and career are mixed up with these four different designs and they culminate in this garden because it is the most mature formulation of my theories on Post-Modernism, architecture, and science. So I'd much rather end on that note than my Thematic House in London—which is the third stage of my thinking.*

Scottish Garden by the Brook Designed by Maggie Keswick, 1997. "This area I had conceived as a riotous wilderness of overgrown and dying vegetation, a primeval swamp, a place where the excess of untended nature would show, at once, death and renewal." — Charles Jencks.

I had seen neither Jencks' Thematic House nor his Scottish garden. I had only experienced his studio and was still feeling the power of that place. "I think the studio was about more than Post-Modernism—it seems to show both the feeling and thinking part of you. To me that single-room structure symbolizes the head, the heart and the body together."

I agree and Maggie and I worked on it together, her heart, my head. I've always thought one shouldn't create without a woman. Maggie made the room really like the old place on School Street in Wellfleet, a cozy wonderfully warm room and yet it has that high style.

"It was the perfect combination of those two strands which you experienced in childhood."

What you're saying reveals that to me but I hadn't thought about it. I agree it's embedded in my past—you're right.

I asked Jencks, "What does all this that I've been revealing mean for architecture?"

It means that the production of architecture may be more than the average production of architecture.

I nodded in agreement:

"Yes, and this is what else I think it means. When we talk about the various styles people have and the style wars, we're looking at superficial 'isms'—Post-Modernism or whatever. But underneath the 'isms' are these personal stories. Just as Michael Graves' story is shown in his house, so his story is also shown in his buildings. If I went to other famous architects, I'm sure I'd find their stories shown in their public buildings as well. So when we talk about symbolism, I disagree with Venturi because he emphasized sign over symbol. As such, for instance, the importance of Caesar's heads would have been overlooked. But I also see what you've written is only the top layer. That the real symbolism is these deeper symbols underneath, the symbols of selfhood. When you talk about this bungalow or the Thematic House, you talk about symbolism of culture, but you haven't explored, for example, the deeper meaning of your studio which has nothing to do with culture *per se*, although it's not like it has to be one thing or another.

"Let me just take it a little further and explain why I think it's just as important to look at symbolism my way as it is to see it your way. Let's just say everything I've said about your environmental autobiography is the case or even three quarters of it is the case. Then, perhaps, what I've done over the last three days is bring it to consciousness. The next step for you, or an architect or any person going through this process would be to ask, 'How do I bring these things consciously together in the future?' How do you continue to bring the heart and the head together further as in the studio? Are you bringing them together in the garden in Scotland?"

*Yes, but again I did that with Maggie . . .. When you talk about
emotions you're talking about a level of design and control which is
the amplification and direction of ideas. The rational things have to
be designed one way, and then you allow the emotional things to
accrue and modify them. You may become arbitrary if you start off and
continue to design within a feeling perspective. There are people that
can do this, such as Frank Gehry. That's why Maggie worked beautifully
with Frank. The best thing she ever did was a garden design with him.
So I won't put rationality above emotion as a design principle. But
often, if you start off and continue to work within a feeling perspective,
you generate horrors. You'll either end up with wicker and pillows and
"nice pretty, pretty" or drown in kitsch.*

"It isn't that! When you described that last house on School Street, that had
nothing to do with wicker furniture."

Yes, that's right. That came straight out of a tradition.

"Forget tradition. The studio! What was totally lost in pictures of it was the
feeling in that house and it had no wicker furniture!"

*Maggie's problem as a designer, and why she was not a very good
designer until she worked with Frank Gehry was that her decisions were
eclectic and going from one image or ambience to another. Frank works
entirely differently, although he works out a feeling tone. He sculpts,
mixes and he's very intuitive—he likes to work out of control. He loves
the intuitive and worked brilliantly with Maggie, so I'm not denying this
method for some people. All I'm saying is that usually, if people allow
expression to dominate, they end up with clichés of self-expression.
Before I came along in Maggie's life, she was designing things that were
standard of living packages for the upper middle class.*

"She contributed to you, but you contributed to her."

That's right.

"So the challenge for you is: She's gone, so how do you carry on?"

*I have other women who I collaborate with and who I can bounce ideas
off. I think the female sensibility is extremely important.*

"That sensibility can be discovered in *you*."

Frank Gehry and I can do it together.

**The next step for
you or an architect,
or any person
going through
this process would
be to ask, "How
do I bring these
things together
consciously in the
future? How do I
continue to bring
the heart and the
head together?"**

"*You* have the early experiences of love and affection and it's very evident in yourself and your family as well, so it's not so remote a part of yourself. *You* have the potential to explore that for yourself."

Perhaps this was again a case where our views were not mutually exclusive. Jencks could explore his "feeling" part by himself, yet he could also gain a balance from someone else. Jencks went on:

> Let me put the worst case scenario to you. You start a game of noughts and crosses and you fill in all these spaces of the past and then you say, "Ah! There are certain links." Therefore you read a link. But in the nature of the case there will always be some connections because architecture always relates to other architecture. They have similar structures, will always generate parallelisms. But the problem is you can't know which are the correct ones, and which are the ones that just happen to pop out of the pre-structured game of architecture. I accept that you are sometimes right about me, but I'm not convinced of your method. You take the past and locate things and then take the present and locate similar things and then say, "Ah! I see, there are links!" There may be deep connections, but it may be only fortuitous appearances. How do you tell the difference?

"I've gone through this process so many times with architects and non-architects. You said, 'Good Heavens!' as I brought your environmental story to consciousness, but I've had people say variations on "Good Heavens" to me for years! Let me put it back to you. Does it seem to you like I have struck a cord or not?"

Jencks paused and then confirmed:

> I think you are on to something, but the two questions that are on my mind are: a) How can you separate the superficial structure from the deep reality? b) And supposing that it's true that you've got the parallels, how do you translate them into design? What are the implications for design? Suppose this is all true? So what?

"I've put the exercises in the book for people to do themselves. It's basically an opportunity for self-reflection, for people to explore ways they can strive for healthy place–self development."

> But how can you convince someone that what they'll get out of it is important?

"I begin the book by talking about the importance of childhood experience—"

Jencks was quick to interrupt stating that he simply did not believe that childhood was any more important than later experiences.

"I agree. Childhood just has a profound beginning effect. Look at your story here. You had these profound messages and images from childhood. That wasn't the end point. You created the Thematic House but you also created the studio and you are also doing Scotland and you also had a wife who had an influence on you. So it wasn't like this is the beginning, middle, and end. It's not, but the problem is that people don't look at that. They don't look at those stories. They are trained in architecture school in aesthetics and technology and maybe if they're lucky they do one session on environmental psychology, but that is it. They design as either sculpture or function or a combination of the two and the whole human part is left out. The human part is in each of us both in terms of self and in terms of environmental experiences. We've all had environmental experiences. So when we end up in that chair in the lecture theatre we're bringing a host of information with us—a reservoir, a treasure chest. In the same way that *you* have a treasure chest, everybody has a treasure chest—a different one from yours and, perhaps not as rich, but it is there. It is rich for them and it isn't even looked at."

I agree.

"Well, that's what this book is about—getting people to look at that treasure chest. For example, one thing that happens is that people begin to design with high-art input. But, if they're students from working class families, as many of my students were in England, they end up with this conflict between all the messages they got in childhood about what place is and what they're being told place is in architecture school. How do they reconcile those two things? They don't, unless they know Gans. And nobody deals with the environmental knowledge architecture students already come with. It's disregarded and overlays are put on top of it. Then, when they design for somebody else, they think, "This is the high art. This is the right thing," and so they disregard their treasure chests and that of their clients and substitute a high art notion of taste and style. If they went into that reservoir, they could then identify with their clients, but also do what Gans says and give them alternatives, choices, an approach built on cultural democracy— what you might call a respect for, and deeper understanding of pluralism."

I guess we agree. Semiotics and all the work I did on Post-Modernism was an attempt to design within the codes of the user and extend these codes—and they have to do with life experience. I just don't know how the type of learning you're talking about is going to compete for money and time with the study of the symbolic, aesthetic, and functional aspects of architecture.

"What I say in my book is that the ideal place is functional, aesthetic and contains this part as well."

What do you call this area? You'll have to call it something. Give it a name like aesthetics and function: you can't create a new paradigm in architecture and study without giving it a name.

"The idea of environmental autobiography has been around for a long time, so has environmental psychology. Unfortunately these ideas have not been effectively communicated to the public at large, or to architects. Perhaps this book will help convince people that there is a powerful connection between past, present and future sense of home and place and that this connection can be explored through . . . Design Psychology.

"One thing I can say for sure: having done these exercises, when you return to your London house, or any of your homes, for that matter, you will now experience them, see them in a totally different way than ever before."

Our time had run out. As I was leaving, Jencks' family and friends had gathered by the porch and were busy artistically arranging a huge collection of smooth grey stones. They were all very intent yet laughing and enjoying themselves too. Jencks explained that this communal exercise had become a regular Cape Cod ritual for them. I looked back before heading down the road and imagined that these beautiful, carefully placed stones formed a simple monument to Jencks' true legacy of place. A sense which, until now, lay buried so meaningfully below.

Andres Duany

When I turned down the road heading toward my final session with Andres Duany, I was surprised to find that his office was located in a working class, nondescript residential Miami neighborhood rather than in the more predictable high-powered, center-city location usually associated with those of Duany's professional stature. Even more surprising was the office itself. A former warehouse, the outside of the building seemed to be the simplest possible ochre stucco building. Its imposing door set right up to the street was, in fact, not a door at all but a plain, white curtain hanging down across the building's opening. For a moment it appeared as if the facade, complete with curtain, was a stage set—that by slipping past a portion of the drapery which was pulled to one side, I was about to go behind the scenes to see how the newest drama of American planning was being produced.

I passed through the entry to the conventional reception desk and indicated that I was there for a late-afternoon appointment with Duany. First, however, I asked if I could use the ladies' room. The receptionist directed me through a main room and then to the right. As I followed her directions, I enjoyed the drama of this space of high ceilings, open plan offices and drafting tables. I walked on but then hesitated when I realized that the main room I was to pass through was Duany's office and that he was there in the middle of a meeting. Had I gone the wrong way? Returning to the receptionist, she assured me that I had followed her directions correctly and that it was perfectly fine to walk right through the large room even though there was a meeting in progress.

Uncomfortable about this, I tried to pass through unobtrusively and it was only when I returned to meet there with Duany that I understood: in the center of this large room, facing each other, the desks of Elizabeth Plater-Zyberk and Andres Duany touched, forming almost one big table. This was "the room of the table" office style. As Duany and I spoke, staff members came and went freely around us in that familiar swirl I had experienced in his Coral Gables home and *he* had experienced in the homes of the Cuban and Spanish peasants of his past.

Duany suggested that we go to dinner around the block at one of his usual places, an informal Cuban restaurant. The combination of clattering dishes, lively Latin music singing from the radio and the friendly exchange of greetings between waiters and customers made his home and office seem quiet as a tomb by comparison! Duany, of course, was unperturbed and the flavorful quality of our meal and discussion quickly drew me in also.

I began by having Duany complete the Special Objects Inventory Exercise. He had already mentioned that Christopher Alexander's book would be the one thing he would bring to a desert island with him. Another book that Duany mentioned as a special object was Edward Lutyens' *Memorial*, the three volume set. Duany explained that he considered Lutyens a uniquely talented architect working within conventions and went on to talk about the importance of his books to him overall.

Beyond his books, Duany mentioned owning a collection of military pistols made between 1870 and 1950. He considered the pistols "cultural objects," designs that belonged to officers and were associated with national prestige. Duany had an "art historical take" on these guns, pointing out that they were a complete manifestation of the many countries they came from. He easily traced his interest in weaponry back to his youth in Castro's Cuba. Duany could remember those years between 1955 and 1959:

My house was very close to the fighting. We would sometimes have to hide, and sometimes we had to leave Santiago—the shooting was too nearby. There was much more fighting in Santiago during the revolution than [in] Havana. Sometimes our gardener would go out to the field and bring back this military stuff—empty shells, a helmet and at seven, eight, nine years old, I would have a collection.

On my grandfather's farm there were certain places we couldn't go into because there may have been explosives dropped. There was fighting all around the city. There were soldiers in jeeps going up and down the streets. After the revolution triumphed it was tremendously exciting. Very cool guys all around: "The Victorious Revolutionaries."

My family continued to live in Cuba for a year after the revolution. Of course that was a very glamorous situation—the young guerilla fighters. Those were our heroes. My family was quite pro-revolution and I was very taken by these soldiers who gave you souvenir bullets. I had many toy guns which my grandmother would give me. It wasn't this horror of guns that we know now. We got guns for presents. That's the way it was.

Duany's memory of those revolutionary years was fascinating. Trying to make sense of those recollections in terms of Design Psychology, I reflected back to him:

"What I'm hearing is this story of a lot of changing territory. I hear of this very stable situation—your grandfather, your father laying out the city. They were the ones who created this city. Then the territory of the hill, the battle. Then the plantation that your grandfather laid out . . .."

Duany quickly interrupted:

But I never said that was stable . . .. Even before the revolution it was unstable . . .. My grandfather tried to sell it in 1929. He already knew Cuba was unstable. That it would not end well. My other grandfather, the doctor was in exile three times. That's how much revolutionary activity there was in Cuba. Bombs. Coups d'état. I don't think stability is something my family had ever known. My grandmother's family who lives here lost everything in the war of 1868 to '78.

Listening but reflecting further, I continued:

"I was going to say: they laid out this place. They established territory. You were in Cuba. Then you were in America. Then you weren't in America anymore—you were in Barcelona. America. Cuba. All this back and forth. What if I said to you, that the underlying motive for you to create timeless towns is to create stability in the city?"

Sure. Except that we've lived in this house for twenty-four years.

"Perhaps all this history is part of why architecture is less interesting to you—because architecture is not where the challenge was. Perhaps in your life story the challenge was to create stable land."

I think that may be so.

Later he also reflected:

You have to understand that it was very glamorous. The revolution was not a traumatic experience. It was exciting . . . and it could be that the appeal of the CNU[35] could be the search for that kind of excitement.

It was amazing to think that the seeds of an American planning revolution had actually been planted by a Cuban revolutionary war.

I moved us on, asking, "What other special objects or collections do you have?"

I've always had a good car! I really like them!

I laughed then asked him, "Are there any other special objects for you? In fact, if there were a fire and you could only save one thing in your house, what would that one thing be?"

It was amazing to think that the seeds of an American planning revolution had actually been planted by a Cuban revolutionary war.

Probably the painting of my mother, which is a great work of art. When I was in Cuba on the last trip, I brought it out.

"Where did you get it?"

When we left, we gave it to the painter, the artist, who then gave it to his administrator. When I was in Cuba, I heard that he still had it so I bought it from him. I had it restored in Havana and brought it out just recently. It had been missing for forty years.

"That's amazing. So tell me the history of the painting."

It was done in '57. It always had a central place in our living room. The artist was very much a friend—perhaps even a best friend of the family so he was very real to me. He has done other paintings of members of the family in exile which I have. This missing painting of my mother became a mythological piece . . .. It was unbelievably exciting that we found it! . . . So this would be the object.

Remembering the painting clearly, I said, "I kept looking at that painting off and on when we were in your dining room. I thought it was a painting of Liz. Do you think there's a similarity?"

Oh yes.

"Also, aside from looking at it as an object of design, it certainly seemed to me like it told a story."

A very enhanced story.

"What's the story to you?" I asked.

Lost and recovered. It could be the recovery of the history of our family in Cuba. It could be the first step in that direction. The things we left in Cuba—the houses, are very damaged so this was the prime object.

"Besides conveying the drama of lost and found, just looking at the painting and not knowing any of that, it is still a very dramatic painting. If you could disassociate from all the history that you know and just free associate and say, 'this woman . . ..' Now put the adjectives in."

I really like the way she looks as an object. I really like the colors and the composition.

"And who is she?"

A Greek. She's Hellenized aesthetically.

"Hellenized as what?"

Her hair and posture. It's a classic version/interpretation of my mother.

"An ideal?"

Yes, an ideal.

"An ideal of what?"

A classic and aesthetic ideal. There's something interesting in front of her in the painting. I don't know what it is.

"If I remember correctly, it looked like she's drawing a curtain back."

I hadn't thought of that. Opening the curtain. I hadn't seen that.

"What was she drawing it back to—symbolically?"

No one knows, perhaps my mother knows.

Maybe not, but there seemed to be a convergence of the "poetics of space" here: the curtain drawn back in this painting and the curtain drawn back at the entrance of Duany's office seemed remarkably similar! To me, both suggested mystery and impending drama—perhaps loss and recovery of some place like home in Cuba and in . . . America. Once again Bachelard's words came back to me: "Through the brilliance of an image, the distant past resounds with echoes, and it is hard to know at what depth these echoes will reverberate and die away."[36]

As Duany moved on to the final Homestyle Exercise and Home as Actualization Exercise, themes that we had already discussed were reinforced: Duany saw his ancestors as coming from an upper middle-class taste culture, yet he now associated his taste structure (i.e. Arts and Crafts design) with lower middle culture. He seemed deeply satisfied with his home on an aesthetic, social and psychological level yet very dissatisfied with Coral Gables and Miami as places of social or psychological growth. Overall he commented that it was true, adding:

Churchill said, "We shape buildings and then our buildings shape us."
Design does effect behavior.

With this in mind, Duany remarked:

One of the things that worries me about your thesis is that the
interviews if you do them with people who've grown up not

> ". . . through the brilliance of the image, the distant past resounds with echoes, and it is hard to know at what depth these echoes will reverberate and die away."
> —Gaston Bachelard

*in interesting houses, but with the suburban product? The highly
manipulated product. If you show them a house with good proportions
and a house with bad proportions, an increasing number of people
will choose the house with bad proportions. I'm really worried about
the kids who have experienced nothing but that. There's a generation
that is now in college that doesn't know what a real street feels like.
It's typical here in Miami. We have to take kids to older cities and
show them what a street is.*

"A lot of my theories come from child development theory. I believe that the
seeds of one's environmental preferences are planted in childhood. We talk about
heredity and environment and speculate about which is more important, but we
are usually talking about the social environment. We don't think about the physical
environment, but the physical environment has a profound effect."

Duany continued:

*So what is going to happen to these kids who have grown up in really
mediocre environments?*

"I say my mission is to show people that a whole part is missing—the middle
of the triangle. We just can't look at design magazines . . .. For example, often
when I do these exercises, when I ask them to remember transcendent places—
the places that come to the fore may have nothing to do with architecture. They
may be outdoor places, for example, that have some powerful quality for them.
They realize, 'Oh my God, there's none of that here! The kind of place that means
so much to me is absent!' It's getting people to realize that."

Thinking about what I had said, Duany suggested:

*I always try to take a good idea and multiply it because nothing in the
modern world is important unless it's done massively. To figure out how
to do it on a large scale—not just how to build one town, but how do we
build hundreds of towns. One of the techniques to do this is to give
away the knowledge. How does Design Psychology become national?*

I explained:

"In the book are all these exercises you've done that others can actually do as
well. They are also written so that they can be used in schools of design with first
year design students, for example, rather than having them just learn all about
the great design gurus. That way they learn from the beginning how to tap into
the great reservoir of environmental knowledge that *they*, themselves, possess but
which is usually dismissed."

Duany agreed:

*In fact it's not dismissed, it's removed. The schools cut the kids off
from what they know. Architecture professionals are not the least bit*

interested in that. They are interested in whatever is the latest thing and that does not come from within. It's about surface.

I think that our clients would be interested in this (although I'm no longer building houses). They would be flattered. It would offer a great deal of efficiency in focusing the client—many people who are having houses designed all over the map. People who have been thinking about building a house for a long time often have a pile of clippings which are contradictory. You have to point out to them that this room that is full of windows with mullions is not like this cantilevered glass wall. Actually it would be a session for the client to focus. It would be efficient for the architect to have someone do that.

However, this is a very high-end operation. The luxury of having nine hours. Although from the point of view of how much time the architect wastes, it's very efficient. Actually nine hours is nothing.

I was pleased that Duany could envision the practical application of Design Psychology. Turning back to him, I asked, "What legacy would *you* like to leave for future generations?"

I have the opportunity to actually answer that concretely. I would like to help recover—I think the ideal of urbanism in North America. Well there isn't one ideal . . .. What's happening today is that as the private realm—the houses and yards—improve, the public realm—the streets and squares—decay. One could think that the best public realm of all is in an average twenty-storey city like New York—terrific street life, but the private realm is a bit squeezed. Charleston, on the other hand, is the midpoint of the balance between public and private. That's what I admire about that city.

Finally, I do think that some people do prefer living in larger-lot houses in which neighbors don't play a part. They have a very weak public realm. What I would like to leave is a concept of urbanism in which people have a choice, particularly as their preferences change at different times of their lives. So [I'd like people] to be able to live within these varied environments and preferably within the same city.

What I don't like about suburbia is that it gives none of these choices. Suburbia delivers only a decent private realm. Whatever the density in suburbia—and it can be very high—there's no public realm, and that's the problem.

I would like to restore a model of urbanism that would have within a community all the choices but that you still belong to a community that has a public realm.

Duany's planning vision certainly was clear but did not seem dictatorial. On the contrary, it seemed egalitarian and provided for freedom of choice.

> "I think clients would be interested in this . . .. It would offer a great deal of efficiency in focusing the client."—Andres Duany

Portrait of Enid Duany, Mother of Andres
Duany, which was Recovered from Cuba.

Photograph by Carlos Morales. Courtesy Andres Duany.

Exterior
View of
Duany
Plater-
Zyberk and
Company's
Office.

Photograph by Carlos Morales. Courtesy of DPZ.

As we left the restaurant and drove back to his office, I wondered what city had had the most impact on him as a young man. He replied quickly:

Paris

"Why is that?"

*I studied in Paris just one year but I **constantly** refer to Paris in my mind in terms of what urbanism should be. . .. It's a city that has real conceptual clarity and I understood it when I was first observing and learning.*

"What were you doing there?"

Studying at the Ecole des Beaux Arts, but mostly hanging out. I learned so much.

"Like what?"

Well, first I learned about the city, second I learned French, third of all I learned how an architecture school is supposed to work. Not the stylistics. You see, I was in an atelier that still had the Beaux Arts tradition, a way of learning architecture which had to with older and younger students really meshed into a team.

We were energized by the prospect and the feeling of the atelier competing with other ateliers for the prizes—the kind of bonding that happened as older students taught younger ones and younger ones helped older ones with drafting. To such an extent that, for example, the master, the chef d'atelier, only had to come teach one morning a week to distribute his wisdom and it would filter down through the tradition of having older students with the younger students.

There was a tremendous spirit because of the competition. Every atelier competed for prizes . . .. If the architecture schools were truly competitive these days, the projects would be better. Also there was the efficiency: the tuition was just $70 a semester. Of course there was an extra $140 party fee. I have often thought about how well that system worked. Even though they weren't teaching anything of particular value, they really taught it. The material was terrible. The methodology was superb.

In many ways our office is very much an atelier . . .. Everybody helps everybody else—there are no individual projects. Everybody is as interchangeable as possible in their skills. The teams negotiate. It's efficient, if chaotic.

Stairs Leading to Folly and Beach at Seaside, Florida.

I'm thinking out loud now: I have not made this connection, but the office really does resemble a Beaux Arts. Also the look, the spirit of the office is like an atelier—the way we dress in the office. If you see anyone with a coat and tie, it's because there's a particular meeting with somebody outside of the office. Our clients have to put up with the dogs, the extreme informality. They're not retaining us because we look sharp—we could never get our office to look sharp anyway. It's a wonderful place to work. . .. It's a wonderful experience.

As we reached his office, Duany began talking about plans for what seemed to be building a teaching atelier next to his office. He imagined it as a place where, eventually he would assume more of a teaching role, a place where the latest design ideas would be cross-pollinated with ongoing office projects discussed during meals, of course, around what he envisioned as a huge dining table at the center of a large room.

Duany and I shook hands as I thanked him for the time we had spent together. Then, in a moment, he disappeared behind the curtain. Looking back one more time as I drove down the street, I noticed how well the converted church/office fit in this little neighborhood: somehow it managed to be totally novel and dramatic yet, at the same time, unassuming and respectful to the modest houses which lined the street. In the end, it was a reflection, no doubt, of the Design Psychology of its creators, and of their amazing and dedicated efforts to draw the American streetscape back . . . to the people.

Design Psychology Exercises:
The Future

Our deepest fear is not that we are inadequate. Our deepest fear is that we are powerful beyond measure. It is our light, not our darkness, that most frightens us.

We ask ourselves, "Who am I to be brilliant, gorgeous, talented, and fabulous?" Actually, who are you not to be?

You are a child of God. Your playing small doesn't serve the world. There's nothing enlightened about shrinking so that other people won't feel insecure around you.

We were born to make manifest the glory of God that is within us. It's not just in some of us: it's in everyone.

And as we let our own light shine, we unconsciously give other people permission to do the same. As we are liberated from our fear, our presence automatically liberates others.

Nelson Mandela,
1994 Inaugural Address

Exercise 7   Special Objects Inventory[37]

As well as choosing the building which is our home, we also fill our dwelling with objects which are special to us. These objects also help to express our identity. Many people have collections of special objects—perhaps a coin collection, a stamp collection, a doll collection, etc. Others have favorite individual special objects which they place in their home.

Make a list of the special objects in your home and categorize them below in terms of what they mean to you.

Example: My Special Objects

MEANING: Connection with many cultures
OBJECTS: Tapestries, artifacts from around the world, furniture from foreign countries

MEANING: Love of family and friends
OBJECTS: Photographs, children's drawings, gifts from friends

MEANING: Interest in the environment
OBJECTS: Books, magazines, prints of places lived

MEANING: Love of art
OBJECTS: Art books, artworks, pottery

MEANING: Love of natural beauty
OBJECTS: Rocks, shells, pine cones, plants

Your Inventory/List of Special Objects in Your Home:

Categories they fall into:

MEANING:
OBJECTS:

MEANING:
OBJECTS:

MEANING:
OBJECTS:

MEANING:
OBJECTS:

MEANING:
OBJECTS:

MEANING:
OBJECTS:

1. Do you feel that these objects and categories reflect *you*? Why or why not?

2. Are there other special interests or values you have that are not being reflected in your home? Are there other special objects you could include in your home to reflect *you*?

3. If you could save only *one* of these special objects, which one would it be and why?

Exercise 8   Homestyle

Your own particular aesthetic, your taste, and style may be derived from your past experience, for example, from your ancestor's sense of taste and style—what Herbert Gans called one's "taste structure." Gans identified five "publics"/"cultures" from which these taste structures are drawn:

PAST ————————————————————————————————➤ **PRESENT**

❑   **High Culture**—which includes creators and critics whose emphasis is on construction of a work
      of art. They think they provide the "proper culture" for the rest of society.   ❑

❑   **Upper Middle Culture**—are the upper middle-class professionals who are not concerned with
      form but borrow and alter from high culture.   ❑

❑ **Lower Middle Culture**—represents America's dominant taste culture— teachers, accountants, etc. who value traditional morals and values. The art they prefer is romantic and representational. ❑

❑ **Low Culture**—includes skilled and semi-skilled factory and service workers. They reject culture and prefer lavish ornateness, what Gans calls "Hollywood Modern." ❑

❑ **Quasi-Folk Culture**—consists of poor, unskilled workers. They are not catered to by the mass media but find expression in church or street festivals. ❑

❑ **Fringe Cultures**—include youth, black and ethnic American cultures that rely on a variety of alternative traditions and expressions. ❑

1. Although these categories may seem to pigeonhole or stereotype people, it may also be possible to recognize that we each do come from certain taste cultures which may have influenced our present sense of taste and style. With this in mind, put an X in any left hand boxes you feel represent your family's taste culture during your childhood. Put an X in any of the right hand boxes which you feel represent your taste structure in the *present*.

2. Looking at the categories you checked, discuss any similarities and differences between your family's sense of taste in the past compared to your present home style, i.e. does one represent high culture versus popular culture?

3. How do you account for any similarities or differences?

4. Is your present home style one that you feel comfortable with? If not, how would you like to change it?

5. If you are a designer, do you see any differences between your taste culture and that of your clients? Do you think it is important to bridge those differences? If so, how do you see yourself doing that?

6. Do you have any further reflections on the connection between your past, present and/or future "homestyle?"

Exercise 9   Creating Some Place Like Home

How close have you come to creating "Some Place Like Home?" Thinking about your *home setting* (city, suburbs, town, village, etc.), your *house* (dwelling) and *special objects*, use the chart below to see whether you have been able to "actualize" a home environment that truly feels like home to *you*.

On the next page mark how closely your home setting, house and special objects come to fulfilling your need for home as a place of aesthetic pleasure, social growth, psychological growth and shelter by using a "✓+" a "✓" or a "✓-":

1. Looking at your answers, how satisfied are you that you have created home as a place for *shelter*? Are there any changes you could make to help you fulfill this need further?

2. How satisfied are you that you have created home as a place for *psychological growth*? Are there any changes you could make to help you fulfill this need further?

3. How satisfied are you that you have created home as a place for *social growth*? Are there any changes you could make to help you fulfill this need further?

4. How satisfied are you that you have created a home as a place for *aesthetic pleasure*? Are there any changes you could make to help you fulfill this need further?

5. Draw a picture/reflect further on your ideal home in terms of shelter, psychological and social growth and aesthetic pleasure. Draw/write about *Some Place Like Home* for *YOU*.

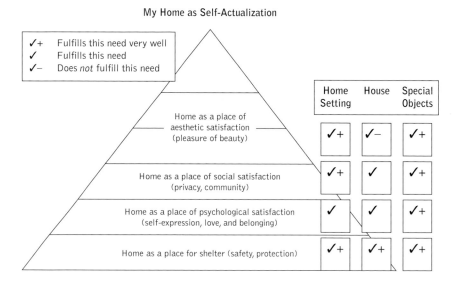

CHAPTER 4

Some Place Like Home

Some Place Like Home

I am overwhelmed with emotion as I drive to the lawyer's office for the closing on the house. This move has now taken on a bittersweet quality. My purchase of the house broke open questions about the long term future of my relationship with Bill and we've split up. Still, my sadness is overshadowed by feelings of the most profound satisfaction and joy: it seems a miracle to me that two years ago I left England with such an uncertain future and now the children and I have a house we can call our own.

Few people reach complete self-actualization in their lives or in their homes. How far we climb up Maslow's hierarchy is dependent on a complex interplay of the physical, emotional, social, and aesthetic forces we have experienced. It is to be hoped, however, that by exploring our environmental autobiographies via Design Psychology we can become more conscious of our profound place in the world.

> And after we are in the new house, when memories of other places we have lived in come back to us, we travel to the land of Motionless Childhood, motionless the way all Immemorial things are . . .. Memories of the outside world will never have the same tonality as those of home and, by recalling these memories, we add to our store of dreams; we are never real historians, but always near poets, and our emotion is perhaps nothing but an expression of a poetry that was lost.[1]

As near poets we can be creators. While our childhood may be motionless, our lives can move on. We *can* go into the storehouse of memory and come as close

As near poets we can be creators. While our childhood may be motionless, our lives can move on. We *can* go into the storehouse of memory and come as close as possible to retrieving the poetry of lost home.

as possible to retrieving the poetry of lost home. In doing so, some of us will retrieve the transcendent images of uniquely designed buildings like Graves' stockyards, Jencks' grandmother's house or Duany's grandfather's house. Many more will remember the gift of places not designed at all—open spaces like Jencks' Cape Cod field, or my Big Woods.[2] Among these places of light also will be our homes of shadowed memory, homes that we never lived in as we had hoped or homes of darkness that should not have been inhabited at all.

Though perhaps momentarily overwhelmed by the clarity of such memories, we can use them to reflect upon our past place stories. Those reflections can help illuminate our present sense of place. With clearer vision, we can strive to create homes and other places that mirror our most fulfilled selves. Thus we can embrace our warm, grandmotherly shawls of home. We can escape from the gulags of the past prisons which have been our dwelling places.[3]

In so doing, we set aside all images labeled "ideal home" or "ideal place." We dispense with the emperor's new clothes syndrome of architecture syndrome that allows us to believe that good, true, or beautiful architecture comes dressed in any *one* golden robe. Instead architectural trends and "isms," while certainly influential need to remain just that—an influence rather than a prescription. On the domestic level, especially, some place like home must reflect the best of each of *us* uniquely, not the best of someone else.

Outside the home, the best buildings are also those which have embraced our individual and collective need for shelter, for psychological and social growth as well as our need for beauty. Homes, public buildings, and overall settings that achieve this may rely on principles of technology and aesthetics. They may also rely on familiar cultural signs or symbols. In the end, however, technology, aesthetics, and cultural signs and symbols also must be combined with the design *psychology* that is our world. This means that architecture must speak to all our *human* needs. It must challenge us to assimilate and adapt to new forms but must do so in a way that does not overwhelm or diminish us. We must be able to achieve an equilibrium between the security of shared, familiar, conventional signs *and* symbols around us *and* the unlabeled experience of place that resonates as a poetry without words. In this way we can be challenged and motivated to continue the process of world discovery which we began at birth.

What will such architecture actually *look* like? In the public domain, Wright's Guggeheim Museum is such a masterpiece, "a round temple to art"[4] that is pure poetry. It has become an unconventional landmark that continues to inspire as well as orient us as the city threatens to overwhelm. Similarly Michael Graves wove his private world of place into the very public, unconventional Portland Building, now a city landmark.

In the private domain, Frank Lloyd Wright captured the spirit of his time and his most existential sense of place in Fallingwater. Charles Jencks' Cape Cod Gargeola studio achieved the same unity of cultural, personal, and aesthetic expression.[5] Yet all of these places look as different from each other as Chaplin's cane compared to Monroe's red lips. However, like Chaplin and Monroe, they speak in languages that can be heard by all, revealing universal human experience.

Thus such fulfilling architecture can take innumerable forms. In this sense it would be fascinating to learn more about the environmental autobiographies of other famous architects, planners, and interior designers with contrasting styles and backgrounds, to hear what tales their buildings tell. For example, what private language does a Modernist like Richard Rogers speak in his controversial public buildings? Does Frank Gehry's wildly imaginary and original "Deconstructivist" home tell the tale of a self-actualized place and person? To what degree have the roots of Zaha Hadid's Middle Eastern family tree or Denise Scott Brown's South African genealogy influenced their groundbreaking architectural styles and perspectives?[6]

My sense is that the stories of all the standard-bearers of the great "isms"—Deconstructivism, Post-Modernism, Modernism, Classicism, etc.—would all reveal the same secret of "good" design that Graves', Jencks', Duany's and my own story revealed: ultimately the most fulfilling buildings are those which embody the designer's and dweller's fully expressed self.

In this context, it must be remembered that when the style and perspectives of these architectural trendsetters become public, they are making not only a public statement about place but a unique and private statement about themselves as manifested in place. When expressed, this public and *private* sensibility affects our own notion of taste and style. The fact that this is so puts special responsibility upon the architect to build places that reinforce a universal, not just personal, self–place bond.

> . . . dispense with the emperor's new clothes architecture syndrome that allows us to believe that good, true, or beautiful architecture comes dressed in any *one* golden robe.

My Children, Liam and Sarah, Preparing the Pond at Our New Home.

The process of Design Psychology provides both designers and their clients—all of us—with the opportunity to explore and express the whole entity that is self and place. Such exploration is essential for any architecture education to be complete. It is environmental education in the most profound sense. Of course, both designers and non-designers can create authentic, transcendent places by *unconsciously* climbing the pyramid of self-actualized place and home. However, the potential for reaching this peak seems greater if one can more clearly see the paths ahead and thereby choose the most promising trail.

In the end, however, in order to uncover our most intimate connection to the world, our environment must offer opportunity for such intimacy. Children, especially, must be given the chance to experience more than just cloned shopping centers, soulless mass housing, or distressing homes. We must provide them with an environmental reservoir of healthy indoor and outdoor places where they can grow along with us. In this way we can all write our own book of treasured environments, read our own stories of place and conclude with chapters in which our *deepest* dream of some place like home can come true.

*We have lived here one week today. There **is** a focus to this house: it is the small pond and waterfall right behind the house in our back garden. The children are excitedly getting ready to transfer their goldfish into the pond and have been reading up on pond ecology. I sit here on the porch writing these final words and listening to the calm and gentle sound of the waterfall which fills the house. I see two butterflies, a squirrel and then a beautiful red bird all resting in turn on the cherry tree next to the pond. I close my eyes and then open them again. Two deer are standing only feet away. Where have they come from? I live in the suburbs, not the forest! They are my neighbors who have simply come to visit and wish me good luck. I am in the big woods again. . . .*

CHAPTER 5

Applying Design Psychology

Applying Design Psychology

The Design Psychology exercises that Michael Graves, Charles Jencks, I and, hopefully, you, the reader, did in the preceding chapters, illustrated the importance of exploring the lush, overgrown trail of one's own very personal history of place. Yet, how can the insight gained about connections between past, present, and future sense of place be translated into design? What are the implications of Design Psychology for the world of design? In order to understand how to apply this new field, the following chapter describes three projects—a residential, an institutional and a workplace—that incorporate the practice of Design Psychology.

The choice of a residential case study was simple: it made sense to use the Design Psychology process not only to help me *find* my "ideal" house, but to continue to use the process to help me design and renovate its interior space. Thus this continuing story of the transformation of my house into home illustrates how the Design Psychology process can be embedded in the process of creating fulfilling *residential* design.

Although a main focus of this book has been the creation of some place like *home* (home here meant to imply literally "home" as a place to live), some place like home also connotes the primal, transcendent sense of being truly *at home in the world* as perhaps most purely experienced in childhood. In fact, since a main thesis of this book is that childhood environments have a powerful, long-lasting effect upon us, it also makes sense to explore ways Design Psychology can be applied to the design of schools—the place where children spend the most time in besides their home. As such, the second case study describes how Design Psychology can be used to help create the institution that is school.

The final case study example highlights the use of Design Psychology in the design of a workplace as part of a training process for this new discipline. Of particular interest, both here and in terms of institutional design, is the challenge of translating the personal place experience of many users, not just one person, into a final, fulfilling design for all.

While these case studies represent three entirely different contexts, it is important to recognize that the Design Psychology process in each case involved similar steps:

1. The client first remembered his/her past experience of place.

2. The client then identified the "highest positive" associations they had with remembered place(s).

3. The client used these "high positives" to help forge a holistic vision of the design ideal they wished to achieve ("actualize") in their design project.[1]

4. The client recognized and articulated a comprehensive pyramid of functional, psychological, social, and aesthetic needs they wanted met in order to achieve that ideal design.

5. Using this pyramid of needs as a touchstone, the designer translated the client's vision into a fulfilling, final design.

As you can see, this model correctly suggests that there must be client/user as well as designer involvement in any Design Psychology process. Still, as the following case studies will show, the exact nature of that involvement—of user/client participation and of the designer/client relationship—can vary depending upon the particular project.

For example, the designers involved in these case studies came to the table with simply a willingness to be open to a new way of working, a way which inevitably required them to put their own egos on hold, to listen and respond to their client's needs.

This was a brave thing to do. Since Design Psychology is still in its infancy, it required a real leap of faith on the part of the designers who worked with me. It would have been easy for them to worry that Design Psychology was simply an ephemeral process that would gobble up their project time and budget, impinge upon their artistic vision, and even compromise the very nature of a given project.

In fact, as I hope the following case studies show, the Design Psychology process:

➤ helps focus both the client and the architect;

➤ provides a strong foundation upon which to build a solid design;

➤ saves time rather than wastes it;

➤ offers a desirable added-value service that, in at least one case, was the key piece used to market and win the design commission for the firm;

➤ proves inspirational not only in terms of the final design, but is professionally and personally meaningful for the client and designer.

Author's Residence, Princeton, New Jersey

The Project

Five years have now passed since I moved to my "ideal" home in Princeton. In terms of community, my neighborhood has been the village helping to raise my children. Liam and Sarah have grown up here playing ball in the street, biking to school, and exploring the nearby shopping center oasis of pizza parlor, video store, and library. On weekends they scoop up their friends around the corner and, under the watchful eye of our parent safety net, walk to the center of down-town Princeton. A yearly block party celebrates our good fortune to live in a neigh-borhood with old and young teachers, doctors, electricians, nurses, architects, and others who have lived here for years or have moved here from England, Hungary, Yugoslavia, India, China, Tibet, Czechoslovakia, and from other far-off homelands. In my mind, we have found an idyllic suburban neighborhood.

Our house, too, has fulfilled its promise. It is well built, roomy, light-filled, and easy to maintain. In the spirit of Design Psychology we are slowly making the house our home. The biggest challenge was the kitchen. Unchanged since the house was built in 1950, it was cramped, dated, ill designed and ugly. From the beginning, also, I lamented that it was not an eat-in kitchen: the outdoor porch/eating space could only be accessed by going out the back door and down the alleyway between the house and shed. Thus a kitchen re-design was the only major renovation the house required.

The Architect

Although I felt confident that I could re-design the kitchen workspace myself, I also wanted to extend the space and connect it to the shed wall, thereby creating an eating area. In doing so, I knew that any necessary architectural drawings would be well beyond my level of expertise.

Thus I asked Ray Heinrich (AIA), a long time friend and practicing architect for many years, to help on this aspect of the project. Ray had much more technical expertise than this small design scheme required. Still, it was not only that I wanted someone to do technical drawings; I wanted to work with a designer who would be sensitive to the Design Psychology process.

In this sense Ray was perfect. It was he, in fact, who had introduced me to the world of environmental psychology twenty-five years earlier. He had long been attuned to approaches which mirror his own vision of the architect as a "people-concerned creator of a better world." The former Director of the New Jersey Division of Housing and Development and long term Co-Adjunct Professor at Rutgers University, Ray's projects included numerous public and private sector buildings ranging from community centers and office complexes to urban designs.[2]

The Client/Users

On this job I was both Ray's client and my own client: Ray's role was to focus on the kitchen extension. By the time he joined the project I had made most of the major decisions about the kitchen workspace myself. Still, as the job progressed, I eagerly sought Ray's advice on a variety of decisions regarding finishes as well as the overall integration of the cooking and eating areas. Ray was able to strike a balance between actively giving me the professional advice I needed and stepping back while I continued on the journey of integrating the best of my past, present, and future sense of place into the kitchen design. In this latter sense, this residential project evolved as an ideal collaboration between an architect and a "Design Psychologist" client.

Still, where "the client" was concerned, there were other users of this space to consider. My small children who had looked with wonder into our little pond that first week were now teenagers. They, too, had their needs and preferences when it came to the kitchen design. To what extent should they participate in decision making about this renovation? My son was already taking high school architecture courses and talking about being an architect. My daughter had exhibited an astounding, seemingly innate, sense of design since she was a small child. Nevertheless, they were hardly trained professionals. This could simply be an opportunity for them to observe and learn about the design/build process.

This project would form part of *their* childhood experience of place and home. Given what I now knew about the confidence that comes—the sense of self that is nurtured—when children are able to participate in the creation of space, it seemed right that I should appropriately involve my own children in the kitchen design.

The Process

If I had been simply a Design Psychologist working with a client on *their* residential design, I would have begun the process by taking my client through the Design Psychology exercises in the main body of this book. Since I was my *own* client, I had already taken myself through this past, present, and future environmental exploration. I now had reached the jumping off point from where the next step was to translate such environmental self-reflection into a program that would lead to a fulfilling design.

My "high positive" associations with home/place

Thus I began the Design Psychology process by looking back into the past. I examined the results of my Environmental Family Tree and Environmental Visualization exercises to identify my "high positive" associations with past place. Of course, the environment that remained my favorite place from childhood was "The Big Woods", that dark, moist world of onion grass and apple blossoms, the place where we, the neighborhood children, had reigned supreme.

When it came to my environmental genealogy, the *kitchen* that loomed largest was my great-grandparents' kitchen in Hungary. In fact, that kitchen *was* their house. Their home had consisted of three rooms—a large living room/bedroom, a large kitchen/bedroom, and a third room called "the oven" where they baked those delicious cakes and breads. Although my grandmother was happy to leave this crowded dwelling of mud and straw behind and come to America, stories about this village home and kitchen held a kind of romance for me. From the safe haven of my modern American home, I had filtered out family tales of poverty and listened instead to stories of this hearth as the center of my ancestors' earthy, lively, close-knit existence.

A trip some years earlier to Szentendre, a re-constructed Hungarian village, encouraged this vision. The whitewashed, wood-beamed kitchens with mud floors there had a simple charm. Overall, the village's vernacular of thatched homes set near each other and close to the street generated a feeling of community that New Urbanists could only dream about. Then, too, in the more recent past, I still fondly remembered my British Beverley eat-in kitchen where we all used to gather round and tell stories together.

My "ideal" kitchen/home design

Now, however, I live in a modern, suburban New Jersey home on a ¼ acre lot. How could I—and why would I—want to re-create a Hungarian village, dreamy woods or a quaint English kitchen in this entirely different place?

My project and program were not about reconstructing—reproducing an exact replica of these remembered places. Design Psychology is *not* about nostalgia design. Instead, the point of Design Psychology is to identify the primal, satisfying, existential *essence* of these places in order to use the "high positive" *associations* they trigger as a touchstone from which to design. Thus, for example, it was not a primitive, old-world kitchen I wanted to create but one that was simple, earthy and perpetuated the lively and close-knit quality I wanted my family to inherit. The essential appeal of my Beverley kitchen was that it was a gathering place. The Big Woods was the epitome of beautiful, natural escape; it was a place in which to be free, imagine, and create.

Thus my mission in terms of my "ideal" kitchen design was to create a space that embodied all of these fulfilling qualities. The challenge, though, was how to weave past memory of place into the present reality of my Princeton home and life.

Climbing the pyramid of fulfilling design

Having used my "high positive" association with past place to help forge a vision of my ideal kitchen, what was the next step? According to the Design Psychology model, the next step was to examine the remaining "present" and "future" Design Psychology exercises I had done to complete my vision of a kitchen that addressed our needs in the four major areas:

➤ functional;

➤ psychological;

➤ social;

➤ aesthetic.

Conventionally, a project like this one begins by discussing the practical/ functional as well as aesthetic improvements the client wants to make. For example, I knew that I needed to change totally the layout of the kitchen work-space and replace all the cabinets, countertop, appliances, and flooring. I also had to tear down the existing wall to create my desired eat-in space.

When it came to the "look and feel" I wanted to achieve, however, rather than referring to kitchen magazines showing the latest trends, those words "simple," "earthy," "natural," and "escape" formed my aesthetic collage. As I began to translate these words into visual imagery, I realized that by tearing down the kitchen wall I could open up the kitchen not only to the existing porch but also to the pond and graceful cherry tree beyond. That pond and its waterfall, the dense ferns and wildflowers, the smell of blossoms all gave this place a magical quality. It was the same magical quality as the Big Woods of my childhood! The cherry tree that bowed low hugging the pond was, in fact, the same shape as the apple tree/childhood meeting place deep in the middle of my much-cherished woods. This beautiful, natural space set deep in the core of our house could also be a touchstone, a focal point when it came to the kitchen design.

While it was possible to argue that this special little woods held memory and meaning only for me and not, for example, for my children, I knew full well that they had also been enchanted by this little outdoor spot. In fact, all visitors to the house were drawn to this half-hidden space.

Had I digressed? A minute ago I was talking about the practical aspect of this renovation. Suddenly I was talking about the aesthetics of this mystical place. As you can see, the Design Psychology process I was applying here was not rigid. I intuitively stepped back and forth as I walked myself up the pyramid of functional, aesthetic, social and psychological needs to be addressed by the kitchen design. The order in which I considered each of these needs was not crucial. What seemed important was that I examined them all with equal diligence.

For example, in reviewing the results of my Personality and Place Exercise, I remembered that I had scored as a "feeling" person, slightly more extravert than introvert. Thus I increasingly imagined the kitchen as the social center of my house. I wanted it to be not just an eat-in kitchen but also a "sit-in" one—a special space where my friends could come to sit and chat while I cooked.

Still, the introverted part of me wanted time and space to be alone. Hectic times as a single, working mother often made this need for retreat even more pressing. Of course my bedroom was the private place on my "Environmental Sociogram." But I could have more. Perhaps I could devise a way to adapt the new eat-in area so it sometimes could be separated from the main kitchen. Thus, adjacent to my little pond and woods, I could escape again to a sacred oasis. This public/private dimension of the kitchen became part of the Design Psychology program for the space I wished to create.

Having thought through the project thus far, the next practical step was to choose the type of new cabinets I wanted. My budget was modest so rather than getting a custom kitchen designer to work with me, I simply visited the kitchen showrooms of various mega stores to try to find a cabinet design I liked. A Mission-style kitchen made of oak caught my eye. The cabinetry seemed earthy, of simple craftsman-style and was certainly in vogue at the moment.

My son thought the cabinets looked much too heavy and not slick enough for his taste. Instead he pointed out a more modern, sleek looking kitchen. Its cabinets had a warm, high gloss, orange veneer that gave the kitchen a simple yet striking effect. A black kick-toe and black feature strip running along the front of the cabinets had an almost Japanese lacquer feeling. This feeling seemed to fit with the indoor/outdoor Japanese quality created by the house's Wright-inspired open plan and large windows.

Simple craftsman or simply oriental? Unsure, I referred back to the Taste Cultures and Special Objects exercise I had done to help me clarify further the "look and feel" I wanted to create. In thinking about the taste cultures I had inherited, I saw that my grandmother, mother and aunt had *not* tried to reproduce the earthy quality of my great-grandparents' home.

Instead, the beautiful things they gravitated towards were often oriental in design. In fact an exquisite, fanciful, black lacquer oriental breakfront my aunt had purchased became the prize example of the sophisticated upward mobility my larger family had achieved since the days of their peasant ancestors. My relatives had reworked their past history of place to communicate "success" by placing these special objects, valuable antiques, in their homes.

I admired and, no doubt, was influenced by the oriental quality of this branch of my environmental family tree. Yet my generation had learned to be more *inquisitive* than *acquisitive*.[3] I had not amassed things—just ideas—and the idea here was to see if I could blend together the simplicity that was the best of these oriental and Hungarian traditions with the sleek and modern kitchen my son envisioned for the future!

The Design

I chose the Japanese-style kitchen. The rich orange of the cabinets was not unlike the warm ochre colored buildings I had seen all over Hungary. Perhaps I was also drawn to this warm color because of the "feeling" aspect of my personality type. By choosing a slate-colored porcelain tile for the floor I hoped to create the deep, earthy quality I had envisioned for the kitchen and the porch. The bright white walls Ray recommended echoed the purity of both classical Japanese design and Hungarian hut-house. A backsplash made of black bulletin board rubber became an art gallery where I could display the drawings and photographs of our evolving lives. A shoji ceiling fixture Ray selected further emphasized the oriental quality of the space. Shoji blinds I installed between the kitchen workspace became an instant way to separate the public kitchen from the private refuge that was now the kitchen extension.

Ray had designed the extension to maximize not only the view out but also view up: two huge skylights brought bright sunlight into the kitchen during the day and moonlight and stars into view at night. A trapezoid window he designed for one wall repeated the rhythm of the sloping carport and perfectly framed another, Japanese flowering cherry tree across the street. Most importantly, a sliding glass door between the kitchen and the porch emphasized the tree and pond as the focal point of the kitchen and the core of the house.

Kitchen furniture was the next thing to select. I continued the oriental theme by purchasing a Japanese cabinet for use as a breakfast bar. With my son's sleek kitchen in mind, I placed stylish chrome bar stools around the table so my children and friends could swivel and chat while I cooked. I put wheels on the cabinet so it could also serve as a table when pushed into the new eating nook. Yet pushed up to what? I had struggled to decide how to furnish that small kitchen extension. I wanted it to be a social, eat-in space so it did require some type of table and chairs. Since I also wanted it to function as my sometimes retreat, it needed to contain a piece of furniture to lie down on, too.

Tony Bisogno, the contractor carrying out the work, began bringing beautiful old pieces of wood to show me as the project progressed. Tony was more than just a workman doing a job, he was a craftsman who loved trees.[4] The old beams and varnished off-cuts he brought gradually began to occupy my kitchen space and mind and I dreamed of a thousand ways to re-create "The Big Woods" inside and not just outside my house.

Tony became as enthusiastic as I was about my tree conspiracies and, with his encouragement, I finally visited a nearby tree farm. Wandering among a wonderland of timber, I spotted a huge tree trunk on its side, which I realized could be cut to size and sliced to form a bed to lie or sit upon. Tony worked with dedication to

Author's Kitchen Before
Renovation.

Author's Kitchen
After Renovation.

"Spirit Seat" Designed
for Author's Kitchen.

Planter/Face Selected by
Author's Daughter,
Sarah Golightley.

transform the log's beautifully barked body into a "spirit seat." When he had completed it, Tony, my son and half the school soccer team lugged the tree into the kitchen and centered it under the skylights. With a down futon placed on top, it proved an irresistible draw to all those who entered the kitchen, smiled at the tree and lay down on it with child-like fascination.

Long ago my grandmother had promised to give me a marble statue of a simple peasant girl pouring water from a jug. I placed it on a high pedestal so the girl faced both the waterfall next to the porch and looked down on my sylvan bed. I lay down on my spirit seat, closed my eyes and dreamed of past, present, and future.

The only decisions remaining related to the exterior of the house. The new extension had created a backdoor entryway. Most backdoors are regularly used as *front* doors in America, so I wanted this space to be as welcoming as I hoped the kitchen would be. With this in mind, Ray chose some wonderful Japanese-type paving stones and embedded them in a new path as part of the enhanced entrance.

Then it was my daughter's turn to make the final design decisions regarding the material to go around the stones. I had tried placing little pebbles around the pavings but they looked terrible. Sarah came up with the simple suggestion that we plant grass around the path's edges. This sounded like a great idea so we went to search for the right seeds.

Once at the garden store, Sarah looked fifty yards across the bags of pebbles, seeds, and plants and, pointing to an unusual, concrete planter in the shape of a face, she said, "Look mom! Let's get that! There isn't anyone who wouldn't love it!" She was right. We brought that simple, expressive pot/face home and placed it on the front step where it looked best. When it is spring we will put plants in it. This life will continue to grow, giving the house a human face.

The University Academy Charter School, New Jersey City University Jersey City, N.J. KSS Architects

The Project

The University Academy Charter School, a high school for 500 students, grades 9 through 12, will be based at New Jersey City University (NJCU), in Jersey City, N.J. The school's charter expresses clearly its deep commitment to education, community, and service:

> The mission of the University Academy Charter School is based on the philosophy that everyone can make a contribution to the betterment of the world and that individuals working together can truly help to make a significant difference. The school is dedicated to engaging young people in an academic experience designed to encourage a need to explore their world, a deep desire for knowledge and a passionate commitment to justice and service to others.

The charter school will be housed in buildings around NJCU and within an existing industrial laundry building near the university's main campus. Although vacant and in disrepair, the two-storey laundry building, set in a local neighborhood, is a character-filled example of industrial architecture. It required adaptive reuse in order to accommodate both the high school which would occupy half of the building's 60 000 square feet, as well as a business incubator to occupy the other half. The refurbishment of the laundry building was the major step to be taken to create this vital, community-centered school within the university neighborhood.

The Architects

I contacted KSS Architects at about the same time that New Jersey City University issued a Request for Proposals (RFP) for the renovation of the laundry building. I was aware that KSS, a 35-person architecture firm with offices in Princeton and Philadelphia, had established a reputation for producing sensitively designed, high quality work. Their experience included almost twenty years of designing new buildings, renovations, interiors and planning studies for academic, municipal, corporate and developer clients. I knew that they were interested in undertaking more school projects. I was also particularly impressed by the KSS firm ethos description:

> [The] spirit of collaboration pervades our approach and is centered on the client. We begin by taking the necessary time to understand your organization, its goals and needs, and only then begin exploring a design solution. For this reason, while we emphasize good design, our portfolio does not show a single "KSS look," but contextual, thoughtful design solutions, which respond to our client's existing contexts . . ..

> We understand that architecture is more than shelter: it speaks to your mission, and enhances the experience of those who live in, work, or use the structure . . ..

I approached KSS about undertaking a school project incorporating Design Psychology procedures. Michael Shatken (AIA), the KSS principal I met first, had a thoughtful and open demeanor which suggested (as did the firm's description) that he would be receptive to exploring new ways of working. Although I never

Laundry Building
to be Renovated and
Occupied by
University Academy
Charter School.

used the term Design Psychology, Michael recognized that an approach involving user participation could be particularly appropriate when it came to school design: the University Academy Charter School project might be a good place to start, especially given its avowed mission of empowering the students and local community.

We began to formulate a proposal for the charter school project with the two other architects from this KSS team. Merilee Meacock (AIA) had been a project architect with KSS for twelve years. She had managed the design, construction, and renovation of buildings including schools, university buildings and laboratories. Merilee would be responsible for the daily management of this commission if it were awarded to KSS. Petar Mattioni, who had been with KSS for one year, would be her assistant. Although a young, recent architecture school graduate, Petar exhibited the same qualities of dedication, reflection, and sensitivity as the others on this KSS team.

The Client/Users

The client, New Jersey City University, is an urban, state funded institution located directly across the Hudson River from lower Manhattan in aging industrial Jersey City, New Jersey. With over 10 000 students enrolled in pre-college to graduate studies, the mission of the university is to provide educational opportunity for a diverse student body. In order to achieve this, the university recognized the importance of reaching out to at-risk teenagers. The university's aim was to foster this young adult community by establishing the charter high school to help prepare and motivate students to go on to college.

In their presentation to the NJCU selection committee, KSS described their clear work plan for the project, shared initial design ideas and pointed to their impressive track record. Then we moved on to propose running six "visioning" sessions with user representatives including parents and students. We further offered to run an eight-week Architect-in-Residence program with 8th grade students scheduled to attend the charter school. We explained that this would be a structured participatory process that would allow people to express their needs and preferences when it came to the school design.

In the spirit of participation, I then asked the committee to put down their pencils and simply remember back to the best school environment they had ever experienced. I asked them to briefly share what it was about that school that made it special. In keeping with Design Psychology, by so pausing to reminisce, the committee members stepped out of their "business as usual" personas and, in that moment, re-entered their most satisfying school time and place. I explained that this five-minute exercise was a mini-version of similar exercises we would carry out as part of the participatory design process. We were awarded the commission. The committee later explained that they had chosen us because we offered this unique design *process*, not just a finished product approach to design.

As a first step, we needed to draw together those who would take part in this participatory process. We hoped to ensure genuine participation in the design decision making rather than just achieve "degrees of tokenism" or "non-participation."[5] However, the "clients" with whom designers work on a project are typically official *representatives* of the users—facilities managers, VPs, and other official decision makers rather than the day to day building users. Even when user participation is more broadly based, designers often struggle to draw a line between appropriate user involvement and common denominator decision making that leads to compromised, banal architecture. Then, too, in the deadline-driven business of design, there is always the fear that a long, drawn out decision-making process will stall the drive needed to propel a project ever forward.

Michael expressed his thoughts on the participatory design process:

> *The classic dilemma with the process is whether we are really seeking participation in the design process or more thoughtful exchange with the client. I still believe that when it literally comes down to manipulating space—architecture—that's what we do very, very well but we tend to overlook; we tend to design things around **our** criteria, **our** understanding of the problem . . . . At what point do we move over to the place where client becomes architect, and is that ultimately appropriate?*

Once convened, the visioning session group included a vice president of the university, three staff members from the office of Facilities and Construction Management, two deans of the College of Education, a parent, one community member, the three KSS architects and myself. As with any facility not yet built, it was difficult to reach out to any future building users: neither the school's principal nor teachers were yet hired. Students seemed reluctant to attend sessions in an unfamiliar place with adults whom they did not know.

This situation made an Architect-in-Residence component of the program all the more important as these sessions would provide the only opportunity for the KSS architects to have direct contact with future student users. NJCU identified a core group of about seven 13-year-old boys and girls to attend the weekly sessions. All were enrolled in the charter school for the following year.

The Process

Visioning sessions

The Design Psychology visioning process included a series of six, two-hour meetings held every two weeks with the 12 adult participants mentioned above. At first glance, the agenda for those sessions seemed to conform to a conventional series of programming and schematic design meetings. Embedded in each session, however, was a different Design Psychology exercise: the Time Line, Mental

Map, Guided Fantasy, Environmental Sociogram, Taste Cultures—all exercises that Graves, Jencks, Duany, you, the reader, and I have had a chance to do. In this context, however, each exercise was adapted for use by the client/user *group* rather than for use by the individual. The exercises were presented in the deliberate progression typical of the Design Psychology approach, enabling participants to

➤ explore their past history of school environments;

➤ identify the "highest positive" associations they had with those past schools;

➤ use these "high positives" to help envision their "ideal" charter school;

➤ recognize and articulate the pyramid of functional, psychological, social, aesthetic and growth needs to be addressed by the school design; and to

➤ use the pyramid to express those needs to the designer so they could be translated into a fulfilling charter school design.

Now that I was dealing with an institutional rather than residential setting, however, I created a pyramid using terms coined by Fred Steele, an organizational theorist, who had identified the six functions any *organization* needs to address in order to create their ideal physical environment:[6]

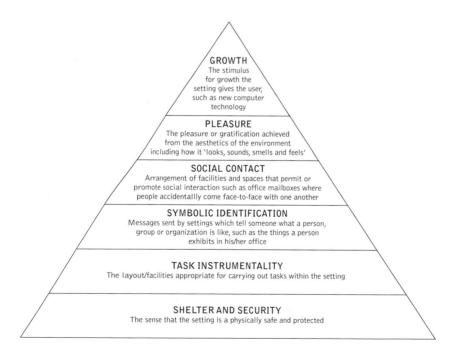

GROWTH
The stimulus for growth the setting gives the user, such as new computer technology

PLEASURE
The pleasure or gratification achieved from the aesthetics of the environment including how it 'looks, sounds, smells and feels'

SOCIAL CONTACT
Arrangement of facilities and spaces that permit or promote social interaction such as office mailboxes where people accidentallly come face-to-face with one another

SYMBOLIC IDENTIFICATION
Messages sent by settings which tell someone what a person, group or organization is like, such as the things a person exhibits in his/her office

TASK INSTRUMENTALITY
The layout/facilities appropriate for carrying out tasks within the setting

SHELTER AND SECURITY
The sense that the setting is a physically safe and protected

Thus, by creating the Six Functions of Physical Settings pyramid, I cross-pollinated Steele's six functions and Maslow's pyramid of needs suggesting, as I had in terms of residential environments, that all of these functions must be addressed in order to create an "actualized," fulfilling institutional setting.

Merilee reflected on the reality illustrated by the pyramid:

The nature of the pyramid is that the functions on the bottom are considered requirements. The functions on the top are less tangible, however just as vital to human fulfillment. These aspects are many times overlooked.

Each exercise the group did corresponded with a different level of the pyramid, thereby helping the group identify and articulate the building blocks upon which the charter school vision would rest. In doing so I reached into what I have now come to call the Design Psychology Toolbox (see Appendix), a sequence of generic exercises used as part of the programming, schematic design, and even design development process.

Exercises undertaken at each level were deliberately interwoven with discussion of issues such as square footage requirements so that both practical decisions and higher vision could be forged together in a time-efficient yet meaningful way. In fact the exercises served as a catalyst via which the project's conventional programming and schematic design issues were explored.

Michael described the process:

*By everyone going through a series of exercises that were similar in nature and dealing with how we had experienced places in our own past, it kind of leveled the playing field with regard to roles . . .. I think the process allowed us to be a lot more thoughtful and to go back to an earlier step in regard to design and what the place **could** be.*

Using the Design Psychology toolbox

I began the first visioning session by picking up where I had left off during the selection interview: I asked everyone again to take off their "official" hat, step out of their role as meeting representative and simply draw a Time Line of Schools they had attended from the earliest one they could remember to the present. I then asked them to circle the school they liked most and write down nouns or adjectives that described what they liked about that particular school.

Participants then introduced themselves by describing their favorite past school place. "Light," "wood," "community gathering space," "open space," "clean floors and hallways"—all were phrases participants used to describe the urban/rural, Northeast/Midwest/Yugoslavian/Caribbean kindergarten/high school/dorms that made up the kaleidoscope of their best past history of school place. Even though everyone came to the table with a different background, personality and position, all were willing and able to share their treasure chest of favorite past schools.

Similarly, in keeping with Design Psychology, the exercise enabled everyone to remember their "highest positive" association with school place. No matter how far back in time participants had to go, each could recall in detail and describe with delight their favorite school environment. Thus the exercise re-framed the design problem at hand and gave it a higher purpose: the challenge before us was not just to create the ideal environment for the University Academy Charter School, but to create a school environment as positive and memorable as the ones participants themselves had experienced.

Michael's verdict:

> I thought this exercise was brilliant. It allowed everyone to introduce [themselves] from the standpoint of where they were from—not focus them on their particular background but focus on their interest with regard to what was successful in their educational experience. It got people to think about their positive experiences.

I began the next session by introducing and explaining the Design Psychology pyramid of needs chart. At the peak of the chart I wrote that the goal of our sessions was to achieve "The actualized philosophy, mission and method of the charter school."[7] I then took out playing cards with the words "friendly,"

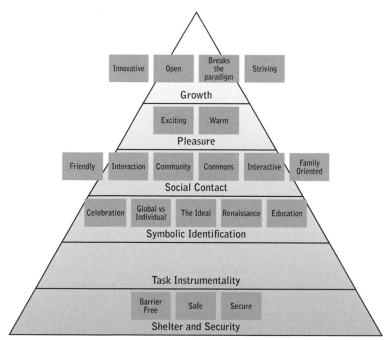

Courtesy KSS Architects.

Innovative | Open | Breaks the paradigm | Striving

Growth

Exciting | Warm

Pleasure

Friendly | Interaction | Community | Commons | Interactive | Family Oriented

Social Contact

Celebration | Global vs Individual | The Ideal | Renaissance | Education

Symbolic Identification

Task Instrumentality

Barrier Free | Safe | Secure

Shelter and Security

The Actualized Philosophy
Mission and Methods of the Charter School

Pyramid of Needs Envisioned by University Academy Charter School Visioning Session Participants.

"community," "family-oriented," "common (gathering) space," "interaction" on the back of them. These were words participants had written down at the end of our last visioning session—words they hoped students would use to describe the charter school when *they* looked back years after *their* graduation.

Petar's assessment:

*This process allowed everyone to move away from his or her professional position or role and as **people** say, "This is what we want to do." It was more relaxed and allowed us to explore certain issues— how we occupy a place, how we make a place. It allowed us to put ourselves in [the] shoes of people who were going to be in [the] building.*

I added these red rectangle cards to the chart as visual metaphors for the bricks to be used in building the NJCU vision. What became apparent immediately was that most of the "bricks" had to do with "social contact." Thus the group confirmed that a real priority for them was a design that supported the community/social aspect of the school. Yet these bricks were pinned on halfway up the chart; other levels of need still had to be considered before the charter school vision was complete.

Starting back at the bottom of the pyramid to consider "shelter and security," the next step was for participants to do a Mental Map of Jersey City to understand the larger context surrounding the school. Noise, traffic, student safety and supervision, storage for personal items, were all issues of shelter and security to be considered in terms of design for this Jersey City school.

Merilee commented:

As architects we draw mental maps but don't include the client in that aspect of the project until we have conclusions. Clients might not see value in an exercise examining relationships to their surroundings— they just want their building.

Michael added:

In the back of my mind was that one day people would be drawing mental maps of the school.

When then asked to complete the Ideal School Plan, visioning session members could bring their magnifying glass down to focus on the laundry building itself. They could use their imaginations to draw the types of spaces they felt would be needed inside the building. This enabled them to think further about "task instrumentality" in relation to the school—the facilities and layout appropriate for carrying out tasks in the building. Classroom, faculty, and administrative offices, common facilities were all program requirements. At the same time, it brought to the fore the challenge that KSS faced placing a wish list of requirements into a restricted space.

During the next session, the Guided Visualization Exercise "walked" participants in their mind's eye from the city street into and through the spaces they wanted to include in the charter school. This led to further group discussion and fine-tuning of program requirements. Words used to describe what they "saw" in their imagined new school—wooden floors, white pillars, etc—became further bricks/playing cards providing insight about how the need for visual "pleasure" could be satisfied as we continued to climb the pyramid of needs.

Using information that had been gleaned thus far, KSS created a schematic design of the school, a draft version of how the school could be laid out in the two-storey space. Committee members critiqued the floor plan, questioning issues such as the placement of bathrooms and the size of classrooms.

Then, in an effort to analyze "social contact" within the school they completed the Environmental Sociogram Exercise. They drew on the initial floor plan KSS had created: coloring spaces used by the public in blue, semi-private spaces in yellow, and private spaces in red. What this exercise immediately illustrated was that staff "owned" all of the private space with their offices dominating the central core of the school. Semi-private places consisted of highly structured classrooms and corridors constituted the dominant public space.

Referring back to the pyramid, it was obvious that this design solution ran contrary to participants' fundamental desire to create a school environment that encouraged social contact. KSS went back to the drawing board and reconfigured the space by pushing back the faculty spaces (retaining the square footage required) thereby creating instead a large informal, multimedia area for faculty and students at the heart of the school.

Public Spaces
Semi-Private Spaces
Private Spaces

Courtesy KSS Architects.

Sociogram - Before

Environmental
Sociogram of Charter
School Layout—
BEFORE.

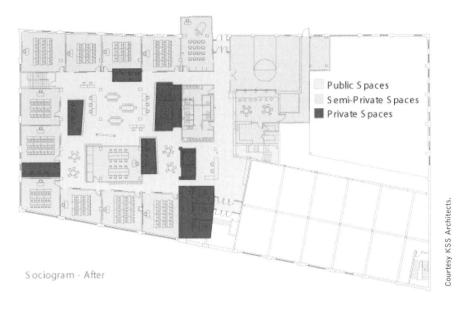

Public Spaces
Semi-Private Spaces
Private Spaces

Sociogram - After

Merilee commented:

*This exercise tested the program and layout—who belongs in what
space. It made us go back to the mission statement and ask, does this
still apply to this physical space? That's when we discovered that the
faculty had everything and the students had nothing . . .. It was like a
light bulb went off in everyone's head.*

With major decisions made about the school's layout, the group returned to
thinking about the sense of place they wanted to achieve. Participants completed
the Organizational Personality Test, characterizing the school's "personality" as
the ENFP type—extraverted, intuitive, feeling, perceiving. Thus the words
"warm" and "exciting" became the new cards/building blocks of "pleasure" added
to the pyramid of design needs. Similarly, the words "innovative," "open,"
"striving," "breaks the paradigm" were added to describe the "growth" they envisioned—an options-open, fluid description which fit the "perceiving" aspect of
the school's personality type.

Yet how far out on to the innovative edge should KSS go in terms of design?
Clearly the group wanted to maintain the industrial aesthetic of the school.
However, within that shell, the Taste Culture Exercise helped the group further
articulate the symbolic message they wanted to communicate. Rather than seeing
the Charter School as a place of "high" or "low" culture, participants wanted it
to be "culturally inclusive—an environment that everyone feels familiar with yet
still makes a statement."

Exactly what would that place look like? KSS showed the group visual examples of different design styles. Participants began to pull out a variety of preferred

images—industrial looking railings juxtaposed against wood or carpeted floors, openness created by glass walls and skylights, and brick exposed to preserve historic character. In the end, participants were most enthusiastic about the example of an industrial building renovation of MASS MoCA (Massachusetts Museum of Contemporary Art), which KSS also preferred.

Merilee was struck by the effectiveness of the exercise:

> *The biggest piece of information I got out of this exercise was that they liked MASS MoCA. If they hadn't seen that image, to this day I would still have been nervous about what it was we were giving them.*

The committee's vision, the building blocks needed to "actualize" the charter school philosophy, mission and method were now gathered together. Merilee remarked:

> *The way the pyramid related back to a bigger picture was clearer in this process.*

Reflecting on the usefulness of the Design Psychology approach, Michael summed up his feelings:

> *In a big sense what the process did was took us through a program confirmation stage where we went back in and challenged the project's conceptual design and not just at the end but all the way through with regard to the philosophy, mission statement, goals and objectives— experientially how the project would perform. So in a big sense that whole process is much better than the process we normally go through.*

Yet the needs articulated were those of the NJCU client *representatives*. The process of getting input from the *users*, the students attending the Architect-in-Residence sessions, was not yet complete.

Architect-in-Residence sessions

Of particular importance in terms of the overall school design would be any cross-pollination of ideas between the adults in the visioning sessions and the future charter school students attending the residency sessions. Petar and I co-taught the sessions once a week for an hour and a half over eight weeks. Our goals, method, and curriculum had been devised with the NJCU's mission of student empowerment in mind.

Although our adult visioning sessions began by having participants reach back into their past history of school place, the students attending the residency sessions were still children, albeit teenagers. We hoped their *present* experience of the environment still retained the primal, transcendent magic of childhood. Michael articulated our feelings:

MassMoCA Interior
Image Similar to the
Interior Envisioned for
the Charter School.

*The kids experienced things in a pure fashion you could tap into, less
encumbered by the laws of society. With the adults you really do need to
bring back to a historical perspective not encumbered by the things the
adults think about.*

When the students did the Mental Map Exercise we realized that their contribution would be invaluable. They created unbelievably lively and detailed drawings of Jersey City's streets, shops, and homes. The students, rather than the adults, were the experts as far as the charter school environs were concerned. In fact, the adults' perception of the physical environment of Jersey City was limited: they were commuters into the city with knowledge of highways that led to the university campus. It was these students with their intimate knowledge of the Jersey City streets, who educated us about the rich flavor of the city.

Petar was impressed by the students' input:

*I think what was really neat about it was that it went both ways: They
educated us as much as we educated them. I learned so much about
their life in Jersey City.*

Merilee felt that the students' input would have a profound effect on the charter school's architectural design:

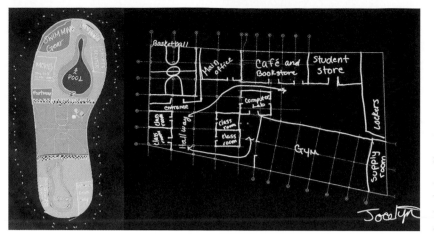

After doing this exercise, we started to trust the instincts of the kids . . ..
Through the residency the kids became architects.

We then asked the students to help us "Walk in their Shoes"—literally to take their shoes off, trace around them on a piece of paper, and fill them in, pretending to step on one area of the city they wished to change. They were able to do this immediately, to think "out of the box" and create drawings of their ideal new place. Their exuberance enthused and inspired the architects, Petar admitting that the immense success of the students' contribution had by no means been anticipated:

> *I had mixed feelings when I got there. I was nervous. I was amazed how*
> *much energy and commitment the kids had. They were always there*
> *and willing to do work. In the same way it helped bridge this gap*
> *between this project and the community itself, because we got the kids*
> *involved and the kids' parents and, for that matter, neighbors and*
> *cousins who even lived around there—people who were able to hear*
> *about and participate in the project indirectly through the kids. People*
> *were expressing their concerns through the children and the children*
> *had some concerns of their own because they were critical of the school*
> *they were going to now. They were doing the drawings and writing stuff*
> *and working with us to tell us what they wanted.*

Places and images that appeared in their mental maps and shoe drawings later re-emerged when we asked the students to draw their Ideal Floor Plan and imagine a Place Visualization through the school. Basketball courts, music, food were all the "high positives" of their imagined ideal environment. Through this weekly contact with the students, KSS and the visioning committee learned about the nuances of student life. As their understanding of the students' needs evolved, the school program and schematic design evolved too. Basketball courts were added to the plan. The music room was placed in a central location.

Tapping further into the students' energy and creativity, the last four sessions were spent having students build a scale model of the school and design an environmental artwork to go in it. The environmental artwork was meant to express both their individual identity and the charter school's essence. One student proposed a giant Claes Oldenberg type purple trumpet sculpture to be placed in the main lobby. It seemed to sum up all the exuberance of this user group. The students, their parents, the visioning session participants and KSS designers all gathered together to celebrate the students' proposals during the final session. The entire process was summed up by Merilee:

> It was much less about product and more about process. Normally clients are trying to tell us, "Move that wall to the left." Because people weren't thinking like that—they were thinking about the kids feeling like they belonged to a greater organization. They didn't care about where the walls were. This process was interesting in that way.

The Design

The challenge for KSS was to weave together all the input they had received from the adult visioning sessions and the student architecture residency and translate those ideas into a final design. In fact, however, the very nature of this partici-patory process meant that translation of vision into design had been ongoing as the adult and student sessions had progressed. Commenting on the difference between conventional architectural practice and the opportunity for enhanced vision created by incorporating Design Psychology, Michael felt that

> People very readily default to a menu of design options: we want the classroom this way; we want this many offices. What happens is the focus is on the pragmatic and not the idea of the philosophy but what this [Design Psychology] enabled us to [do was to] swing back and forth between philosophy and the program—rather than have the philosophy isolated. What we kept coming back to is, "What is this place trying to be as a place and how are people going to experience it?

When it came to the interior layout of the school, a key piece of the floor plan design puzzle fell into place when KSS reconfigured their original floor plan to create that large, informal, multimedia area for faculty and students at the center of the school. During the visioning sessions adults could see that this arrangement of facilities and space was crucial to promoting the social interaction, the sense of community which figuratively and literally formed the heart of the school.

Meanwhile as a result of the residency, KSS architects picked up the beat of the moving, dancing, talking, and exuberant students and juxtaposed the music room with the main/rear entrance. Such placement had a symbolic intention. The hope was that the students, who so strongly identified themselves with music culture, would get an immediate message upon entering that this school was a place that was about *them*—that it was a place with which *they* could identify. Once again, Merilee articulated the significance of the student residency for the creation of a fulfilling design:

> Through the residency and meeting the kids we found out how much larger than life they really were. We knew that we had made a big mistake and that we had to bring that media room back into the project, and that it needed to be much larger than we thought. That revelation was a key part and big turning point for this project. Usually we build these buildings and we never meet the kids. We meet the faculty, we meet the principal, but we never meet the kids. This residency really enhanced this project.

Once the floor plan was agreed, the challenge remained to create a look and feel for the school with which students could identify and feel comfortable which at the same time inspired them to grow. Then too, as good architects, KSS felt charged with the responsibility of creating a space that was of the highest aesthetic quality.

The decision to design the interior of the laundry building in a manner that maintained and, in many ways, accentuated its industrial quality appropriately "actualized" everyone's best hopes and "highest positive" associations with this place. Sliding, corrugated, industrial doors gave classroom spaces flexibility, an openness and novelty that could never be achieved via more conventional classroom doors. This flexibility, openness, and novelty fit the "extraverted" "innovative," "feeling," "warm," "exciting" organizational personality that the adult participants had envisioned for the Charter School. Then, too, the use of corrugated doors juxtaposed with rough, exposed brick walls maintained the building's jaunty, city feel—a rich, urban gusto revealed in the students' mental maps.

Similarly, from the architectural standpoint, KSS felt that they had maintained the integrity of the laundry building's character. For them

> Part of the design intention was to articulate the "time" or history of the building by preserving certain characteristics of the found condition. By taking advantage of the specific nuances of the existing building; aging or weathering, special aspects of the building's presence were revealed.

As parents and students began to attend orientation meetings about the Charter School, some remarked that a number of students' grandparents had actually worked in the laundry building when it was operational. With this in mind, KSS began to consider ways in which the oral histories of these community members could be embedded in artwork created for the building. Such a direction was in keeping with the "culturally inclusive" taste culture and aesthetic that had been embraced here in order to realize an environment that "everyone feels familiar with yet still makes a statement."

In terms of aesthetics, KSS also helped achieve the school's goal of "breaking the paradigm" by eliminating the traditional long corridors of lockers and their associated institutional feel. Merilee explains:

> One of the first things they did **not** want to see is hallways with lockers. Normally we would be hesitant to break the rules. In this case we broke the rules with them and we broke them to enhance something else that was more important.

Finally, then, the inclusion of wood floors, open space and light-filled skylights in the Charter School design echoed the best memory of participants' favorite past school place, reverberating as a gift for generations of students yet to come. An enthusiastic Petar summed up the process:

> The process that we went from was really amazing. It took a whole group of people and it brought us all to one point but it actually challenged everyone within the group and allowed them to develop . . .. This process allowed us to bring the project to a higher level than is conventionally done.

The Mufson Partnership, New York, New York

The Project

The Mufson Partnership is a Manhattan-based architecture and design firm specializing in corporate and residential projects. Located in an office building near Fifth Avenue, the firm consists of two principals and approximately thirty-five employees. After hearing a talk about Design Psychology, one of those employees, designer Randi Larowitz, became interested in incorporating this approach into a Mufson project. After discussion with Larowitz and Principal Larry Mufson, they decided to focus on training the Mufson staff in the use of Design Psychology rather than working on a client-based design project.

With this in mind, I conducted a series of six Design Psychology training sessions with a small group of Mufson Partnership designers. The purpose of those sessions was to:

➢ enable participants to explore their own personal history of place thereby increasing their awareness of their self–place connection;

➢ identify ways in which such awareness can help participants more consciously create satisfying environments for themselves and their clients;

➢ develop and test with participants Design Psychology exercises appropriate for use as part of Mufson's programming and schematic design process;

➢ advise on the use of those exercises that enable designers to address social and psychological as well as aesthetic and functional design considerations.

The Designers

Founded in 1994, the Mufson Partnership describes itself as grounded "in the principle that good design is about appropriateness, integrity, and a certain timelessness."[8] Mufson also believes that their work is not about developing a "stylistic signature." For them it is about "creating a product which is appropriate and unique to each client."[9]

In fact, in terms of their approach with corporate clients, Mufson seemed already attuned to the Design Psychology approach, stressing the relationship between the *spirit* of a corporate culture and its design:

> We seek to three-dimensionalize the culture of a corporation, manifesting it in architecture. By developing a clear picture of who our clients are and how their businesses operate we are able to determine how a thoughtfully designed facility can foster harmony, efficiency and growth while personifying the spirit of an organization.[10]

The Process

Training sessions

The training sessions first included a one-hour lecture that provided an overview of the theory and methods of Design Psychology. All Mufson staff members attended this session. Out of this group, approximately eight people volunteered to attend five further training sessions, lasting approximately two hours each, to be held over the next five weeks.[11]

During one portion of each of these sessions, participants completed the same Design Psychology exercises that had been completed by Graves, Jencks, and Duany. During the other portion of sessions, Mufson staff used the Design Psychology process to envision a hypothetical office design—the interior design of the Mufson Partnership office itself. To do this, the group completed exercises from the Design Psychology Toolbox (see Appendix below) which were similar to the ones used during the NJCU Charter School visioning process. In this case, however, those exercises were adapted for use in a workplace rather than a school setting. The hope was that staff could then embed these exercises in future Mufson programming and schematic design processes.

As had been the case with the NJCU sessions, the exercises were presented in the deliberate progression typical of the Design Psychology approach, enabling participants to

➤ explore their history of past work environments;

➤ identify the "highest positive" associations they had with those past workplaces;

➤ use these "high positives" to help envision their "ideal" design for Mufson's offices;

➤ recognize and articulate the pyramid of functional, psychological, social, aesthetic, and growth needs to be addressed by the office design;

➤ translate the Mufson's staff vision into a fulfilling workplace design, using the pyramid of needs as a touchstone.

Using the Design Psychology Toolbox

As a first step in thinking about the Mufson office re-design, I had the workshop participants explore their past history of *work*places by doing the Workplace Family Tree Exercise. I asked the Mufson staff members to fill in a blank family tree (see Appendix, Tool 2 below) by using words to describe the work, work values and/or workplaces of their forebears. Then I asked them to analyze their workplace family trees to discern patterns from the past that may have influenced their own perspectives and values when it came to work and workplaces. Larry explained his perception of his career in the context of second generation immigrant aspirations:

> *I looked at my relatives who were farmers. Both of my families were*
> *Jewish farmers. My paternal grandfather died in a pogrom. The next*
> *generation all became business owners. Tire business on my father's*
> *side; garment center business on my mother's side. I never realized until*
> *this moment—why would I do this [job as an architect]? It's interesting.*
> *I'm the first professional in my family. They were all business owners.*
> *It's so generational—so second generation immigrant mentality. Such a*
> *hardworking background. You come here dirt poor and you're rated on*
> *your success. So my success was I got to go to college.*

Given this Workplace Family Tree, it also seemed a natural progression for Larry to become not just the family's first professional but also a business owner like his forebears.

Another Mufson designer, Brian, had absorbed the work ethic of his parents:

> *I do creative work and no one in my background did creative work.*
> *I come from really non-creative stock. A lot of them might have been*
> *creative but they didn't have opportunities. They worked to put food*
> *on the table. They were diligent, reliable, and loyal. I got those work*
> *habits from my parents.*

After other participants had also shared their Workplace Family Tree, I asked all to choose one or two words to describe their highest positive association with work, based on the workplace perspective and values passed down to them by their family. The group then brainstormed further to suggest other words they would associate with a workplace of real value.

We continued to create a collage of words to describe the highest positive association with past workplaces by doing the Workplace Timeline. I asked the

Mufson designers to recall all the places where they had worked. Then I asked each staff member to pick just one word out of all the words we had listed that represented their highest positive association with workplace. The point was to build from each person's very personal ideal a collective vision of the ideal Mufson workplace. The staff could then compare the ideal they had envisioned with the public image projected in the Mufson mission statement. By the end of the session we could see that there was some overlap between the personal ideal each had articulated and Mufson's public image.

Which vision of Mufson, the personal or public, should any design speak to? Often designers begin working with a corporate client by asking them about their project goals and company mission. Here we were taking a step even further back by identifying participants' very basic sense of the ideal workplace—any workplace—not just the office of the Mufson Partnership. Designers need to come to terms with this key issue of workplace identity as an initial step in any holistic design process. Becker and Steele in their book, *Workplace by Design*, suggest a way forward:

> The necessity to make spatial choices also provides a fallout benefit in terms of the discipline that comes from examining one's vision of the organization and style. It is all too easy to put off such self-examination in keeping with day-to-day operations, but a new headquarters project forces the question. It is very hard to proceed without choosing or confirming an identity as the basis for determining the building form and space planning decisions.
>
> There is an inherent tension in this area between, on the one hand, choosing an image to project and then making headquarters that will project this image, and, on the other, choosing desired ways of working as an organization, making a good workplace to support that, and letting the result be the image statement, reflecting how the system really works.
>
> We strongly support the latter approach—making workplaces that reflect your goals and work style, thereby letting the image speak for itself. Doing it the other way around requires too much "staging" of scenes for the benefit of observers. This places too much pressure on workers to follow scripts so they look right in terms of the desired image, which in many instances is different from getting on with doing a good job.[12]

Was it possible to take the best of the personal workplace ideal that participants had articulated and combine it with the most authentic aspects of the Mufson public image statements to come up with a "whole/actualized-workplace" vision? Once the sea of words that had been brainstormed by the group was distilled in this way, one phrase emerged that encapsulated that vision:

The Mufson Partnership Whole-Workplace Vision
A workplace that is awe-inspiring, stimulating, allowing for privacy and flexibility as we do creative work of integrity.

Having explored participants' history of past workplace and used their highest positive associations with workplace to meld this whole-workplace vision, the next step in the Design Psychology process was to use these "high positives" to envision ideal design. With this in mind, during the next session, I had group members do the Mental Map Exercise (see Appendix, below). In this context I asked them to draw a mental map of the path they took from home to the Mufson office, a mental map of the entire office layout and a mental map of their own workstation layout. When the three maps were completed, I asked participants to go back to their maps and add words to the maps to describe the look and feel of these environments (i.e. colorful, friendly, noisy, crowded, etc.).

We then charted their impression of the Mufson site, office, and workstation layout by categorizing their descriptions in terms of the pyramid of needs that must be satisfied to create "The Mufson Partnership Whole-Workplace Vision." At the suggestion of workshop participants, however, I also simplified the terms used by Steele, for instance changing the categories "Task Instrumentality" to "Functional Needs" and "Symbolic Identification" to "Identity":

The workshop group was then able to step back, look at these three triangles and assess how well needs on the rungs of their ladders were being met, especially in relation to the ideal vision they had formulated for Mufson. They could see, for example, that the location of the Mufson office seemed fairly satisfying— convenient and richly urban. Yet the Mufson office space itself, while a hard-working hive of activity, did not live up to the Whole/Actualized Workplace Vision staff members had articulated. Rather than being "awe-inspiring," for example, staff members described the office space as simply "pleasant." Also, while Mufson's open space plan encouraged a communal, egalitarian spirit in which the firm took pride, it offered staff no privacy.

Such methodical assessment of their workspace enabled the group to develop project goals for this hypothetical re-design of their office. Those goals included the creation of

> a more awe-inspiring environment;

> a space that achieved a more satisfying balance between privacy and openness;

> extra meeting rooms, including project rooms, teams rooms and an informal space;

> an improved library space;

> an area for display of projects;

> more storage space.

Had this been a real project, the next step, of course, would have been to carry out a more conventional programming process which would identify the "Functional Needs" and those related to "Shelter and Security." Instead the group

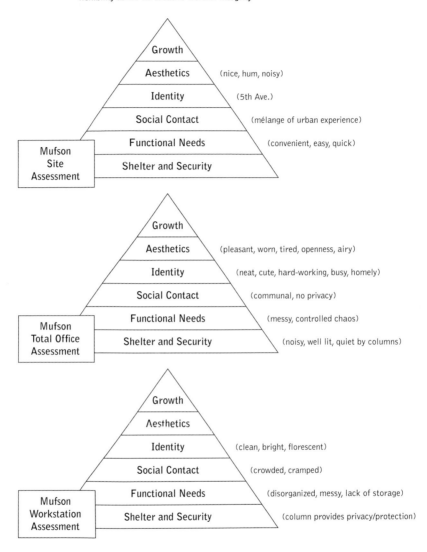

Mufson Whole-Workplace Vision:
A workplace that is awe-inspiring, stimulating, allowing for privacy and
flexibility as we do creative work of integrity

Mufson Site Assessment

- Growth
- Aesthetics — (nice, hum, noisy)
- Identity — (5th Ave.)
- Social Contact — (mélange of urban experience)
- Functional Needs — (convenient, easy, quick)
- Shelter and Security

Mufson Total Office Assessment

- Growth
- Aesthetics — (pleasant, worn, tired, openness, airy)
- Identity — (neat, cute, hard-working, busy, homely)
- Social Contact — (communal, no privacy)
- Functional Needs — (messy, controlled chaos)
- Shelter and Security — (noisy, well lit, quiet by columns)

Mufson Workstation Assessment

- Growth
- Aesthetics
- Identity — (clean, bright, florescent)
- Social Contact — (crowded, cramped)
- Functional Needs — (disorganized, messy, lack of storage)
- Shelter and Security — (column provides privacy/protection)

began to climb the pyramid of needs by doing exercises which corresponded with each level of the "Whole-Workplace Triangle."

When doing the Ideal Workplace Exercise (see Appendix) each participant created floor plans suggesting different solutions for the above issues. I then asked the group to do the Environmental Sociogram Exercise which helped them analyze to what extent the new floor plans they had drawn (see Appendix, below) did achieve the desired balance between openness and privacy.

The group then set aside this initial brainstorming regarding their workplace layout in terms of "Social Contact" to move further up the pyramid of needs and consider the "Identity" they wanted to achieve for the space. Toward this end, staff members completed the Organizational Personality Test. Results suggested that the Mufson Partnership, just as the NJCU Charter School, was an ENFP type organization—extraverted, intuitive, feeling, perceiving.

We then talked about the importance of matching the office environment with the *personality* of the organization as well as matching that environment with an organization's work patterns. Of interest in this regard were four different work setting types presented in the book *New Environments for Working:*[13]

<table>
<tr><td>

Den
- Group process work
- Low autonomy
- High interaction
- PC, specialized equipment
- 9 to 5 hours, some variation
- Complex timetabling

</td><td>

Club
- Varied work (individual and group)
- High autonomy
- High interaction
- Elaborate IT

</td></tr>
<tr><td>

Hive
- Individual process work
- Low autonomy
- Low interaction
- Networked PC
- 9–5 hours, shift work

</td><td>

Cell
- Isolated work
- High autonomy
- Low interaction
- Elaborate IT
- Individual timetabling

</td></tr>
</table>

Currently, Mufson seemed to be organized as a "hive" with multiple work-stations and a shortage of areas set aside for team interaction. As an extraverted organization, a "club" configuration might prove more appropriate, allowing for both the "high interaction" essential in team-based design projects and the high autonomy needed to do concentrated, individual design work.

In our final workshop session, in order to help participants imagine the aesthetics of this new space, I conducted the Workplace Visualization Exercise (see Appendix) with them. As designers, they were able freely to imagine in their mind's eye a newly created imaginary office space with revolving red doors, glass walls for privacy, a grandfather clock, etc.

Workshop participants produced a final collaborative drawing that borrowed from each of their visualizations to create a final office layout and interior design that addressed the pyramid of needs we had been discussing over the past five weeks. That layout included a large, awe-inspiring, elliptical-shaped reception area and a gallery for Mufson's project work. Also envisioned was a corridor with a series of meeting/presentation rooms, each with a worktable. Additionally configured was a series of glass-enclosed private offices for senior personnel and two new team meeting rooms. In this way they had used the pyramid as a touchstone for translating the "Mufson Whole-Workplace Vision" into a fulfilling office design.

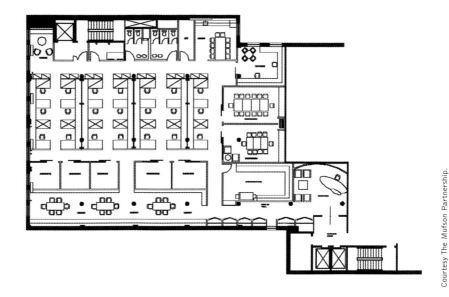

Courtesy The Mufson Partnership.

Applying Design Psychology to Real Workplace Design Projects

Building the case for the Design Psychology process

The Mufson office design project described here was a hypothetical exercise undertaken as part of Design Psychology training workshops. Thus it is appropriate to ask to what extent can the Design Psychology process be applied successfully to real workplace projects? The main motivation of corporate clients, unlike residential clients, for instance, is to make a profit rather than create holistic environments. As Larry Mufson suggested, "It's about making money. It's not necessarily about making this great space. It's about the bottom line." Why, then, would companies be motivated to engage in a process approach to design?

Workshop participants felt that a case would first have to be made to show the importance of matching people and their workplace in terms of productivity and/or attraction as well as retention of employees. Such findings do exist.[14] Then, too, the group felt that designers whose services included creating "The Actualized Workplace," a workplace that realized its full potential in terms of physical setting and organizational function, might be appealing to clients as an "added value" approach.

Appropriateness

Another concern was that the personal exploration inherent in the Workplace Family Tree Exercise might be inappropriate in a formal corporate setting. Mufson designers agreed that much depended on the client. Certain clients (like both the Mufson Partnership and the NJCU Charter School group) who are by nature "intuitive," "feeling," "perceiving" organizations or simply open-minded and innovative, might be more receptive to this approach than more conservative organizations. Then, too, the group suggested that the Design Psychology exercises should be "seamlessly embedded" in the regular programming process, creating an acceptable balance between a more open-ended exploratory approach and routine discussion of such integral issues as square footage requirements.

One should also not assume that *all* of the Design Psychology exercises presented here need to be conducted with the client in order to complete the process. Depending on the circumstances, completion of even one or two exercises may contribute to thoughtful examination of the psychological/social design dimension of an office's design, which otherwise might not be considered.

For example, Dr. Susan Painter, a psychologist and interior designer working with the firm of A.C. Martin and Partners in Los Angeles, adapted the "Favorite Objects" exercise[15] and used it as a springboard for the design of offices and laboratories for a biotech company doing groundbreaking work in DNA research.

During her interview with the CEO, Dr. Painter found that a biosphere on his desk was his favorite object. A biosphere is a self-contained glass environment filled with shrimp and algae, which live by being placed in sunlight. While discussion of square footage requirements with him proved a necessary but uninspiring exercise, discussion of the biosphere was what really enthused him and touched an inspirational chord. The biosphere seemed to be a metaphor for the biological and organic nature of the work on which the company was engaged. It made sense that the design of the firm would showcase this world of nature in this man-made office.

Thus the focus of the design of the new office is the reception area. Its oval shape is symbolic of the biosphere—the introduction of a shape that is more organic than geometric. In this way, the design is imbued with symbolic and psychological value. It is design that speaks to the poetics of space rather than just being the literal translation of a company's mission.

Participation

Of course, in this example, it was one person only, the CEO, with whom Painter conducted this Design Psychology interview. Thus the office design was primarily an interpretation of the deeper meaning of the company for *him*. This can be appropriate since often a company is a realization of one key person's inspiration/vision.

Yet often it is also appropriate to involve other employees in design decision making. This may be particularly true, for example, when the CEO does not want to be directly involved in the design process. In fact, the type of client representative(s) with whom the designer works on any given project may vary from job to job. Research shows, for instance, that it is usually managers and supervisors who participate more frequently and get to make more design decisions than any other job type. Similarly, although participants have higher job satisfaction and satisfaction with the environment, less than one in five employees has a chance to participate in design decisions, although most would like to do so.[16]

As an alternative, Mike Brill of BOSTI Associates suggested, "Rather than imposing decisions on workers, organizations might consider systematically incorporating workers' views."[17] How can this be done using Design Psychology? The Design Psychology training sessions I carried out with Mufson staff members involved the firm's principal, supervisors *and* employees. As such, it provides one example of collaborative visioning and decision making in relation to design.

Facilitation

When designers and their clients are committed to such participation, especially as it involves Design Psychology, who should facilitate such a process? As the training process here did not include using the Design Psychology exercises on a "live" project, it is not possible to assess to what extent the Mufson designers gained the ability to apply this process on their own. In fact, KSS architects felt they needed my expertise as a Design Psychologist to facilitate any such process. However, another designer, Morris Stafford from Seattle, who simply heard me speak about Design Psychology, was able readily to apply its precepts to a residential project. He wrote:

> Several days prior to your [talk] I was hired to design a house for a client who wanted to build a stone house, with lots of references to castle details. I did a quick design for him for "talking paper" but missed the mark, as far as he was concerned. He was rather cool. After your program, I met with my client and I started asking him about his upbringing, with lots of questions about why he wanted a building that seemed so incongruous to our region.
>
> He told me he grew up in Portland, Oregon and described neighborhoods that I was familiar with, which led to even more confusion on my part. Maybe he really didn't want a castle. I showed him some historical references. One was in a book about shingle style homes, which are mingled with many of the fine older craftsman style homes in Portland.
>
> I was thinking his interest may also have some roots in Richardsonian Romanesque brownstones. Even though he works in Europe and made reference to the castles there, I doubted their influence over him as an adult could lead to such a strong desire.
>
> I knew of a house that had some of the characteristics of what he was looking for. It really was a shingle style house, with stone masonry walls up to the second floor. I had a book with an illustration of the house. His jaw about hit the tabletop. This house had the turret and the stone and the Richardsonian arches. But what was key was that this house was located across the street where he attended elementary school in Portland. He talked with great animation about how he spent hours gazing out the windows of his school, admiring this house.
>
> After that moment, we absolutely clicked. I came back with a revised design in a similar genre and it was immediately accepted.
>
> Your illustrations of how designers work are interesting, but the real power to me is in understanding my clients.[18]

Of course, this architect was talking about a one-to-one client-architect relationship in the context of *residential*, not workplace design. Yet, what seems an important starting point is that designers are at least exposed to the idea that we all experience a deep psychological connection to place that can reverberate for both designer and client for years to come. Perhaps the best way for designers to understand the significance of that link is to examine their own self–place connections.

It is to be hoped that in this sense the Mufson training sessions were equally valuable in terms of the personal insights participants gained from them. In some instances, the Mufson designers I worked with saw what I hope Graves, Jencks and Duany recognized: how they unconsciously had reworked elements of important past places into their current designs. Larry described his amazement when he realized how relevant the Design Psychology process was in revealing his own past place influence:

> Right now we are doing a building called The Beresford, a very fancy
> building on Central Park West. When I was growing up I had relatives
> who were living there. All my work is in this building. It's amazing the
> effect this building had on me! It was like a kid from New Jersey going
> to Versailles Palace. As you walk down this hallway there was this
> arch, this processional thing.

> Amazing how unconsciously my take on what the rich and glamorous
> want is the vocabulary of this building. Even my doodling—all these
> little sketches for years, all were about this place. I saw this when I
> started doing the Taste Culture Exercise. I just went "Wow!"

We expect symbolism from *artists'* personal lives to reverberate in their work. Why would not we, naturally, expect to see the same reverberation in *designers'* work?

Then, too, Larry recognized how the process of early homebuilding, his family life and later career all may have been subconsciously intertwined:

> When I did the Favorite Childhood Place Visualization, I went to where
> my house in New Jersey was being built. I never thought about this. It
> was a split-level 1959 and my mother made these great lunches and we
> had picnics on the concrete slabs while they were building this house.
> I was so happy over the new construction. I was so happy there at that
> moment, but I wasn't happy living there but the **construction**—I was
> miserable living there but the **anticipation**. Ironically, I constantly
> renovate houses. I wonder if there's a connection with my happiness.[19]

Another workshop participant, Anne, also made the connection between her childhood experience of place and the creation of her present home:

> My mother was a communications officer on board a ship. My father
> was the captain. I spent the first two years of my life aboard a ship.
> I was pampered by the sailors. The ship was a plain white/gray color.

*We just moved house and I picked out all these colors for rooms and
when I was painting the walls I noticed even though it is a slightly blue
color or purple color, there is gray in it. In certain light you see more of
the gray rather than the actual color that I picked. It's possible that it
goes all the way back to the time on the ship.*

Yet these are just quick glimpses of connections. The real value of the Design Psychology process comes with asking, "Why do these design elements continue to resonate? Can I follow their echo through my life and work? Can I harness their symbolic power so it rings with an even deeper timbre in the world of places I inhabit and create?"

Randi seemed to be following the echo in this way, making connections between her personal and professional growth:

*I thought it was interesting when we had gone through the entire
Workplace Timeline Exercise and all the jobs that I had, that I
completely left off being a singer, because that was a huge part
of my life.*

In fact she described herself as " a life-change expert":

*At thirty years old I completely re-invented myself. Until then I had
defined myself one hundred percent as a singer. I loved it . . . . Then I
decided OK, I am going to stop singing. This is not the life that I want . .
. . From thirty until forty I became Randi the designer . . . I just decided
to transition myself. From forty until now I became Randi the mother
which has changed my life tremendously.*

Now she felt she had very few "favorite objects" in her house, explaining, "Now that my daughter is here, she's the jewel in the crown. Now the interior is a lot less important." She described this present time as a period of real happiness:

*There's no such thing as a perfect life but my life now is as near perfect
as it gets.*

Still, she remembered that the theme of ongoing change/transition had also emerged in her design work:

*When I was at school we had this project and there was this Egyptian
reference I wanted to make. It was about change . . . . I built this big
round thing. When I saw it, I thought, "It's all about transition." I was
thinking about life and death transitions. Life in like: as we grow we are
transformed.*

Randi realized that the same theme of transition had echoed more recently:

We did this project last year for Right Management and it was also about change . . .. It was about how the physical manifestation of change would be walking in a circular path. Sort of like at the Guggenheim but I didn't realize that until later. We designed these sort of "operas" that we made people go through where they would eventually cross into each other. I just realized that I'd done that before [in the school project].

Randi went on to recognize that the source of this recurring circular design element was her childhood experience of place:

I don't know where it comes from. There is one thing: where I grew up in the front of the building there's a reinforced concrete parabolic curve. There's a circular driveway in front of my parent's apartment building where you have to drive to get out. So to me that is a very familiar transition. My home as a child and their current home was a happy place for me. The first thing I draw will always be this kind of curve. I've always drawn that even when I'm just sort of brainstorming and connecting lines. That's interesting.

A week later Randi wrote to me:

Monday night I was at the Metropolitan Opera and outside of the auditorium pretty much alone in the space. I was blown away by the realization that all of my adult "singing" life, the Met represented to me all that was beautiful, great, important. Two things came to mind—how much this was like the structure of my c. 1960s apartment building (same period of the Met's construction) and how that love of the function of the Met had translated to my version of beautiful space as a designer. Thanks for the clarity!

Rather than seeing her singing life as now past, Randi realized that she had simply made the transition to singing in another form—that she had integrated the visual symbolism of her happy childhood home and the exuberance/meaning she brought to her life and song into her design work. In the future, then, she could continue to honor her own voice. Rather than seeing the interior of her home as not very important, for example, she could seek to create an interior design for it that harmonized her own identity with her role as a dedicated mother.

When Randi spoke with me again in another week, she was aware of the wider ramifications of this direction for the future:

In this period of time now I'm ready to bring the singer back. I had to sublimate that to be Randi the designer. In the early part of my career I was designing for someone else—executing other people's designs. I was designing by what you learn is, quote, "good taste." As you get more confident and secure you try to meld who you are, how to become the client and what came before you historically in terms of good taste. Now I have to get myself out.

I asked her what she meant by "get myself out." She explained by referring to wisdom passed on to her by an old acting teacher:

She used to say, "The only thing you have to bring as a creative person is yourself. You can't try to be someone else. If you are successful at art you bring yourself—everything else is meaningless." Getting myself out? I'm just at a point where my life has come full circle. I'm at the point where I'm confident enough to be able to say and express that . . ..

Given the very pressured, deadline-driven nature of this business, Randi concluded:

For a while I thought, "Just do the work" and don't put so much of my "self" into it, but that just wasn't me. I am evolving and I refuse to stop.

Continuing to "actualize" herself in this way, Randi could help clients evolve as well. With a greater awareness of the deeper power of design, through the Design Psychology process, she could help them recognize and integrate the *meaning* of place with the *design* of place, thereby creating fulfilling home, school, work or other settings for those clients.

The hope is that other designers will also see the compelling connections that exist between the construction of their "self" and the building of place. I hope that designers will be energized by the challenge of integrating the essence of their work with the story that is their life. In this way they open themselves to the opportunity to move toward greater wholeness rather than greater fragmentation in the face of the daily time pressures intrinsic to the profession.

Design Psychology offers designers, clients, and users a means of gaining such insight. It provides them with a new method of creating, together, deeply satisfying places. To this end, those involved in the design process can reach into the Design Psychology Toolbox provided at the end of this book and meaningfully weave these exercises into their programming, schematic design, and design development process. Then, too, as this new field grows, it can be included as part of the formal training and further education of designers.

Though still in its infancy, I believe in the power and promise of Design Psychology:

Today I listened as the latest round of superstar architects unveiled their proposals for Ground Zero. "Memory," "Soul," and "Hope" were words they used again, and again and again.

What memory? What soul? What hope?

*Architects, planners and politicians: remember the worst day of your life—perhaps a day of someone dearly loved, suddenly lost . . .. What places soothed **your** soul? Were they places to be alone? To gather? To hear water fall or see light rejoice? . . . Has no place soothed you yet?*

*Lift your veil to be present in the most poignant moment, just as the widow lifts her veil to receive the folded flag. Design and build **together** from the truth of that past pain as ceremony healing loss and as celebration, despite loss, of the meaning and promise that life holds.*

Appendix
The Design Psychology Toolbox

The following Design Psychology Toolbox includes a series of nine "tools" derived from the exercises laced throughout the main portion of this book. However, while the exercises previously presented are for use by individuals, these exercises can be done by groups. In particular these exercises form a toolbox into which designers can reach as they facilitate a visioning process that helps client groups brainstorm ideas for schools, workplaces, institutions and other places including even large scale environments that users will feel connected to in the deepest possible way.

How to Use the Toolbox

With the above purpose in mind this Design Psychology Toolbox for designers includes:

A chart of "Design Psychology Steps"
The flow chart on the next page shows the steps I used to carry out the case study design of my kitchen project, the University Academy Charter School, and the Mufson Partnership office space. I provide this flow chart with the caveat that I do not believe in pat formulas. Thus it would be a huge mistake simply to apply a route Design Psychology formula to all projects.

A chart showing an "Overview of the Design Psychology Toolbox"
For example, in this second chart which shows the relationship between each Design Psychology step and the eight tools, I stress that the exercises need not be

STEP 5: Using the pyramid as a touchstone, translate vision into fulfilling design

Growth
Aesthetics
Identity
Social Contact
Functional Needs
Shelter and Security

STEP 4: Climb the pyramid of needs to be satisfied to envision ideal design

STEP 3: use 'high positives' to envision ideal design

STEP 2: Identify 'high positive' associations with past place

STEP 1: Explore past history of place

done in the order given. They can be done in any order that makes sense in terms of the project at hand. Similarly not *every* exercise needs to be completed, only those that are appropriate given the project and client/user group.

Sample Design Psychology visioning session agenda

This agenda gives one example of how the Design Psychology tools can be used as part of their conventional programming, schematic design, and design development process. Every designer has their own toolbox—their own approach to project development. The point is for designers to adapt and embed some or all of these tools in their own working process. Then, too, the agenda example shown here is for an interior renovation project. The Design Psychology process, however, can be applied equally to a planning or architecture project. No matter what the project context, the guiding principle should be to expand the conventional design process to encompass people's deepest, most authentic connection to place.

The tools

Each tool/exercise is presented here in a generic form so that it can be adapted for use depending upon the particular circumstances. Some exercises may be

Design Psychology Tools		
Steps	*Tools*	*Tips*
Step 5: Translate vision into fulfilling design ↑	*Schematic and final design completed by designer*	To ensure the group's vision is fully translated, it is important that the Design Psychologist or group facilitator continue to have input into the project's design phase
Step 4: Climb the pyramid ↑	**Growth** *Actualized Place Exercise* **Aesthetics** *Taste Culture Exercise* *Place Visualization Exercise* **Identity** *Group Personality Exercise* **Social Contact** *Place Sociogram Exercise*	Visual images can be a useful prompt to help group members to talk about/confirm their design ideas. Although these five exercises should generally be done in their "climbing" order, that order need not be rigid
Step 3: Use "high positives" to envision ideal design ↑	**Functional Needs** *Ideal Layout Exercise* **Shelter and Security**	Conventional program information such as square footage requirements and adjacencies should be added to information considered at this stage
	Mental Map Exercise	The Mental Map Exercise is crucial to understanding the setting/context of a given project
Step 2: Identify "high positive" associations with past place ↑	*Place Family Tree Exercise*	This exercise may be appropriate only for use with groups that are very open and innovative
Step 1: Explore past history of place ↑	*Place Timeline Exercise*	It is good to begin the Design Psychology process with the Place Timeline. This exercise is easy to do and not highly personal

more appropriate for one context than another—a school project as opposed to a corporate project, for instance.

Finally, then, as with the exercises done on an individual basis, the group exercises here should be done only on the level that is comfortable for participants. With this in mind, designers may wish to take part in Design Psychology further education opportunities which provide training on the use of these techniques.[1]

Design Psychology Visioning Session Agenda Example

Programming

Visioning Session 1   The Vision

➤ Discuss the mission and characteristics of the project

➤ Establish general project goals and objectives

Tool 1: Place Timeline Exercise

➤ Formulate vision of "Whole-Place Vision" to be supported by design

➤ Compare "Whole-Place Vision" with the mission, goals, and objectives of project

➤ Finalize "Whole-Place Vision" statement

Visioning Session 2   Shelter and Security/Functional Needs

➤ Establish space requirements and adjacencies to support the Whole-Place Vision

Tool 2: Mental Map Exercise

Tool 3: Ideal Place Exercise

➤ Identify opportunities and constraints of design of site, interior layout, etc. in order to support Whole-Place Vision

Visioning Session 3   Social Contact: Organization of People and Places

➤   Refine desired space adjacencies and criteria for organizing of programmatic elements

➤   Develop design ideas for the interior layout

   Tool 4: Environmental Sociogram Exercise

➤   Refine interior layout

➤   Review/refine final program document

Schematic Design
Visioning Session 4   Place Identity: A Sense of Place

➤   Review floor plans

➤   Review preliminary cost priorities

   Tool 5: Organizational Personality Exercise

➤   Develop design concepts that affect the exterior and interior of the building

Visioning Session 5   Place Aesthetics

➤   Review elevations

➤   Establish final budget and project phasing

   Tool 6: Taste Cultures Exercise

   Tool 7: Visualization Exercise

➤   Establish final budget and project phasing

Visioning Session 6   Parts Equal the Whole

   Tool 8: Whole/Actualized Place Exercise

➤   Confirm final layout of the floor plan, building footprint and potential phasing

➤   Plan detailed interviews regarding every room of the project

TOOL 1: PLACE TIMELINE

1) Thinking about the type of setting your group is envisioning (i.e. school, workplace, vacation spot, neighborhood . . .), create a timeline of other environments of that type you have experienced from birth to present.

Example: MY SCHOOL TIMELINE:							
Place:	Englewood Nursery	Cleveland School	Englewood Middle School	Dwight Morrow High School	Trinity College	Rutgers University	CUNY
Age: in years	3–5	5–10	11–13	14–17	18–21	23–26	28–35

YOUR PLACE TIMELINE:	
Place:	
Age: in years	

2) Draw a circle around the place you liked the most on your timeline. Write down words describing why you liked it.

3) Share your answers with the group and together create a "Whole-Place" Chart listing the special qualities of the places each person circled on their timeline.

4) Once the "Whole- Place" Chart is completed, compare the qualities listed on the chart with any already existing mission statement, or statement of project goals and objectives.

   a) In what way does the group's vision of "whole" place match the official project mission, its project goals, and its project objectives?

   b) In what way is the group's vision different from that mission, goals, objectives?

   c) Which words best sum up the special qualities of place which the group really wants the new design to support?

5) Through group discussion, arrive at one sentence that summarizes the "Whole-Place Vision" that epitomizes the type of place you want the project design to reflect.

Whole-place Vision Statement:
Example: A workplace that is awe-inspiring, stimulating, allowing for privacy and flexibility as we do creative work of integrity.

TOOL 2: PLACE FAMILY TREE*

Depending on the type of place/project you are designing, fill in the blank Place Family Tree below by using words that describe the workplace or other place* your ancestors experienced.

Place Family Tree

© Copyright Toby Israel

Place Family Tree

---

* This tool may be used instead of Tool 1: Place Timeline or it may be eliminated altogether depending upon the nature of the project. For example, if one were designing a retirement community, it might be more appropriate to have users think back to their *ancestors'* retirement experience rather than have them do a timeline of their own retirement experience—especially if they are not retired yet![2]

1. In what way(s), if any, did your family's experience of this type of place differ from generation to generation?

2. In what way(s), if any, was your family's experience of this type of place the same from generation to generation?

3. In what way(s), if any, do you think your family tree influenced your own perspective and values when it came to this type of place experience?

4. In what way(s), if any, do you think that influence was positive or negative?

5. Referring back to the Place Timeline Exercise and the "Whole-Place" Chart created in the previous exercise, work with your group to add words to the "Whole-Place" Chart that would describe the legacy of place that you want to pass down to the next generation.

Decide with the group if this changes the "Whole-Place Vision" you developed in the Place Timeline Exercise. If it does, revise that "Whole-Place Vision" to sum up the type of place you most want the new design to support.

TOOL 3: MENTAL MAP

1) Draw a map of your project's setting/context. The map does not have to be perfect, exact, or even accurate. Just draw this place as you experience it—almost as if you were drawing a map for someone who has never been to that place and wants to visit it.

2) When you have finished, go back to the map and annotate it with words which might give a visitor an accurate impression of how that setting looks and feels. For example label the map with words that say what you like the most/least about that setting (i.e. warm, friendly, noisy, crowded, etc.)

3) Have members of the group discuss their maps by describing the good and bad impressions they had of the project's setting.

4) Answer the following questions to become more aware of those qualities of the area surrounding your project which are especially pleasing or significant to you.

   a) Overall what are the most positive associations that group members have with this setting?

   b) Are there qualities of this setting that make it particularly distinctive, i.e. landmarks, districts, paths, edges, or major transition points i.e. bus or train terminals that are particularly distinctive? In what way(s) are they distinctive?

4) Are there ways in which your project's design can address/incorporate the most positive aspects of this setting to support the "Whole-Place Vision" the group has devised?

5) If your project includes the re-design of an existing building or space (i.e. the re-design of a school or office space), ask the group make another map of the *interior* layout of that place—as if drawing a map to help a visitor find their way around the building's interior. Label your positive and negative impressions of that space.

6) Discuss the positive and negative qualities of this interior with the group.

7) Are there ways your project's interior layout and design can address/incorporate the most positive aspects of the current interior to support the "Whole-Place Vision" the group has devised?

TOOL 4: IDEAL PLACE EXERCISE

1) After discussion has taken place about the project's functional requirements (space and adjacency requirements, for example) as part of the conventional programming process, examine the pyramid of needs to be addressed to make this new place truly fulfilling. At the top of the pyramid, write the statement the group previously formulated (see Tool 1) to describe the group's "Whole-Place Vision" for the project:

THE WHOLE PLACE VISION STATEMENT:

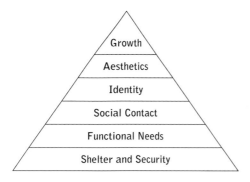

Growth
Aesthetics
Identity
Social Contact
Functional Needs
Shelter and Security

2) Each group member then should receive a blank plan showing the perimeter of the space to be designed to create the group's vision of the "ideal" new place. Make sure the plan shows only the boundaries, walls, or other fixed features that will not be changed by any new design.

3) Use your imagination to fill in the plan in a way you think the newly designed place could best be arranged. You do not need to be a designer to do this exercise. Ideas do not have to be perfectly drawn or even drawn to scale. Just consider how to

   a) establish agreed upon functional requirements;

   b) achieve the "Whole-Place Vision," project mission and goals;

   c) consider the pyramid of needs to be addressed given the project's Whole-Place Vision.

4) Share your ideas for the Ideal Place plan with the rest of the group.

5) Discuss with the group:

   a) Which group member(s) suggestions seem similar and/or different from one another?

   b) Which ideas do they like best?

   c) Do the suggestions the group likes address:

      i   the project's functional requirements?

      ii the Whole-Place Vision and project's mission and goals?

      iii the pyramid of needs to be met?

4) Work with other group members to arrive at an informal schematic design that meets all of the above criteria. Use this collaborative first draft as a springboard for the next draft of a more formal schematic design which the designer will create.

TOOL 5: PLACE SOCIOGRAM

Once a schematic design of the new place has been completed by the designer, analyze the plan by doing the following Place Sociogram to see if it meets place needs in terms of social contact.

1) Each group member should receive a copy of the designer's schematic design for the new place.

2) Group members should then use 3 different color magic markers to color in the different areas of the plan using one color each for:

   a) **Public space**   "belonging" to all those in the place;

   b) **Semi-private space**   "belonging" to sub-groups within the place;

   c) **Private space**   "belonging" to one person only in the place.

3) Discuss the following issues with the group:

   a) Does the newly designed place have an equal division of public, semi-private and private space? If not, what type of space predominates? Does this division make sense given the ideal place you imagined?

   b) Does one person or group of people "own" more space than others? If so, is this appropriate given your ideal/Whole-Place Vision?

   c) What are any conflict areas?

   d) How could the social space/plan be adapted to more closely fit the ideal place vision?

TOOL 6: ORGANIZATIONAL PERSONALITY

The "Organizational Character Index" I use during the visioning groups I conduct appears in the book, *The Character of Organizations: Using Personality Type in Organization Development* by William Bridges. The following exercise represents a more general series of questions to help you match the personality of your organization/users and the sense of place to be designed.

1) How would you describe the personality or group identity you want your project's design to reflect? For example, would you want the design to reflect an identity that is more:

   a) thinking or feeling?

   b) innovative or traditional?

   c) introverted (subdued, reflective) or extraverted (exuberant, open)?

2) Are there any other personality characteristics you want the project's design to reflect?

3) In what way(s), if any, do you think that personality/identity is reflected in the current schematic design for the project?

4) In what way(s), if any, do you think that personality/identity is *not* reflected in the schematic design?

5) In what ways (if any) could the schematic design be changed to best reflect this personality/identity?

TOOL 7: PLACE VISUALIZATION

The following script should be read slowly to the group by the group's facilitator. This reading should include pauses as indicated to allow for imagining in between sentences. Before the facilitator reads it, however, he/she should edit the script by filling in the blanks so it will be specific to the project at hand.

Relax. Listen to your breathing. Close your eyes. Make sure you are comfortable. Breathe easily . . ..
Begin to imagine that you are resting comfortably on a carpet . . . that the carpet is small . . . your own special carpet.

Feel that you are sitting on it in the middle of a huge field. Now imagine the carpet become magical. Let it begin to float safely upward, off the ground, moving effortlessly right into the sky, higher and higher, gently, safely . . .. Look down as you move over the tops of trees, of buildings . . .. See everything become smaller as you float higher . . .. Feel relaxed, happy.

Now begin to recognize landmarks below you . . . See the* _____, and _____. Float gently lower and see the _____, _____, _____ and other landmarks, other streets, whatever . . .. See this building . . .. Float down lower and see this room.

---

* Facilitator should fill in the blanks with word/images which are part of participants' Mental Map of the project area

Now imagine that you see the entrance to the new space we are designing in front of you. Float your carpet gently down and come to rest at the entrance to that place. Walk into the space and notice that everything is completely new—changed now. What do you see? . . . Look carefully all around . . . . Notice the colors . . . the shapes . . . the objects . . . the textures . . . the light . . . Look at the different things there . . .

Move on into another part of the newly designed space . . . . Look carefully all around. Notice the colors, textures, shapes—anything that tells you that this is a* _____ place. What do you see as you walk towards that space . . .? Notice what you are walking on, what's in front of you and above you.

Walk on through the new place, perhaps to the area where you will spend the most time. What do you see? . . . Notice anything that has now made this place special.

Now walk out of your space and into another newly created part of this place . . . . What do you see there? . . .

Notice that the "Whole-Place Vision" we have been talking about really has been achieved to make this place seem like a** _____ place . . . . Look all around . . . . Notice the colors . . . the shapes . . . the textures. . . .

Sit down next to someone you know. Have them say something to you . . . . Answer them . . . . Look carefully around one more time. Notice a special object you didn't notice before in that place . . . .

Then imagine that your seat is magical once again, that is no longer a seat in the new space . . . . It is in this room. Imagine that you are back in this meeting and when you are ready, open your eyes . . . .

After you have completed the visualization, answer the following questions:

1) Were you able to imagine the newly designed place? Take a few minutes to draw the place you visualized. There is no right or wrong to this exercise—you do not need to be a designer to draw this. Include whatever helps you re-create the look and feel that you imagined for the newly designed place: the shapes, color, textures, objects, people, etc. that you imagined.

2) When everyone's drawing is complete, have the group share what each of you visualized in terms of:

    a) the overall look and feel of your newly designed place;

    b) the shapes, color, textures there;

    c) objects, furniture, lighting, etc.;

    d) the way people occupied the new space.

---

* Facilitator should fill in the blanks using words participants previously used (Tool 6) to describe the personality/identity they want the project to express.

** Facilitator to fill in the blanks with words participants previously used to describe their "Whole-Place Vision."

3) Discuss with the group:

   a) which suggestions seem similar and/or different from one another;

   b) which ideas the group likes best;

   c) which ideas best match the project's mission, goals, and Whole-Place Vision;

   d) which ideas address the pyramid of needs to be met.

4) Work with other group members to arrive at design ideas that meet all of the above criteria. Have your designer use this collaborative brainstorming as a springboard for creating drawings/elevations to be considered in terms of the aesthetics for the new space.

TOOL 8: TASTE CULTURES*

Cultures	Designers	Clients	Users
High Culture includes creators and critics whose emphasis is on construction of a work of art. They think they provide the "proper culture" for the rest of society			
Upper Middle Culture are the upper middle class professionals who are not concerned with form but borrow and alter from high culture			
Lower Middle Culture represents America's dominant taste culture—those who value traditional morals and values. The art they prefer is romantic and representational			
Low Culture includes skilled and semi-skilled factory and serviceworkers. They reject culture and prefer lavish ornateness, what Gans calls "Hollywood Modern"			
Quasi-Folk Culture consists of poor, unskilled workers. They are not catered to by the mass media but find expression in church or street festivals			
Fringe Cultures include youth and ethnic American cultures that may rely on a variety of alternative traditions and modes of expressions			

Your own particular aesthetic, your taste and style, forms what Herbert Gans called one's "taste structure." Gans identified five "publics"/"cultures" from which these taste structures are drawn (see table above.)

Although these categories may seem to pigeon hole or stereotype people, it may also be possible to recognize that we each do come from certain taste cultures which may influence our sense of taste and style. With this in mind, put an X in the columns you feel represent the taste culture of the project's designer(s), the client representative(s) and the project's users.

1) Looking at the categories you checked, discuss any similarities and differences between the taste culture of the project's designers, clients and/or users.* Does one represent high culture versus popular culture, for example?

2) Given the project's mission and goals and your "Whole-Place Vision" for it, which taste culture or combination of taste cultures do you think is/are most appropriate for the design of this project?

3) Do the group's previous ideas about how the project should look and feel express this/these taste culture(s)? Are there aspects of that design that need to be changed/developed further to express this culture(s)?

4) If so, work with other group members to brainstorm further suggestions for the look and feel of your project which your designer can translate into further design ideas.

TOOL 9: ACTUALIZED PLACE

Once the design for your new space is almost finalized, analyze how close the group has come to creating the actualized "Whole-Place" you all envisioned.

1) Fill in below the sentence that expressed your Whole-Place Vision.

THE WHOLE-PLACE VISION:

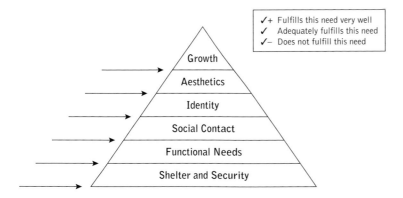

✓+ Fulfills this need very well
✓ Adequately fulfills this need
✓− Does not fulfill this need

Growth
Aesthetics
Identity
Social Contact
Functional Needs
Shelter and Security

---

* In conducting this exercise, a high degree of sensitivity is particularly important in order to avoid any perception of cultural stereotyping. The point of the exercise is just the opposite — it is to envision a design that addresses Gans' goal of cultural diversity/inclusion.

2) Fill in a ✓, ✓ +, or ✓ – next to each rung of the ladder above to assess how well needs on that rungs are being met by the proposed new design:[3]

3) Discuss your ratings with the rest of the group. How confident is the group that the design being proposed
   a) Satisfies the need for shelter and security?
   b) Addresses the functional requirements of the project?
   c) Satisfies the need for social contact?
   d) Communicates the desired personality or identity of the group that will occupy the new place?
   e) Satisfies the need for aesthetic pleasure in a way that speaks to the identity of the client group/users?
   f) Allows for and encourages growth, development, and change within the group and the space it will occupy?

4) Overall, to what extent is the "Whole-Place Vision" you devised being fulfilled in terms of:
   a) the project's setting?
   b) exterior design?
   c) interior design?

5) What needs (if any) require further addressing in terms of design?

6) What design changes can be made to address these needs?

7) Which of these design changes do you consider a priority?

Notes

INTRODUCTION

1. Gaston Bachelard, *The Poetics of Space* (Boston: Beacon Press, 1964), p. 5.
2. These exercises formed the basis of many of the exercises that now appear in this book.
3. Although not included here, Design Psychology sessions were also conducted with Margo Grant Walsh, the Vice Chairperson of Gensler Worldwide.
4. The interviews were conducted on three separate days and each lasted approximately one to three hours.
5. Bachelard, *Poetics of Space*, p. 8.
6. Ibid., p. xxxiii.
7. Of course, the reality of our physical world can also be shaped by other forces such as the political and economic, though I have not chosen to address these influences directly here.
8. For a useful discussion of the challenging of applying Environmental Psychology, see Frances E. Kuo, "Bridging the Gap: How Scientists Can Make a Difference" in R. Betchtel and A. Churchman *Handbook of Environmental Psychology*, (New York: John Wiley & Sons, 2002).
9. Searching for an appropriate name for this new field, I initially dubbed it "Topoanalysis," then "Design Insight." Finally I called it Design Psychology at the suggestion of a colleague of Constance Forrest, Ph.D. Forrest contributed a major portion of the definition of Design Psychology which appears here.
10. "Thinking Big: A Plan for Ground Zero and Beyond." *New York Times*, September 8, 2002, pp. 32–58. In this design exercise, sponsored by the *New York Times*,

fifteen famous architects were asked to create ideas that would "re-establish New York's skyline as the most thrilling in the world." A later proposal (December 2002) by a team including Eisenman, Richard Meier, Charles Gwathmey and Steven Holl, was commissioned by the Lower Manhattan Development Corporation. Thankfully, the five-tower grid the group proposed did not at all echo the traumatic moment of the Twin Towers' collapse.

11. In his book *Place and Placelessness*, Relph commented on the difficulty of conducting such analysis: "Place and sense of place do not lend themselves to scientific analysis for they are inextricably bound up with all the hopes, frustrations, and confusions of life, and possibly because of this social scientists have avoided these topics" (Preface). Still, since this was written in 1976, environmental psychologists have continued to conduct many studies that have contributed to our knowledge of people–place relationships.

12. Bachelard, *Poetics of Space*, p. 16.

13. This is true not only for Design Psychology but for psychoanalysis as well. For an interesting discussion of the nature of autobiography see Jerome Bruner, *Acts of Meaning* (Cambridge, Mass.: Harvard University Press, 1990), especially chapter 4.

THE PAST

1. Kimberley Dovey, "Home and Homelessness" in I. Altman and C. Werner, *Home Environments: Human Behavior and Environment: Advances in Theory and Research* (New York: Plenum Press, 1985), p. 53.

2. Clare Cooper, "The House as Symbol of Self" in H. Proshansky, W. Ittelson, and L. Rivlin, (eds.), *Environmental Psychology: People and their Physical Settings* (New York: Holt, Rinehart & Winston, 1976), pp. 435–48.

3. Ibid., p. 436.

4. Ibid.

5. See Charles Jencks, *Post-Modernism: The New Classicism in Art and Architecture* (New York: Rizzoli, 1987).

6. Robert Venturi, Denise Scott Brown, and Steven Izenour, *Learning From Las Vegas* (Cambridge, Mass.: MIT Press, 1977).

7. Robert Venturi, *Complexity and Contradiction in Architecture* (New York: Museum of Modern Art, 1966).

8. Charles Jencks, *Towards a Symbolic Architecture: The Thematic House* (New York: Rizzoli, 1985), p. 11.

9. Piaget identified the following stages:

➤ **sensorimotor** (ages 0–2)   At this stage the child moves beyond reflex action to gain the ability to coordinate movement and internalize thought—they become less passive and more active. Thus the child moves beyond awareness of their own body parts to perception of outward space, depth and objects.

➤ **Preoperational** (ages 2–7)   During this stage the child begins to think on a basic level. They now begin to represent the world in symbols though this is still in an intuitive and partially coordinated way. At this stage children remain egocentric with their sense of the environment still seen from their own point of view.

➤ **concrete operations** (ages 7–12) At this stage children are capable of logical thought. They are less egocentric and able to conceive of space as more mobile, flexible, and reversible.

➤ **formal operations** (ages 11–14) Having reached this stage, adolescents are able to reason on a higher, abstract level. Children of this age are able to understand the range of spatial possibilities.

Further description of these stages and their environmental relevance can be obtained from the same sources used in the above summary of stages including: Irwin Altman and Martin M. Chemers, *Culture and Environment* (Cambridge: Cambridge University Press, 1980), pp. 64–71; Roger Hart and Gary Moore, *Image and Environment* (New York: Aldine Publishing Company, 1973).

10. In their paper, "The Development of Children's Concern for the Environment," given at the International Institute for Environment and Society (Berlin, 1980), geographer Roger Hart and environmental psychologist Louise Chawla commented on this debate:

> Piaget's theory of development has come under growing criticism. Central to this criticism is the charge first made by the Soviet development psychologist Vygotsky that the developmental uniformities Piaget found amongst his Swiss children are not laws of nature but are "historically and socially determined" . . .. However, the misinterpretations of reality that Piaget first described have been repeatedly found. Piaget first revealed, as he has termed it, that young children are "both nearer to and farther from the world of objects than we are" . . .. They are nearer to the world through a "fidelity to fact," a tendency to accept the world as it is given in observation. They are also nearer to it through a projection of their own feelings and abilities into it. At the same time, these tendencies create the confusions that distance them from the world of objects in which adults live.

11. Hart and Chawla, "The Development of Children's Concern for the Environment."
12. Edith Cobb, *The Ecology of Imagination in Childhood* (New York: Columbia University Press, 1977).
13. Ibid., pp. 54–5.
14. Ibid., p. 89.
15. Louise Chawla, "Ecstatic Places," *Children's Environments Quarterly* 7, 4, 1990.
16. Quote from Cobb, *The Ecology of the Imagination in Childhood* as cited by Louise Chawla, *In the First Country of Places: Nature, Poetry and Childhood Memory* (Albany: State University of New York Press, 1994), p. 154.
17. I was first taken through this exercise by Mark Francis, a landscape architect who was then a professor at the Environmental Psychology Program of the City University of New York. Similar visualization exercises have been used by a variety of those working in the realm of environmental autobiography.
18. Ernst Schachtel, *Metamorphosis: On the Development of Affect, Perception, Attention, and Memory* (New York: Basic Books, 1959).
19. Ibid., p. 83.
20. Ibid., p. 177–8.

21. Louise Chawla, "Childhood Place Attachments" in I. Altman and S. Low, (eds.), *Human Behavior and Environment Advances in Theory and Research: Place Attachment* (New York: Plenum Press, 1992), p. 70.

22. A study by Anthony ("Moving Experiences: Memories of Favorite Homes," 1984) found that when subjects did actually return to their favorite home after moving away, 88 percent expressed negative feelings about that return including anger, disappointment, and/or sadness.

23. Chawla, "Childhood Place Attachments," p. 75.

24. Quote from Gaston Bachelard, *The Poetics of Space* as cited by Nora J. Rubinstein, "There's *NO* Place Like 'Home.' Home as 'Trauma': The Lessons of the Unspoken" in *Proceedings*, 24th Annual Meeting, EDRA. (Oklahoma City: EDRA, 1993), p. 268.

25. Nora J. Rubinstein, "Environmental Autobiography and Places of 'Trauma": The Lessons of the Unspoken" in *Proceedings*, 24th Annual Meeting, EDRA. (Oklahoma City: EDRA, 1993), p. 263.

26. When exploring environmental autobiography, Chawla (1995) cautions:

Not knowing what the process will initiate . . . it is critical for teachers and researchers to communicate safety within the classroom or research setting, interrupt memories when it appears that unmanageable pain may surface, and be prepared to recommend opportunities for therapy. (p. 35)

27. Clare Cooper Marcus, "Environmental Memories" in I. Altman and S. Low (eds.), *Human Behavior and Environment: Advances in Theory and Research: Place Attachment* (New York: Plenum Press, 1992), p. 110.

28. Quote from Yi-Fu Tuan (1974) as cited in Rubinstein, "There's *NO* Place Like 'Home,'" p. 269.

29. Erik H. Erikson, *Childhood and Society* (Harmondsworth: Penguin Books, 1950), pp. 239–66.

30. Ibid., p. 259.

31. In fact cognitive psychologists assume that each person has interpreted the world in their own, unique way. Each person's world is the world that *they* experience. That is, it assumes that the world is seen through the speaker's eyes. In this regard cognitive psychology, like Design Psychology, is autobiographical. See Michael T. Vallis, Janice L. Howes, and Philip C. Miller, *The Challenge of Cognitive Therapy: Applications to Nontraditional Populations* (New York: Plenum Press, 1991), p. 5.

32. Andrew I. Schewbel and Mark A. Fine, *Understanding and Helping Families: A Cognitive-Behavioral Approach* (Hillsdale, N.J.: Lawrence Erlbaum Associates, 1994), p. 48.

33. In a related exercise, therapists asked clients to complete a family tree as part of a "Psychohistory Exercise" intended to help these clients discover cognitions that have been handed down from generation to generation. "As the exercise unfolds, they [the clients] also recognize that hand-me-down cognitions that worked to help their parents meet the challenges of their times may not be effective in their household in today's world" (p. 149). See Schewbel and Fine, *Understanding and Helping Families*, pp. 149–62.

34. Kitty Frank, Tamarac Florida, 1992.

35. Gloria Shapiro, Tamarac, Florida, 1992.

36. It may be helpful to think of types of place lived in terms of "Big Town," "Small-Town" or "Out of Town" settings as defined by city planner Sydney Brower:

Big Town settings emphasize near-home spaces that are active, lively, varied, changing: places to see and be seen. Facilities are regional and a great many of the users come from outside the area. It is the type that attracts self-styled "city people," people who enjoy activity, diversity, fashion, and new ideas. This is the place for chance discoveries. It is the place to live if one wants to change one's life, meet someone new, try something different. It includes a large representation of young people who are starting out, and older people who are starting again. Because it is open and tolerant it offers many opportunities, but it can also be uncontrolled and dangerous; it is stimulating but it can also be crowded and competitive; it offers companionship but it also offers anonymity and the risk of loneliness.

Small-Town settings emphasize near-home spaces that blend home and social life. Facilities, institutions, eating places, and meeting grounds tend to be settled, familiar, stable, and locally run . . .. Service is personal, shopkeepers call customers by name and banks do not ask for identification. Residents are not necessarily all of the same income or class, but they get along because of accommodations that have been worked out over time. They tend to hold on to established ways and resist change. This type of setting offers companionship and support, but it discourages non-conformity.

Out-of-Town settings use near-home spaces as a backdrop for the unit and a buffer between the unit and its neighbors. The appearance and spaciousness of near-home spaces, as seen from the unit, are therefore important. Out-of-town settings are effectively removed (although not necessarily distant) from the hustle and bustle of city life. There is little pressure to socialize or join anything. Being off the beaten track, residents depend upon relatively self-contained units and good transportation. Out-of-town settings are for people who want to be alone or to enjoy, undisturbed, the company of family and friends; for those who are self-sufficient, introspective, detached; for seekers after a slower pace, a simpler and more direct way of life, or the natural order. In exchange for privacy, they accept inconveniences in getting to other people, stores, services, and cultural and educational facilities.

Reprinted from Clare Cooper Marcus, *House as Mirror of Self* (Berkeley: Conari Press, 1995) pp. 218–19 by permission from Conari Press.
37. Gaston Bachelard, *The Poetics of Space* (Boston: Beacon Press, 1964), p. 11.
38. Kevin Lynch, *The Image of the City* (Cambridge, Mass.: MIT Press, 1960) pp. 46–90. Reprinted by permission from MIT Press.
39. Amos Rapoport, *House, Form and Culture* (Englewood Cliffs, N.J.: Prentice-Hall, 1969).
40. Amos Rapoport, "Cross-Cultural Aspects of Environmental Design" in I. Altman, A. Rapoport, and J. Wohlwill (eds.), *Human Behavior and Environment Advances in Theory and Research: Environment and Culture* (New York: Plenum Press, 1980), p. 9.
41. Ibid., p. 11.

42. Rapoport, *House, Form and Culture*, pp. 18–45.

43. Rapoport, "Cross-Cultural Aspects of Environmental Design," p. 16.

44. Rapoport, *House, Form and Culture*, p. 7. Even when architects have the sensitivity to develop houses that will respond to users' needs, they may also be subject to constraints including, "those imposed by density and population numbers, and the institutionalization of controls through codes, regulations, zoning, requirements of banks and other mortgage authorities, insurance companies, and planning bodies" ibid., p. 59. However, choice still exists.

45. Rapoport, "Cross-Cultural Aspects of Environmental Design," p. 42.

46. Kenneth Powell, *Graves Residence: Michael Graves* (London: Phaidon Press, 1995), p. 8.

47. Powell, *Graves Residence*.

48. Ibid., p. 24.

49. Design Psychology Exercise 4.

50. What I actually saw in the studio was the sculptural head which eventually became part of an 11 foot bronze stone statue of Eleanor Roosevelt by Penelope Jencks which was installed in Riverside Park, NYC in the Fall of 1997.

51. In later correspondence, Duany commented, "There are three town centers: South Miami, Coconut Grove and Merrick Park *exactly* one mile away in different directions. One of them *should* be within a quarter mile of our house in New Urbanist practice."

THE PRESENT

1. Abraham Maslow, *Motivation and Personality* (New York: Harper & Row, 1954).

2. Ibid., p. 163.

3. Ibid., p. 35–46.

4. Other thinkers in the realm of psychology and environment have also adapted Maslow's theory of motivation including Clare Cooper Marcus (1975) and Fred Steele (1973).

5. Lee Rainwater, "Fear and the House-as-Haven in the Lower Class" in R. Gutman (ed.), *People and Buildings* (New York: Basic Books, 1972), p. 299.

6. Ibid., p. 305.

7. Ibid., p. 310.

8. Pruitt-Igoe, a low income, modern high rise housing complex dynamited in St. Louis in 1972, remains perhaps the best known example of this phenomenon.

9. However, those living in even the most marginal circumstances still dream about some place like home. In her research, environmental psychologist Leanne Rivlin has found that "Whether they are squatters, people in shelters or in temporary, limited quarters, people do make attempts to create homes for themselves and their families. Since we asked them about their past histories, preferred places and plans for the future, we know that they have ideas for setting up their homes. We also saw their attempts to create places, sometimes with the most limited physical contexts and always with very limited resources" (letter to Toby Israel, Winter, 1997).

10. Clare Cooper Marcus, *House as Mirror of Self: Exploring the Deeper Meaning of Home* (Berkeley: Conari Press, 1995), p. 437.

11. Brian R. Little, "Personality and the Environment" in D. Stokols and I. Altman (eds.), *Handbook of Environmental Psychology*, Vol. 1 (New York: John Wiley & Sons, 1987), p. 264.

12. Carl G. Jung, *Psychological Types* (Princeton: Princeton University Press, 1971).

13. Ibid., Chapter X.

14. David Canter, *Psychology for Architects* (New York: John Wiley & Sons, 1974), p. 105.

15. David Keirsey and Marilyn Bates, *Please Understand Me: Character and Temperament Types* (Del Mar, CA: Prometheus Nemesis Books, 1984), p. 14–15.

16. Irwin Altman and Martin Chemers, *Culture and Environment* (Cambridge: Cambridge University Press, 1984), pp. 82–3.

17. Jeffrey D. Fisher, Paul A. Bell, and Andrew Baum, *Environmental Psychology* (New York: Holt, Rinehart & Winston, 1984), p. 149.

18. Edward T. Hall, *The Hidden Dimension* (New York: Doubleday, 1966), pp. 110–20. Hall identified these four zones based on observations and interviews with middle class Americans. Hall stressed that these zones and personal space dynamics differ in other cultural contexts.

19. Fisher, Bell, and Baum, *Environmental Psychology*, pp. 152–3.

20. Rachel Sebba and Arza Churchman, "The Uniqueness of Home," *Architecture and Behavior*, Vol. 3, no. 1: 16.

21. Ibid., pp. 7, 11, 18.

22. Gaston Bachelard, *The Poetics of Space* (Boston: Beacon Press, 1964), p. 136.

23. Sebba and Churchman, "The Uniqueness of Home," p. 22.

24. Cooper Marcus, *House as Mirror of Self*, p. 136.

25. Ibid., pp. 135–6.

26. Oscar Newman, *Defensible Space: Crime Prevention through Urban Design* (New York: Macmillan, 1972).

27. Ibid., p. 3.

28. Christopher Alexander, "The City as a Mechanism for Sustaining Human Contact" in R. Gutman *People and Buildings* (New York: Basic Books, 1972), p. 409.

29. Ibid., p. 415.

30. Ibid., p. 416.

31. Christopher Alexander, Sara Ishikawa, and Murray Silverstein, *A Pattern Language*. (New York: Oxford University Press, 1977).

32. Herbert Muschamp, "Can New Urbanism Find Room for the Old?" *New York Times*, June 2, 1996.

33. Ibid.

34. Ibid.

35. "Bill Linder and His City of Hope," *New York Times*, February 18, 1996.

36. Kenneth Powell, *Graves Residence: Michael Graves* (London: Phaidon Press, 1995), p. 13.

37. Ibid., p. 17.

38. Charles Jencks, *Kings of Infinite Space* (New York: St. Martin's Press, 1983), p. 67.

39. Ibid., p. 67.

40. In correspondence to the author, November 22, 2002, Jencks wrote that the "Thematic House is not 'sweeping staircase' but a very tight, pre-cast concrete stair cylinder that works simultaneously to hold up walls to either side. It is very different in use and appearance to the one in Baltimore."

41. Comments in correspondence to the author, March 24, 1997.
42. Charles Jencks, *Towards a Symbolic Architecture: The Thematic House* (New York: Rizzoli, 1985), p. 182.
43. Bachelard, *Poetics of Space*, pl. xii.
44. Keirsey and Bates, *Please Understand Me*, pp. 178–9.
45. "Charles Jencks", *Architecture and Urbanism*, January 1985, p. 27.
46. Ibid.
47. Mark Linder, *Rap Sheets, The Duany Tapes*. Volume One, Number Five, March 30, 1987.
48. Alexander, Ishikawa, and Silverstein, *A Pattern Language*, p. 437.
49. Ibid., p. 438.
50. Ibid., p. 439.
51. Keirsey and Bates, *Please Understand Me*, p. 178.
52. Ibid., pp. 178–9.
53. Ibid., p. 178.
54. Ibid., p. 179.
55. Ibid., p. 178.
56. Ibid., p. 179.
57. *Please Understand Me: Character and Temperament Types* can be obtained by writing to: Prometheus Nemesis Book Company, P.O. Box 2748, Del Mar, Ca, USA 92014.
58. These are the categories established by Sebba and Churchman in their study, "The Uniqueness of Home." *Architecture and Behavior*, Vol. 3, no. 1, (1986): 7–14.

THE FUTURE

1. Gaston Bachelard, *The Poetics of Space* (Boston: Beacon Press, 1964), p. 61.
2. Clare Cooper Marcus, *House as Mirror of Self: Exploring the Deeper Meaning of Home* (Berkeley: Conari Press, 1995), p. 254.
3. "Understanding Mobility in America" in I. Altman and C. Werner, *Home Environments: Human Behavior and Environment: Advances in Theory and Research* (New York: Plenum Press, 1985), pp. 237–40.
4. For a comprehensive discussion of these issues see William Michelson, *Environmental Choice, Human Behavior and Residential Satisfaction* (New York: Oxford University Press, 1977).
5. Ibid., pp. 34–5.
6. Cooper Marcus, *House as Mirror of Self*, p. 11.
7. Brian R. Little, "Personality and Environment" in D. Stokols and I. Altman (eds.), *Handbook of Environmental Psychology* (New York: John Wiley & Sons, 1987), p. 221.
8. Ibid.
9. Cooper Marcus, *House as Mirror of Self*, p. 74.
10. Abraham Maslow, *Motivation and Personality* (New York: Harper & Row, 1954), p. 51.
11. Ibid.
12. Portions of the following summary of aesthetic schools of thought are from Toby Israel, "The Art in the Environment Experience: Reaction to Public Murals in England" (Ph.D. dissertation, City University of New York, 1988).

13. Herbert Gans, *Popular Culture and High Culture: An Analysis and Evaluation of Taste* (New York: Basic Books, 1974), pp. 69–103.
14. Ibid., see Chapter 3.
15. Ibid., pp. 133–4.
16. Ibid., p. 102.
17. The "fish brick" was given to me by the Public Arts program of Humberside County Council as part of the dedication of their city wide "Fish Trail."
18. During a subsequent first trip to Hungary I was amazed to find a similar color used on the facades of many Hungarian buildings. Had this actual color been passed down to me as part of my environmental inheritance?
19. Charles Jencks, "Leap-frogging the Cultural Pyramid," *Guardian Review*, January 15, 1994.
20. Ibid.
21. Denise Scott Brown, *Urban Concepts* (London: St. Martin's Press, 1990), p. 45.
22. Gans, *Popular Culture and High Culture*, p. 110.
23. Herbert Read, *Art and Society* (London: Faber and Faber, 1936), p. 88.
24. Erwin Panofsky, *Meaning in the Visual Arts* (Chicago: University of Chicago Press, 1955), pp. 26–41.
25. *The Random House Dictionary of the English Language* (New York: Random House, 1967).
26. Panofsky, *Meaning in the Visual Arts*, p. 39.
27. Frank Lloyd Wright, *An Autobiography: Frank Lloyd Wright* (New York: Horizon Press, 1932), p. 42.
28. Bachelard, *Poetics of Space*, p. 186.
29. Abraham Maslow, *Towards a Psychology of Being* (New York: Van Nostrand, 1968), p. 64.
30. Edgar Kaufmann and Ben Raeburn (eds.), *Frank Lloyd Wright: Writings and Buildings* (New York: Meridian Books, 1960), p. 106.
31. Charles Jencks, *Kings of Infinite Space* (New York: St. Martin's Press, 1983), p. 78.
32. Ibid.
33. Rybczynski, Witold, *Looking Around: A Journey through Architecture* (New York: Viking, 1992), pp. 155–6.
34. Jencks, "Leap-Frogging the Cultural Pyramid."
35. The Congress for the New Urbanism (CNU) was founded in 1993. As described in their charter, their mission is "the restructuring of public policy and development practices to support the restoration of existing urban centers and towns within coherent metropolitan regions. We stand for the reconfiguration of sprawling suburbs into communities of real neighborhoods and diverse districts, the conservation of natural environments, and the preservation of our built legacy."
36. Bachelard, *Poetics of Space*, p. xii.
37. This exercise was adapted with permission from Clare Cooper Marcus, *House as Mirror of Self*, p. 79.

SOME PLACE LIKE HOME

1. Gaston Bachelard, *The Poetics of Space* (Boston: Beacon Press, 1964), pp. 5–6.
2. Clare Cooper Marcus' research (1978) found that 86 percent of subjects recalled outdoor places as favorite childhood environments. Cooper Marcus concluded:

. . . if we continue to landscape . . . spaces in the "clipped lawn" aesthetic, we will soon find children seeking hiding places under the backstairs, beneath the juniper bushes, and behind the garbage shed. With careful forethought to the needs of the child and the private, daydreaming child, we can revise our views of the urban and suburban landscape to allow for spaces where clubhouses can be built, streams explored, and the trees climbed. If we don't, we are depriving the next generation of environmental experiences whose worth we have only begun to sense (p. 43).

3. Of course for some, especially those with early traumatic experiences of home, such escape may not be so easy. The Design Psychology exercises included here are intended for use by those seeking greater fulfillment rather than those seeking to recover from serious trauma or disorder. Interestingly, the potential for therapists to use such exercises as part of the psychotherapeutic process has been suggested (see M. Godkin, "Identity and Place," in A. Buttimer and D. Seamon (eds), *The Human Experience of Place* (New York: St. Martin's Press, 1980); C. Verheyen, "Using Home and Personal Objects in Psychotherapy," in J. Urbina-Soria, P. Ortega-Andeane, and R. Bechtel (eds), *EDRA 22*, 1991).

4. Charles Jencks, *Kings of Infinite Space* (New York: St. Martin's Press, 1983), p. 56.

5. Also see Relph's description of such essence of a sense of place: *Place and Placelessness* (London: Pion, 1976), p. 142.

6. I invited Richard Rogers, Frank Gehry, Denise Scott Brown and Zaha Hadid to go through the Design Psychology process, but they declined. I also invited Prince Charles to participate but his office politely declined this opportunity on his behalf.

APPLYING DESIGN PSYCHOLOGY

1. The use of the term "high positives" in relation to design was suggested by Constance Forrest, Ph.D., who thereby made reference to a new area of psychology, "positive psychology". In his President's Address which was reproduced in the American Psychological Association's 1998 Annual Report, Martin E. P. Seligman described positive psychology as a "reoriented science that emphasizes the understanding and building of the most positive qualities of an individual: optimism, courage, work ethic, future-mindedness, interpersonal skills, the capacity for pleasure and insight and social responsibility. It's my belief that since World War II, psychology has moved too far away from its original roots, which were to make the lives of all people more fulfilling and productive and too much toward the important, but not all-important area of any mental illness."

2. The project with which I was most familiar was Ray's design of Charleston Place, a seventy-six unit senior citizen complex in South Brunswick, New Jersey. A model in his practice of what he calls "socio-physical architecture," the complex became a physical translation of the multiple needs of the residents. Rejecting the stacked units/institutional corridor approach, Ray designed, instead, socially oriented individual cottages grouped around patio courts that formed a supportive mini-neighborhood. Thirteen essential health, safety, economic, and emotional needs of the residents were addressed in a program supported by twenty-four specific design features.

3. The distinction between an *in*quisitive as opposed to an *ac*quisitive mindset was suggested to me by John Diffey, president of the Kendal Corporation.
4. Tony Bisgno's business, Home-Tech, operates out of Monroe Township, New Jersey.
5. Sherry Arnstein's landmark article (1969), "A Ladder of Citizen Participation" clearly articulated the difference between genuine "participation" and "non-participation":

8	Citizen control	Degrees of citizen power
7	Delegated power	
6	Partnership	
5	Placation	Degree of tokenism
4	Consultation	
3	Informing	
2	Therapy	
1	Manipulation	Non-participation

According to her typology the lowest steps on the ladder, 1) Manipulation and 2) Therapy, are often disguised as genuine forms of participation. On these levels power holders seek to "cure" or "educate" people rather than to allow them to plan or conduct programs. Beyond these levels of non-participation are degrees of tokenism whereby citizens may be 3) Informed, 4) Consulted, or 5) Placated, they "may hear and be heard" (p. 217). Under these circumstances, however, people lack the leverage to ensure that their needs are met. They remain essentially powerless. Decision making power increases further up the participation ladder. At rung 6) Partnership, citizens can "negotiate and engage in trade-offs with traditional power holders" (p. 217). Full citizen power exists at the highest levels, 7) Delegated power and 8) Citizen control, when participants have complete decision making authority.

6. Adapted from Fred I. Steele, *Physical Settings and Organization Development* (Reading: Addison-Wesley, 1973).
7. The University Academy Charter School's philosophy, mission and method can be summarized as follows:

Philosophy:
➤ everyone can make a contribution to the betterment of the world;

➤ individuals, working together, can make a difference.

Mission: To engage youth in academic experiences that encourage:
➤ exploration of the world;

➤ desire for knowledge;

➤ commitment to social justice.

Method: Enable students to:
➤ interact with the City;

➤ interact with New Jersey City University;

➤ participate in service projects.

8. Mufson Partnership marketing brochure.
9. Ibid.
10. Ibid.
11. Although some participants attended all five sessions, others attended just a few.
12. Franklin Becker and Fritz Steele, *Workplace by Design: Mapping the High-Performance Workscape* (San Francisco: Jossey-Bass, 1995), p. 30.
13. Andrew Laing, Francis Duffy, Denia Jaunzens, and Steve Willis, *New Environments for Working: The Re-design of Offices and Environmental Systems for New Ways of Working* (London: Spon, 1998), p. 26.
14. Studies by BOSTI Associates and others, for example, indicate that ". . . the workplace measurably affects job performance, job satisfaction and ease and quality of interaction, which are important bottom-line measures for all organizations. The research suggests that the dollar value of the benefits of appropriately designed offices are substantial, as are the costs of poorly deigned ones." Michael Brill, Sue Weidemann and BOSTI Associates, *Disproving Widespread Myths about Workplace Design* (Jasper, IN: Kimball International, 2001), p. 16.
15. In 1995, Dr. Susan Painter adapted the Design Psychology exercises which were part of my original manuscript for this book for use in the design classes taught by her at UCLA such as "Venice Child Health Clinic: Translating Design Psychological Principles into Design" (syllabus supplied to the author by Forrest Painter Design via E-mail). The Special Objects Exercise which subsequently formed the basis of the office project described here, was included in that syllabus.
16. Michael Brill et al., *Using Office Design to Increase Productivity*, Vol. 1 (Buffalo: Workplace Design and Productivity, Inc., 1984), pp. 298–300.
17. Ibid., p. 274.
18. Letter from Morris Stafford, AIA, July 17, 2002.
19. See Trish Hall, "An Architect Who Enjoys the Act of Renovating," *New York Times* (Real Estate Section), December 15, 2002, for a further discussion of Larry Mufson as a "serial"/"simultaneous" renovator.

APPENDIX   THE DESIGN PSYCHOLOGY TOOLBOX

1. At the time of writing, I am working with Haworth, Inc. to develop Design Psychology training workshops that can be offered for CEU credit.

2. The Kendal Corporation, a Quaker-related nonprofit organization and a pioneer of university-based senior housing, incorporates past history of place in its visioning sessions. Kendal asks potential residents to remember back to their experience of care taking their own parents as those parents aged. Thinking about the positive and negative housing options available to their parents helps future Kendal residents envision the best ("highest positive") retirement housing options they themselves would like to have as they age.

3. In *Physical Settings and Organization Development* (Reading: Addison-Wesley, 1973), F. Steele describes a similar rating system to assess the effectiveness of a given setting. See Chapter 10.

Bibliography

Alexander, Christopher, "The City as a Mechanism for Sustaining Human Contact." In R. Gutman (ed.), *People and Buildings*, pp. 406–34. New York: Basic Books, 1972.

Alexander, Christopher, Ishikawa, Sara and Silverstein, Murray, *A Pattern Language*. New York: Oxford University Press, 1977.

Altman, Irwin, *The Environment and Social Behavior: Privacy, Personal Space, Territory, Crowding*. Monterey, CA.: Brooks-Cole Publishing, 1975.

Altman, Irwin and Chemers, Martin, *Culture and Environment*. Cambridge: Cambridge University Press, 1984.

Altman, Irwin and Low, Setha M., *Place Attachment, Human Behavior and Environment: Advances in Theory and Research*. New York: Plenum Press, 1992.

Altman, Irwin and Wandersman, Abraham, *Neighborhood and Community Environments. Human Behavior and Environment: Advances in Theory and Research*. New York: Plenum Press, 1987.

Altman, Irwin and Werner, Carol, *Home Environments: Human Behavior and Environment: Advances in Theory and Research*. Plenum Press: New York, 1985.

Altman, Irwin and Wohlwill, Joachim T., *Children and the Environment: Human Behavior and the Environment: Advances in Theory and Research*. New York: Plenum Press, 1978.

Anthony, Kathy H., "Moving Experiences: Memories of Favorite Homes." In *EDRA 15 Proceedings*, pp. 141–7. Edited by Donna Duerk and David Campbell. Washington, D.C., 1984.

Arnstein, S. R., "A Ladder of Citizen Participation," *American Institute of Planners Journal*, July 1969.

Ashcraft, Norman and Scheflen, Albert, *People Space: The Making and Breaking of Human Boundaries*. Garden City, N.Y.: Anchor Books, 1976.

Bachelard, Gaston, "The House Protects the Dreamer," *Landscape*, 13, no.3 (Spring 1964): 28–33.

Bachelard, Gaston, *The Poetics of Space*. Boston: Beacon Press, 1964.

Barker, Nicholas and Parr, Martin, *Signs of the Times: A Portrait of the Nation's Tastes*. Manchester: Cornerhouse Publications, 1992.

Bechtel, Robert and Churchman, Arza. *Handbook of Environmental Psychology*. New York: John Wiley & Sons, 2002.

Becker, Franklin and Steele, Fritz, *Workplace Design: Mapping the High-Performance Workspace*. San Francisco: Jossey-Bass, 1995.

Bjorklid, Pia, *Children's Outdoor Environments*. Stockholm: Pia Bjorklid, 1982.

Bridges, William, *The Character of Organizations: Using Personality Type in Organization Development*. Palo Alto: Davies-Black Publishers, 2000.

Briggs Myers, Isabel and McCaulley, Mary H., *Manual: A Guide to the Development and Use of the Myers-Briggs Type Indicator*. Palo Alto: Consulting Psychologist Press, 1985.

Brill, Michael, Weidemann, Sue and BOSTI Associates, *Disproving Widespread Myths about Workplace Design*. Jasper, IN: Kimball International, 2001.

Brill, Michael with Margulis, Stephen T., Konar, Ellen and BOSTI, *Using Office Design to Increase Productivity*. Volume 1. Buffalo: Workplace Design and Productivity, Inc., 1984.

Brill, Michael with Margulis, Stephen T., Konar, Ellen and BOSTI, *Using Office Design to Increase Productivity*. Volume 2. Buffalo: Workplace Design and Productivity, Inc., 1985.

Bronfenbrenner, Urie, *The Ecology of Human Development*. Cambridge, Mass.: Harvard University Press, 1979.

Brooke, Steven, *Seaside*. Gretna: Pelican Publishing, 1995.

Brown, Denise Scott, *Urban Concepts*. London: Academy Group, 1990.

Bruner, Jerome, *Acts of Meaning*. Cambridge, Mass.: Harvard University Press, 1990.

Canter, David, *Psychology for Architects*. New York: John Wiley & Sons, 1974.

Charles, Prince of Wales, *A Vision of Britain: A Personal View of Architecture*. New York: Doubleday, 1989.

Chawla, Louise, "Childhood Place Attachments." In Irwin Altman and Setha M. Low (eds), *Place Attachments: Human Behavior and Environment: Advances in Theory and Research*, pp. 63–86. New York: Plenum Press, 1992.

Chawla, Louise, *In the First Country of Places: Nature, Poetry and Childhood Memory*. Albany: State University of New York Press, 1994.

Clodagh, Aubry, *Total Design: Contemplate, Cleanse, Clarify and Create Your Personal Spaces*. New York: Clarkson Potter Publishers, 2001.

Cobb, Edith, *The Ecology of Imagination in Childhood*. New York: Columbia University Press, 1977.

Cooper, Clare. "The House as Symbol of Self." In H. Proshansky, W. Ittelson and Leanne Rivlin (eds), *Environmental Psychology: People and their Physical Settings*, pp. 435–48. New York: Holt, Rinehart & Winston, 1976.

Cooper Marcus, Clare, *House as a Mirror of Self: Exploring the Deeper Meaning of Home*. Berkeley: Conari Press, 1995.

Csikszentmihalyi, Mihaly and Rochberg-Halton, Eugene, *The Meaning of Things: Domestic Symbols and the Self*. Cambridge: Cambridge University Press, 1981.

Dehler, Katharine B., *The Thomas-Jencks-Gladding House*. Baltimore: Bodine, 1968.

Duany, Andres, Plater-Zyberk, Elizabeth and Speck, Jeff, *Suburban Nation: The Rise of Sprawl and the Decline of the American Dream*. New York: North Point Press, 2000.

Duncan, James S., "Landscape Taste as a Symbol of Group Identity: A Westchester County Village." *Geographical Review*, July 1973: 335–55.

"Environmental Autobiographies," *Childhood City Newsletter*, 14, December 1978.

Eriksen, Aase, *Playground Design*. New York: Van Nostrand Reinhold, 1985.

Erikson, Erik H., *Childhood and Society*. New York: W.W. Norton, 1963.

Fisher, Jeffrey D., Bell, Paul A. and Baum, Andrew, *Environmental Psychology*. New York: Holt, Rinehart & Winston, 1984.

Gans, Herbert, *Popular Culture and High Culture: An Analysis and Evaluation of Taste*. New York: Basic Books, 1974.

Godkin, Michael A., "Identity and Place: Clinical Applications Based on Notions of Rootedness and Uprootedness." In Anne Buttimer and David Seamon (eds), *The Human Experience of Place*, pp. 73–85. New York: St. Martin's Press, 1980.

Graves, Michael, *Michael Graves: Building and Projects 1982–1989*. New York: Princeton Architectural Press, 1990.

Graves, Michael, Vogel Wheeler, Karen and Scully, Vincent, *Michael Graves: Building and Projects 1966–1981*. New York: Rizzoli, 1983.

Gutman, Robert, *People and Buildings*. New York: Basic Books, 1972.

Hall, Edward T., *The Hidden Dimension*. New York: Doubleday, 1966.

Hart, Roger and Chawla, Louise, "The Development of Children's Concern for the Environment." Paper prepared for International Institute for Environment and Society, Berlin, Germany, June 1980.

Hayden, Dolores, *Re-designing the American Dream: Gender, Housing, and Family Life*. New York: W.W. Norton, 2002.

Hutchinson, Maxwell, *The Prince of Wales: Right or Wrong? An Architect Replies*. London: Faber and Faber, 1989.

Ittelson, William H., Proshansky, Harold M., Rivlin, Leanne G. and Winkel, Gary H., *An Introduction to Environmental Psychology*. New York: Holt, Rinehart & Winston, 1974.

Jencks, Charles, *Modern Movements in Architecture*. New York: Anchor/Doubleday, 1973.

Jencks, Charles, *Kings of Infinite Space*. New York: St. Martin's Press, 1983.

Jencks, Charles, *Towards a Symbolic Architecture: The Thematic House*. New York: Rizzoli, 1985.

Jencks, Charles, *What is Post-Modernism?* New York: St. Martin's Press, 1986.

Jencks, Charles, *Post-Modernism: The New Classicism in Art and Architecture*. New York: Rizzoli, 1987.

Jencks, Charles, *The Prince and the Architects and the New Wave Monarchy*. New York: Rizzoli, 1988.

Jencks, Charles, "Leap-Frogging the Cultural Pyramid," *Guardian Review*, January 15, 1994.

Jencks, Charles, *The Architecture of the Jumping Universe*. London: Academy Editions, 1995.

Jencks, Charles and Baird, George (eds.), *Meaning in Architecture*. New York: Braziller, 1969.

Jencks, Charles and Chaitkin, William, *Architecture Today*. London: Academy Editions, 1982.

Jencks, Charles and Silver, Nathan, *Adhocism: The Case for Improvisation.* New York: Doubleday, 1972.

Jung, Carl G., *Man and his Symbols.* London: Aldus Books, 1964.

Jung, Carl G. in *Landscape*, vol. 14, no. 3 (Spring 1965).

Jung, Carl G. *Psychological Types.* Princeton: Princeton University Press, 1971.

Katz, Peter, *The New Urbanism.* New York: Mc-Graw Hill, 1993.

Keckes, Peter (ed.), *The Museum of the Hungarian Village at Szentendre.* Budapest: Covina, 1989.

Keirsey, David and Bates, Marilyn, *Please Understand Me: Character and Temperament Types.* Del Mar, CA: Prometheus Nemesis Books, 1984.

Keswick, Maggie, *The Chinese Garden: History, Art, and Architecture.* New York: Rizzoli, 1978.

Laing, Andrew, Duffy, Francis, Jaunzens, Denia and Willis, Steve, *New Environments for Working: The Re-design of Offices and Environmental Systems for New Ways of Working.* London: Spon, 1998.

Lawrence, Roderick, J., *Housing, Dwellings and Homes: Design Theory, Research and Practice.* New York: John Wiley & Sons, 1987.

Little, Brian R., "Personality and the Environment." In Daniel Stokols and Irwin Altman (eds), *Handbook of Environmental Psychology*, pp. 205–44. New York: John Wiley & Sons, 1987.

Lynch, Kevin, *The Image of the City.* Cambridge, Mass.: MIT Press, 1960.

Marc, Oliver, *Psychology of the House.* London: Thames & Hudson, 1977.

Maslow, Abraham, *Motivation and Personality.* New York: Harper & Row, 1954.

Maslow, Abraham, *Towards a Psychology of Being.* New York: Van Nostrand, 1968.

Matrix. *Making Space: Women and the Man-Made Environment.* London: Pluto Press, 1984.

Meinig, Donald W. (ed.), *The Interpretations of Ordinary Landscape: Geographical Essays.* New York: Oxford University Press, 1979.

Michelson, William, *Environmental Choice, Human Behavior and Residential Satisfaction.* New York: Oxford University Press, 1977.

Muschamp, Herbert, "Can New Urbanism Find Room for the Old?" *New York Times*, June 2, 1996.

Newman, Oscar, *Defensible Space: Crime Prevention through Urban Design.* New York: Macmillan, 1972.

Nordstrom, Maria, "Childhood Environmental Memories—What are They and to What Use Do We Put Them?" *Architecture and Behavior*, Vol. 11, no. 1: 19–26.

Nuttgerns, Patrick, *The Home Front: Housing and People 1840–1990.* London: BBC Books, 1989.

Panofsky, Erwin, *Meaning in the Visual Arts.* Chicago: University of Chicago Press, 1955.

Piaget, Jean, *The Child's Conception of the World.* New York: Harcourt, Brace, 1929.

Pile, Stephen, *The Body and the City: Psychoanalysis, Space and Subjectivity.* London: Routledge, 1996.

Powell, Kenneth, *Graves Residence.* London: Phaidon Press, 1995.

Rainwater, Lee, "Fear and the House-as-a-Haven in the Lower Class." In R. Gutman (ed.), *People and Buildings*, pp. 299–313. New York: Basic Books, 1972.

Rapoport, Amos, *House Form and Culture.* Englewood Cliffs, N.J.: Prentice-Hall, 1969.

Read, Herbert, *Art and Society.* London: Faber & Faber, 1936.

Relph, E., *Place and Placelessness.* London: Pion, 1976.

Rybczynski, Witold, *Looking Around: A Journey through Architecture.* New York: Viking, 1992.

Schachtel, Ernest, *Metamorphosis: On the Development of Affect, Perception, Attention and Memory.* New York: Basic Books, 1959.

Schewbel, Andrew I. and Fine, Mark A., *Understanding and Helping Families: A Cognitive-Behavioral Approach.* Hillsdale, N.J.: Lawrence Erlbaum Associates, 1994.

Scott Brown, Denise, *Urban Concepts.* London: St. Martin's Press, 1990.

Sebba, Rachel, "The Landscapes of Childhood: The Reflection of Childhood's Environment in Adult Memories and in Children's Attitudes." *Environment and Behavior,* Vol. 25, nos. 4–6, 1991: 395–422.

Sebba, Rachel and Churchman, Arza, "The Uniqueness of Home." *Architecture and Behavior,* Vol. 3, no. 1, 1986: 7–24.

Seligman, Martin E. P., *Authentic Happiness: Using the New Positive Psychology to Realize Your Potential for Lasting Fulfillment.* New York: Free Press, 2002.

Sobel, David, "A Place in the World: Adults' Memories of Childhood's Special Places." *Children's Environments Quarterly* 7 (4), 1990: 5–12.

Sobel, David, *Children's Special Places: Exploring the Role of Forts, Dens, and Bush Houses in Middle Childhood.* Tucson: Zephyr Press, 1993.

Sommer, Robert, *Personal Space: The Behavioral Basis of Design.* Englewood Cliffs, N.J.: Prentice-Hall, 1969.

Sopher, David E., "The Landscape of Home: Myth, Experience, Social Meaning." In D.W. Meinig (ed.), *The Interpretation of Ordinary Landscape.* Oxford: Oxford University Press, 1979.

Spain, Daphne, *Gendered Spaces.* Chapel Hill: University of North Carolina Press, 1992.

Steele, Fred I., *Physical Setting and Organization Development.* Reading: Addison-Wesley, 1973.

Strickland, Roy, *Designing a City of Learning: Paterson, N.J.* Roy Stickland, 2001.

Stuart, David, "Modern Movements in Architecture," *Architecture and Urbanism,* January 1985.

Vallis, T. Michael, Howes, Janice L. and Miller, Philip C., *The Challenge of Cognitive Therapy: Applications to Nontraditional Populations.* New York: Plenum Press, 1991.

Van Vliet, Willem (ed.), *Women, Housing, and Community.* Aldershot: Avebury, 1988.

Venturi, Robert, *Complexity and Contradiction in Architecture.* New York: Museum of Modern Art, 2002.

Venturi, Robert, Brown, Denise Scott and Izenour, Steven, *Learning From Las Vegas.* Cambridge, Mass.: MIT Press, 1977.

Verheyen, Carol S., "Using Home and Personal Objects in Psychotherapy." In Javier Urbina-Soria, Paticia Ortega-Andeane, Robert Bechtel (eds), *EDRA 22,* 1991.

Wakefield, Dan, *The Story of Your Life: Writing a Spiritual Autobiography.* Boston: Beacon Press, 1990.

Weinstein, Carol S. and David, Thomas G., *Spaces for Children: The Built Environment and Child Development.* New York: Plenum Press, 1987.

Weisman, Leslie Kanes, *Discrimination by Design: A Feminist Critique of the Man-Made Environment.* Urbana: University of Illinois Press, 1992.

Werkele, Gerda, Peterson, Rebecca and Morely, David (eds), *New Spaces for Women.* Boulder, Col.: Westview Press, 1980.